A Second Treasury of Kahlil Gibran

A *Second* TREASURY OF Kahlil Gibran

translated from the Arabic by

ANTHONY R. FERRIS

THE CITADEL PRESS · NEW YORK

A Second Treasury of Kahlil Gibran

Table of Contents

book I

the
broken wings

Contents

Dedication

To the one who stares at the sun with glazed eyes and grasps the fire with untrembling fingers and hears the spiritual tune of Eternity behind the clamorous shrieking of the blind. To M.E.H. I dedicate this book.

GIBRAN

Foreword

I WAS EIGHTEEN years of age when love opened my eyes with its magic rays and touched my spirit for the first time with its fiery fingers, and Selma Karamy was the first woman who awakened my spirit with her beauty and led me into the garden of high affection, where days pass like dreams and nights like weddings.

Selma Karamy was the one who taught me to worship beauty by the example of her own beauty and revealed to me the secret of love by her affection; she was the one who first sang to me the poetry of real life.

Every young man remembers his first love and tries to recapture that strange hour, the memory of which changes his deepest feeling and makes him so happy in spite of all the bitterness of its mystery.

In every young man's life there is a "Selma" who appears to him suddenly while in the spring of life and transforms his solitude into happy moments and fills the silence of his nights with music.

I was deeply engrossed in thought and contemplation and seeking to understand the meaning of nature and the revelation of books and scriptures when I heard LOVE whispered into my ears through Selma's lips. My life was a coma, empty like that of Adam's in Paradise, when I saw Selma standing before me like a column of light. She was the Eve of my heart who filled it with secrets and wonders and made me understand the meaning of life.

The first Eve led Adam out of Paradise by her own will, while Selma made me enter willingly into the paradise of pure love and virtue by her sweetness and love; but what happened to the first man also happened to me, and the fiery sword which chased Adam out of Paradise was like the one which frightened me by its glittering edge and forced me away from the paradise of my love without having disobeyed any order or tasted the fruit of the forbidden tree.

Today, after many years have passed, I have nothing left out of that beautiful dream except painful memories flapping like invisible wings around me, filling the depths of my heart with sorrow, and bringing tears to my eyes; and my beloved, beautiful Selma, is dead and nothing is left to commemorate her except my broken heart and a tomb surrounded by cypress trees. That tomb and this heart are all that is left to bear witness of Selma.

The silence that guards the tomb does not reveal God's secret in the obscurity of the coffin, and the rustling of the branches whose roots suck the body's elements do not tell the mysteries of the grave, but the agonized sighs of my heart announce to the living the drama which love, beauty, and death have performed.

Oh, friends of my youth who are scattered in the city of Beirut, when you pass by that cemetery near the pine forest, enter it silently and walk slowly so the tramping of your feet will not disturb the slumber of the dead, and stop humbly by Selma's tomb and greet the earth that encloses her corpse and mention my name with a deep sigh and say to yourself, "Here, all the hopes of Gibran, who is living as a prisoner of love beyond the seas, were buried. On this spot he lost his happiness, drained his tears, and forgot his smile."

By that tomb grows Gibran's sorrow together with the cypress trees, and above the tomb his spirit flickers every night commemorating Selma, joining the branches of the trees in sorrowful wailing, mourning and lamenting the going of Selma, who, yesterday, was a beautiful tune on the lips of life and today is a silent secret in the bosom of the earth.

> Oh, comrades of my youth! I appeal to you in the names of those virgins whom your hearts have loved, to lay a wreath of flowers on the forsaken tomb of my beloved, for the flowers you lay on Selma's tomb are like falling drops of dew from the eyes of dawn on the leaves of a withering rose.

THE BROKEN WINGS

1

Silent Sorrow

MY NEIGHBORS, you remember the dawn of youth with pleasure and regret its passing; but I remember it like a prisoner who recalls the bars and shackles of his jail. You speak of those years between infancy and youth as a golden era free from confinement and cares, but I call those years an era of silent sorrow which dropped as a seed into my heart and grew with it and could find no outlet to the world of knowledge and wisdom until love came and opened the heart's doors and lighted its corners. Love provided me with a tongue and tears. You people remember the gardens and orchids and the meeting places and street corners that witnessed your games and heard your innocent whispering; and I remember, too, the beautiful spot in North Lebanon. Every time I close my eyes I see those valleys full of magic and dignity and those mountains covered with glory and greatness trying to reach the sky. Every time I shut my ears to the clamor of the city I hear the murmur of the rivulets and the rustling of the branches. All those beauties which I speak of now and which I long to see, as a child longs for his mother's breast, wounded my spirit, imprisoned in the darkness of youth, as a falcon suffers in its cage when it sees a flock of birds flying freely in the spacious sky. Those valleys and hills fired my imagination, but bitter thoughts wove round my heart a net of hopelessness.

Every time I went to the fields I returned disappointed, without understanding the cause of my disappointment. Every time I looked at the gray sky I felt my heart contract. Every time I heard the singing of the birds and babbling of the spring I suffered without understanding the reason for my suffering. It is said that unsophistication makes a man empty and that emptiness makes him carefree. It may be true among those who were born dead and who exist like frozen corpses; but the sensitive boy who feels much and knows little is the most unfortunate creature under the sun, because he is torn by two forces. The first force elevates him and shows him the beauty of existence through a cloud of dreams; the second ties him down to the earth and fills his eyes with dust and overpowers him with fears and darkness.

Solitude has soft, silky hands, but with strong fingers it grasps the heart and makes it ache with sorrow. Solitude is the ally of sorrow as well as a companion of spiritual exaltation.

The boy's soul undergoing the buffeting of sorrow is like a white lily just unfolding. It trembles before the breeze and opens its heart to daybreak and folds its leaves back when the shadow of night comes. If that boy does not have diversion or friends or companions in his games, his life will be like a narrow prison in which he sees nothing but spiderwebs and hears nothing but the crawling of insects.

That sorrow which obsessed me during my youth was not caused by lack of amusement, because I could have had it; neither from lack of friends, because I could have found them. That sorrow was caused by an inward ailment which made me love solitude. It killed in me the inclination for games and amusement. It removed from my shoulders the wings of youth and made me like a pond of water between mountains which reflects in its calm surface the shadows of ghosts and the colors of clouds and trees, but cannot find an outlet by which to pass singing to the sea.

Thus was my life before I attained the age of eighteen. That year is like a mountain peak in my life, for it awakened knowledge in me and made me understand the vicissitudes of mankind. In that year I was reborn and unless a person is born again his life will remain like a blank sheet in the book of existence. In that year, I saw the angels of Heaven looking at me through the eyes of a beautiful woman. I also saw the devils of hell raging in the heart of an evil man. He who does not see the angels and devils in the beauty and malice of life will be far removed from knowledge, and his spirit will be empty of affection.

2

The Hand of Destiny

In the spring of that wonderful year, I was in Beirut. The gardens were full of Nisan flowers and the earth was carpeted with green grass, all like a secret of earth revealed to Heaven. The orange trees and apple trees, looking like houris or brides sent by nature to inspire poets and excite the imagination, were wearing white garments of perfumed blossoms.

Spring is beautiful everywhere, but it is most beautiful in Lebanon. It is a spirit that roams round the earth but hovers over Lebanon, conversing with kings and prophets, singing with the rivers the songs of Solomon, and repeating with the Holy Cedars of Lebanon the memory of ancient glory. Beirut, free from the mud of winter and the dust of summer, is like a bride in the spring, or like a mermaid sitting by the side of a brook drying her smooth skin in the rays of the sun.

One day, in the month of Nisan, I went to visit a friend whose home was at some distance from the glamorous city. As we were conversing, a dignified man of about sixty-five entered the house. As I rose to greet him, my friend introduced him to me as Farris Effandi Karamy and then gave him my name with flattering words. The old man looked at me a moment, touching his forehead with the ends of his fingers as if he were trying to regain his memory. Then he smilingly approached me, saying, "You are the son of a very dear friend of mine, and I am happy to see that friend in your person."

Much affected by his words, I was attracted to him like a bird whose instinct leads him to his nest before the coming of the tempest. As we sat down, he told us about his friendship with my father, recalling the time which they spent together. An old man likes to return in memory to the days of his youth like a stranger who longs to go back to his own country. He delights to tell stories of the past like a poet who takes pleasure in reciting his best poem. He lives spiritually in the past because the present passes swiftly, and the future seems to him an approach to the oblivion of the grave. An hour full of old memories passed like the shadows of the trees over the grass. When Farris Effandi started to leave, he put his left hand on my shoulder and shook my right hand, saying, "I have not seen your father for twenty years. I hope you will take his place in frequent visits to my house." I promised gratefully to do my duty toward a dear friend of my father.

When the old man left the house, I asked my friend to tell me more about him. He said, "I do not know any other man in Beirut whose wealth has made him kind and whose kindness has made him wealthy. He is one of the few who come to this world and leave it without harming any one, but people of that kind are usually miserable and oppressed because they are not clever enough to save themselves from the crookedness of others. Farris Effandi has one daughter whose character is similar to his and whose beauty and gracefulness are beyond description, and she will also be miserable because her father's wealth is placing her already at the edge of a horrible precipice."

As he uttered these words, I noticed that his face clouded. Then he continued, "Farris Effandi is a good old man with a noble heart, but he lacks will power. People lead him like a blind man. His daughter obeys him in spite of her pride and intelligence, and this is the secret which lurks in the life of father and daughter. This secret was discovered by an evil man who is a bishop and whose wickedness hides in the shadow of his Gospel. He makes the people believe that he is kind and noble. He is the head of religion in this land of the religious. The people obey and worship him. He leads them like a flock of lambs to the slaughter house. This bishop has a nephew who is full of hatefulness and corruption. The day will come sooner or later when he will place his nephew on his right and Farris Effandi's daughter on his left, and, holding with his evil hand the wreath of matrimony over their heads, will tie a pure virgin to a filthy degenerate, placing the heart of the day in the bosom of night.

"That is all I can tell you about Farris Effandi and his daughter, so do not ask me any more questions."

Saying this, he turned his head toward the window as if he were trying to solve the problems of human existence by concentrating on the beauty of the universe.

As I left the house, I told my friend that I was going to visit Farris Effandi in a few days for the purpose of fulfilling my promise and for the sake of the friendship which had joined him and my father. He stared at me for a moment, and I noticed a change in his expression as if my few simple words had revealed to him a new idea. Then he looked straight through my eyes in a strange manner, a look of love, mercy, and fear—the look of a prophet who foresees what no one else can divine. Then his lips trembled a little, but he said nothing when I started toward the door. That strange look followed me, the meaning of which I could not understand until I grew up in the world of experience, where hearts understand each other intuitively and where spirits are mature with knowledge.

3

Entrance to the Shrine

IN A FEW DAYS, loneliness overcame me; and I tired of the grim faces of books; I hired a carriage and started for the house of Farris Effandi. As I reached the pine woods where people went for picnics, the driver took a private way, shaded with willow trees on each side. Passing through, we could see the beauty of the green grass, the grapevines, and the many colored flowers of Nisan just blossoming.

In a few minutes the carriage stopped before a solitary house in the midst of a beautiful garden. The scent of roses, gardenia, and jasmine filled the air. As I dismounted and entered the spacious garden, I saw Farris Effandi coming to meet me. He ushered me into his house with a hearty welcome and sat by me, like a happy father when he sees his son, showering me with questions on my life, future and education. I answered him, my voice full of ambition and zeal; for I heard ringing in my ears the hymn of glory, and I was sailing the calm sea of hopeful dreams. Just then a beautiful young woman, dressed in a gorgeous white silk gown, appeared from behind the velvet curtains of the door and walked toward me. Farris Effandi and I rose from our seats.

"This is my daughter Selma," said the old man. Then he introduced me to her, saying, "Fate has brought back to me a dear old friend of mine in the person of his son." Selma stared at me a moment as if doubting that a visitor could have entered their house. Her hand, when I touched it, was like a white lily, and a strange pang pierced my heart.

We all sat silent as if Selma had brought into the room with her a heavenly spirit worthy of mute respect. As she felt the silence she smiled at me and said, "Many a time my father has repeated to me the stories of his youth and of the old days he and your father spent together. If your father spoke to you in the same way, then this meeting is not the first one between us."

The old man was delighted to hear his daughter talking in such a manner and said, "Selma is very sentimental. She sees everything through the eyes of the spirit." Then he resumed his conversation with care and tact as if he had found in me a magic charm which took him on the wings of memory to the days of the past.

As I considered him, dreaming of my own later years, he looked upon me, as a lofty old tree that has withstood storms and sunshine throws its shadow upon a small sapling which shakes before the breeze of dawn.

But Selma was silent. Occasionally, she looked first at me and then at her father as if reading the first and last chapters of life's drama. The day passed fast in that garden, and I could see through the window the ghostly yellow kiss of sunset on the mountains of Lebanon. Farris Effandi continued to recount his experiences and I listened entranced and responded with such enthusiasm that his sorrow was changed to happiness.

Selma sat by the window, looking on with sorrowful eyes and not speaking, although beauty has its own heavenly language, loftier than the voices of tongues and lips. It is a timeless language, common to all humanity, a calm lake that attracts the singing rivulets to its depth and makes them silent.

Only our spirits can understand beauty, or live and grow with it. It puzzles our minds; we are unable to describe it in words; it is a sensation that our eyes cannot see, derived from both the one who observes and the one who is looked upon. Real beauty is a ray which emanates from the holy of holies of the spirit, and illuminates the body, as life comes from the depths of the earth and gives color and scent to a flower.

Real beauty lies in the spiritual accord that is called love which can exist between a man and a woman.

Did my spirit and Selma's reach out to each other that day when we met, and did that yearning make me see her as the most beautiful woman under the sun? Or was I intoxicated with the wine of youth which made me fancy that which never existed?

Did my youth blind my natural eyes and make me imagine the brightness of her eyes, the sweetness of her mouth, and the grace of her figure? Or was it that her brightness, sweetness, and grace opened my eyes and showed me the happiness and sorrow of love?

It is hard to answer these questions, but I say truly that in that hour I felt an emotion that I had never felt before, a new affection resting calmly in my heart, like the spirit hovering over the waters at the creation of the world, and from that affection was born my happiness and my sorrow. Thus ended the hour of my first meeting with Selma, and thus the will of Heaven freed me from the bondage of youth and solitude and let me walk in the procession of love.

Love is the only freedom in the world because it so elevates the spirit that the laws of humanity and the phenomena of nature do not alter its course.

As I rose from my seat to depart, Farris Effandi came close to me and said soberly, "Now my son, since you know your way to this house, you should come often and feel that you are coming to your father's house. Consider me as a father and Selma as a sister." Saying this, he turned to Selma as if to ask confirmation of his statement. She nodded her head positively and then looked at me as one who has found an old acquaintance.

Those words uttered by Farris Effandi Karamy placed me side by side with his daughter at the altar of love. Those words were a heavenly song which started with exaltation and ended with sorrow; they raised our spirits to the realm of light and searing flame; they were the cup from which we drank happiness and bitterness.

I left the house. The old man accompanied me to the edge of the garden, while my heart throbbed like the trembling lips of a thirsty man.

4

The White Torch

THE MONTH of Nisan had nearly passed. I continued to visit the home of Farris Effandi and to meet Selma in that beautiful garden, gazing upon her beauty, marveling at her intelligence, and hearing the stillness of sorrow. I felt an invisible hand drawing me to her.

Every visit gave me a new meaning to her beauty and a new insight into her sweet spirit, until she became a book whose pages I could understand and whose praises I could sing, but which I could never finish reading. A woman whom Providence has provided with beauty of spirit and body is a truth, at the same time both open and secret, which we can understand only by love, and touch only by virtue; and when we attempt to describe such a woman she disappears like a vapor.

Selma Karamy had bodily and spiritual beauty, but how can I describe her to one who never knew her? Can a dead man remember the singing of a nightingale and the fragrance of a rose and the sigh of a brook? Can a prisoner who is heavily loaded with shackles follow the breeze of the dawn? Is not silence more painful than death? Does pride prevent me from describing Selma in plain words since I cannot draw her truthfully with luminous colors? A hungry man in a desert will not refuse to eat dry bread if Heaven does not shower him with manna and quails.

In her white silk dress, Selma was slender as a ray of moonlight coming through the window. She walked gracefully and rhythmically. Her voice was low and sweet; words fell from her lips like drops of dew falling from the petals of flowers when they are disturbed by the wind.

But Selma's face! No words can describe its expression, reflecting first great internal suffering, then heavenly exaltation.

The beauty of Selma's face was not classic; it was like a dream of revelation which cannot be measured or bound or copied by the brush of a painter, or the chisel of a sculptor. Selma's beauty was not in her golden hair, but in the virtue and purity which surrounded it; not in her large eyes, but in the light which emanated from them; not in her red lips, but in the sweetness of her words; not in her ivory neck, but in its slight bow to the front. Nor was it in her perfect figure, but in the nobility of her spirit, burning like a white torch between earth and sky. Her beauty was like a gift of poetry. But poets are unhappy people, for, no matter how high their spirits reach, they will still be enclosed in an envelope of tears.

Selma was deeply thoughtful rather than talkative, and her silence was a kind of music that carried one to a world of dreams and made him listen to the throbbing of his heart, and see the ghosts of his thoughts and feelings standing before him, looking him in the eyes.

She wore a cloak of deep sorrow through her life, which increased her strange beauty and dignity, as a tree in blossom is more lovely when seen through the mist of dawn.

Sorrow linked her spirit and mine, as if each saw in the

other's face what the heart was feeling and heard the echo of a hidden voice. God had made two bodies in one, and separation could be nothing but agony.

The sorrowful spirit finds rest when united with a similar one. They join affectionately, as a stranger is cheered when he sees another stranger in a strange land. Hearts that are united through the medium of sorrow will not be separated by the glory of happiness. Love that is cleansed by tears will remain eternally pure and beautiful.

5

The Tempest

ONE DAY Farris Effandi invited me to dinner at his home. I accepted, my spirit hungry for the divine bread which Heaven placed in the hands of Selma, the spiritual bread which makes our hearts hungrier the more we eat of it. It was this bread which Kais, the Arabian poet, Dante, and Sappho tasted and which set their hearts afire; the bread which the Goddess prepares with the sweetness of kisses and the bitterness of tears.

As I reached the home of Farris Effandi, I saw Selma sitting on a bench in the garden resting her head against a tree and looking like a bride in her white silk dress, or like a sentinel guarding that place.

Silently and reverently I approached and sat by her. I could not talk; so I resorted to silence, the only language of the heart, but I felt that Selma was listening to my wordless call and watching the ghost of my soul in my eyes.

In a few minutes the old man came out and greeted me as usual. When he stretched his hand toward me, I felt as if he were blessing the secrets that united me and his daughter. Then he said, "Dinner is ready, my children; let us eat." We rose and followed him, and Selma's eyes brightened; for a new sentiment had been added to her love by her father's calling us his children.

We sat at the table enjoying the food and sipping the old wine, but our souls were living in a world far away. We were dreaming of the future and its hardships.

Three persons were separated in thoughts, but united in love; three innocent people with much feeling but little knowledge; a drama was being performed by an old man who loved his daughter and cared for her happiness, a young woman of twenty looking into the future with anxiety, and a young man, dreaming and worrying, who had tasted neither the wine of life nor its vinegar, and trying to reach the height of love and knowledge but unable to lift himself up. We three sitting in twilight were eating and drinking in that solitary home, guarded by Heaven's eyes, but at the bottoms of our glasses were hidden bitterness and anguish.

As we finished eating, one of the maids announced the presence of a man at the door who wished to see Farris Effandi. "Who is he?" asked the old man. "The Bishop's messenger," said the maid. There was a moment of silence during which Farris Effandi stared at his daughter like a prophet who gazes at Heaven to divine its secret. Then he said to the maid, "Let the man in."

As the maid left, a man, dressed in oriental uniform and with a big mustache curled at the ends, entered and greeted the old man, saying, "His Grace, the Bishop, has sent me for you with his private carriage; he wishes to discuss important business with you." The old man's face clouded and his smile disappeared. After a moment of deep thought he came close to me and said in a friendly voice, "I hope to find you here when I come back, for Selma will enjoy your company in this solitary place."

Saying this, he turned to Selma and, smiling, asked her if she agreed. She nodded her head, but her cheeks became red, and with a voice sweeter than the music of a lyre she said, "I will do my best, Father, to make our guest happy."

Selma watched the carriage that had taken her father and the Bishop's messenger until it disappeared. Then she came and sat opposite me on a divan covered with green silk. She looked like a lily bent to the carpet of green grass by the breeze of dawn. It was the will of Heaven that I should be with Selma alone, at night, in her beautiful home surrounded by trees, where silence, love, beauty, and virtue dwelt together.

We were both silent, each waiting for the other to speak, but speech is not the only means of understanding between two souls. It is not the syllables that come from the lips and tongues that bring hearts together.

There is something greater and purer than what the mouth utters. Silence illuminates our souls, whispers to our hearts, and brings them together. Silence separates us from ourselves, makes us sail the firmament of spirit, and brings us closer to Heaven; it makes us feel that bodies are no more than prisons and that this world is only a place of exile.

Selma looked at me and her eyes revealed the secret of her heart. Then she quietly said, "Let us go to the garden and sit under the trees and watch the moon come up behind the mountains." Obediently I rose from my seat, but I hesitated.

"Don't you think we had better stay here until the moon has risen and illuminates the garden?" And I continued, "The darkness hides the trees and flowers. We can see nothing."

Then she said, "If darkness hides the trees and flowers from our eyes, it will not hide love from our hearts."

Uttering these words in a strange tone, she turned her eyes and looked through the window. I remained silent, pondering her words, weighing the true meaning of each syllable. Then she looked at me as if she regretted what she had said and tried to take away those words from my ears by the magic of her eyes. But those eyes, instead of making me forget what she had said, repeated through the depths of my heart more clearly and effectively the sweet words which had already become graven in my memory for eternity.

Every beauty and greatness in this world is created by a single thought or emotion inside a man. Every thing we see today, made by past generations, was, before its appearance, a thought in the mind of a man or an impulse in the heart of a woman. The revolutions that shed so much blood and turned men's minds toward liberty were the idea of one man who lived in the midst of thousands of men. The devastating wars which destroyed empires were a thought that existed in the mind of an individual. The supreme teachings that changed the course of humanity were the ideas of a man whose genius separated him from his environment. A single thought built the Pyramids, founded the glory of Islam, and caused the burning of the library at Alexandria.

One thought will come to you at night which will elevate you to glory or lead you to the asylum. One look from a woman's eye makes you the happiest man in the world. One word from a man's lips will make you rich or poor.

That word which Selma uttered that night arrested me between my past and future, as a boat which is anchored in the midst of the ocean. That word awakened me from the slumber of youth and solitude and set me on the stage where life and death play their parts.

The scent of flowers mingled with the breeze as we

came into the garden and sat silently on a bench near a jasmine tree, listening to the breathing of sleeping nature, while in the blue sky the eyes of heaven witnessed our drama.

The moon came out from behind Mount Sunnin and shone over the coast, hills, and mountains; and we could see the villages fringing the valley like apparitions which have suddenly been conjured from nothing. We could see the beauty of all Lebanon under the silver rays of the moon.

Poets of the West think of Lebanon as a legendary place, forgotten since the passing of David and Solomon and the Prophets, as the Garden of Eden became lost after the fall of Adam and Eve. To those Western Poets, the word "Lebanon" is a poetical expression associated with a mountain whose sides are drenched with the incense of the Holy Cedars. It reminds them of the temples of copper and marble standing stern and impregnable and of a herd of deer feeding in the valleys. That night I saw Lebanon dream-like with the eyes of a poet.

Thus, the appearance of things changes according to the emotions, and thus we see magic and beauty in them, while the magic and beauty are really in ourselves.

As the rays of the moon shone on the face, neck, and arms of Selma, she looked like a statue of ivory sculptured by the fingers of some worshiper of Ishtar, goddess of beauty and love. As she looked at me, she said, "Why are you silent? Why do you not tell me something about your past?" As I gazed at her, my muteness vanished, and I opened my lips and said, "Did you not hear what I said when we came to this orchard? The spirit that hears the whispering of flowers and the singing of silence can also hear the shrieking of my soul and the clamor of my heart."

She covered her face with her hands and said in a trembling voice, "Yes, I heard you—I heard a voice coming from the bosom of night and a clamor raging in the heart of the day."

Forgetting my past, my very existence—everything but Selma—I answered her, saying, "And I heard you, too, Selma. I heard exhilarating music pulsing in the air and causing the whole universe to tremble."

Upon hearing these words, she closed her eyes and on her lips I saw a smile of pleasure mingled with sadness. She whispered softly, "Now I know that there is something higher than heaven and deeper than the ocean and stranger than life and death and time. I know now what I did not know before."

At that moment Selma became dearer than a friend and closer than a sister and more beloved than a sweetheart. She became a supreme thought, a beautiful dream, an overpowering emotion living in my spirit.

It is wrong to think that love comes from long companionship and persevering courtship. Love is the offspring of spiritual affinity and unless that affinity is created in a moment, it will not be created in years or even generations.

Then Selma raised her head and gazed at the horizon where Mount Sunnin meets the sky, and said, "Yesterday you were like a brother to me, with whom I lived and by whom I sat calmly under my father's care. Now, I feel the presence of something stranger and sweeter than brotherly affection, an unfamiliar commingling of love and fear that fills my heart with sorrow and happiness."

I responded, "This emotion which we fear and which shakes us when it passes through our hearts is the law of nature that guides the moon around the earth and the sun around God."

She put her hand on my head and wove her fingers through my hair. Her face brightened and tears came out of her eyes like drops of dew on the leaves of a lily, and she said, "Who would believe our story—who would believe that in this hour we have surmounted the obstacles of doubt? Who would believe that the month of Nisan which brought us together for the first time, is the month that halted us in the Holy of Holies of life?"

Her hand was still on my head as she spoke, and I would not have preferred a royal crown or a wreath of glory to that beautiful smooth hand whose fingers were twined in my hair.

Then I answered her: "People will not believe our story because they do not know that love is the only flower that grows and blossoms without the aid of seasons, but was it Nisan that brought us together for the first time, and is it this hour that has arrested us in the Holy of Holies of life? Is it not the hand of God that brought our souls close together before birth and made us prisoners of each other for all the days and nights? Man's life does not commence in the womb and never ends in the grave; and this firmament, full of moonlight and stars, is not deserted by loving souls and intuitive spirits."

As she drew her hand away from my head, I felt a kind of electrical vibration at the roots of my hair mingled with the night breeze. Like a devoted worshiper who receives his blessing by kissing the altar in a shrine, I took Selma's hand, placed my burning lips on it, and gave it a long kiss, the memory of which melts my heart and awakens by its sweetness all the virtue of my spirit.

An hour passed, every minute of which was a year of love. The silence of the night, moonlight, flowers, and trees made us forget all reality except love, when suddenly we heard the galloping of horses and rattling of carriage wheels. Awakened from our pleasant swoon and plunged from the world of dreams into the world of perplexity and misery, we found that the old man had returned from his mission. We rose and walked through the orchard to meet him.

When the carriage reached the entrance of the garden, Farris Effandi dismounted and slowly walked towards us, bending forward slightly as if he were carrying a heavy load. He approached Selma and placed both of his hands on her shoulders and stared at her. Tears coursed down his wrinkled cheeks and his lips trembled with sorrowful smile. In a choking voice, he said, "My beloved Selma, very soon you will be taken away from the arms of your father to the arms of another man. Very soon fate will carry you from this lonely home to the world's spacious court, and this garden will miss the pressure of your footsteps, and your father will become a stranger to you. All is done; may God bless you."

Hearing these words, Selma's face clouded and her eyes froze as if she felt a premonition of death. Then she screamed, like a bird shot down, suffering, and trembling, and in a choked voice said, "What do you say? What do you mean? Where are you sending me?"

Then she looked at him searchingly, trying to discover his secret. In a moment she said, "I understand. I understand everything. The Bishop has demanded me from you and has prepared a cage for this bird with broken wings. Is this your will, Father?"

His answer was a deep sigh. Tenderly he led Selma into the house while I remained standing in the garden, waves of perplexity beating upon me like a tempest upon autumn leaves. Then I followed them into the living room, and to avoid embarrassment, shook the old man's hand, looked at Selma, my beautiful star, and left the house.

As I reached the end of the garden I heard the old man calling me and turned to meet him. Apologetically he took my hand and said, "Forgive me, my son. I have ruined your evening with the shedding of tears, but please come to see me when my house is deserted and I am lonely and desperate. Youth, my dear son, does not combine with senility, as morning does not meet the night; but you will come to me and call to my memory the youthful days which I spent with your father, and you will tell me the news of life which does not count me as among its sons any longer. Will you not visit me when Selma leaves and I am left here in loneliness?"

While he said these sorrowful words and I silently shook his hand, I felt the warm tears falling from his eyes upon my hand. Trembling with sorrow and filial affection, I felt as if my heart were choked with grief. When I raised my head and he saw the tears in my eyes, he bent toward me and touched my forehead with his lips. "Good-bye, son. Good-bye."

An old man's tear is more potent than that of a young man because it is the residuum of life in his weakening body. A young man's tear is like a drop of dew on the leaf of a rose, while that of an old man is like a yellow leaf which falls with the wind at the approach of winter.

As I left the house of Farris Effandi Karamy, Selma's voice still rang in my ears, her beauty followed me like a wraith, and her father's tears dried slowly on my hand.

My departure was like Adam's exodus from Paradise, but the Eve of my heart was not with me to make the whole world an Eden. That night, in which I had been born again, I felt that I saw death's face for the first time.

Thus the sun enlivens and kills the fields with its heat.

6

The Lake of Fire

EVERYTHING that a man does secretly in the darkness of night will be clearly revealed in daylight. Words uttered in privacy will become unexpectedly common conversation. Deeds which we hide today in the corners of our lodgings will be shouted on every street tomorrow.

Thus the ghosts of darkness revealed the purpose of Bishop Bulos Galib's meeting with Farris Effandi Karamy, and his conversation was repeated all over the neighborhood until it reached my ears.

The discussion that took place between Bishop Bulos Galib and Farris Effandi that night was not over the problems of the poor or the widows and orphans. The main purpose for sending after Farris Effandi and bringing him in the Bishop's private carriage was the betrothal of Selma to the Bishop's nephew, Mansour Bey Galib.

Selma was the only child of the wealthy Farris Effandi, and the Bishop's choice fell on Selma, not on account of her beauty and noble spirit, but on account of her father's money which would guarantee Mansour Bey a good and prosperous fortune and make him an important man.

The heads of religion in the East are not satisfied with their own munificence, but they must strive to make all members of their families superiors and oppressors. The glory of a prince goes to his eldest son by inheritance, but the exaltation of a religious head is contagious among his brothers and nephews. Thus the Christian bishop and the Moslem imam and the Brahman priest become like sea reptiles who clutch their prey with many tentacles and suck their blood with numerous mouths.

When the Bishop demanded Selma's hand for his nephew, the only answer that he received from her father was deep silence and falling tears, for he hated to lose his only child. Any man's soul trembles when he is separated from his only daughter whom he has reared to young womanhood.

The sorrow of parents at the marriage of a daughter is equal to their happiness at the marriage of a son, because a son brings to the family a new member, while a daughter, upon her marriage, is lost to them.

Farris Effandi perforce granted the Bishop's request, obeying his will unwillingly, because Farris Effandi knew the Bishop's nephew very well, knew that he was dangerous, full of hate, wickedness, and corruption.

In Lebanon, no Christian could oppose his bishop and remain in good standing. No man could disobey his religious head and keep his reputation. The eye could not resist a spear without being pierced, and the hand could not grasp a sword without being cut off.

Suppose that Farris Effandi had resisted the Bishop and refused his wish; then Selma's reputation would have been ruined and her name would have been blemished by the dirt of lips and tongues. In the opinion of the fox, high bunches of grapes that can't be reached are sour.

Thus destiny seized Selma and led her like a humiliated

slave in the procession of miserable oriental woman, and thus fell that noble spirit into the trap after having flown freely on the white wings of love in a sky full of moonlight scented with the odor of flowers.

In some countries, the parent's wealth is a source of misery for the children. The wide strong box which the father and mother together have used for the safety of their wealth becomes a narrow, dark prison for the souls of their heirs. The Almighty Dinar* which the people worship becomes a demon which punishes the spirit and deadens the heart. Selma Karamy was one of those who were victims of their parents' wealth and bridegrooms' cupidity. Had it not been for her father's wealth, Selma would still be living happily.

A week had passed. The love of Selma was my sole entertainer, singing songs of happiness for me at night and waking me at dawn to reveal the meaning of life and the secrets of nature. It is a heavenly love that is free from jealousy, rich and never harmful to the spirit. It is a deep affinity that bathes the soul in contentment; a deep hunger for affection which, when satisfied, fills the soul with bounty; a tenderness that creates hope without agitating the soul, changing earth to paradise and life to a sweet and beautiful dream. In the morning, when I walked in the fields, I saw the token of Eternity in the awakening of nature, and when I sat by the seashore I heard the waves singing the song of Eternity. And when I walked in the streets I saw the beauty of life and the splendor of humanity in the appearance of passers-by and movements of workers.

Those days passed like ghosts and disappeared like clouds, and soon nothing was left for me but sorrowful memories. The eyes with which I used to look at the beauty of spring and the awakening of nature, could see

* Kind of money used in the Near East.

nothing but the fury of the tempest and the misery of winter. The ears with which I formerly heard with delight the song of the waves, could hear only the howling of the wind and the wrath of the sea against the precipice. The soul which had observed happily the tireless vigor of mankind and the glory of the universe, was tortured by the knowledge of disappointment and failure. Nothing was more beautiful than those days of love, and nothing was more bitter than those horrible nights of sorrow.

When I could no longer resist the impulse, I went, on the weekend, once more to Selma's home—the shrine which Beauty had erected and which Love had blessed, in which the spirit could worship and the heart kneel humbly and pray. When I entered the garden I felt a power pulling me away from this world and placing me in a sphere supernaturally free from struggle and hardship. Like a mystic who receives a revelation of Heaven, I saw myself amid the trees and flowers, and as I approached the entrance of the house I beheld Selma sitting on the bench in the shadow of a jasmine tree where we both had sat the week before, on that night which Providence had chosen for the beginning of my happiness and sorrow.

She neither moved nor spoke as I approached her. She seemed to have known intuitively that I was coming, and when I sat by her she gazed at me for a moment and sighed deeply, then turned her head and looked at the sky. And, after a moment full of magic silence, she turned back toward me and tremblingly took my hand and said in a faint voice, "Look at me, my friend; study my face and read in it that which you want to know and which I can not recite. Look at me, my beloved . . . look at me, my brother."

I gazed at her intently and saw that those eyes, which a few days ago were smiling like lips and moving like the wings of a nightingale, were already sunken and glazed with sorrow and pain. Her face, that had resembled the unfolding, sunkissed leaves of a lily, had faded and become colorless. Her sweet lips were like two withering roses that autumn has left on their stems. Her neck, that had been a column of ivory, was bent forward as if it no longer could support the burden of grief in her head.

All these changes I saw in Selma's face, but to me they were like a passing cloud that covered the face of the moon and makes it more beautiful. A look which reveals inward stress adds more beauty to the face, no matter how much tragedy and pain it bespeaks; but the face which, in silence, does not announce hidden mysteries is not beautiful, regardless of the symmetry of its features. The cup does not entice our lips unless the wine's color is seen through the transparent crystal.

Selma, on that evening, was like a cup full of heavenly wine concocted of the bitterness and sweetness of life. Unaware, she symbolized the oriental woman who never leaves her parents' home until she puts upon her neck the heavy yoke of her husband, who never leaves her loving mother's arms until she must live as a slave, enduring the harshness of her husband's mother.

I continued to look at Selma and listen to her depressed spirit and suffer with her until I felt that time had ceased and the universe had faded from existence. I could see only her two large eyes staring fixedly at me and could feel only her cold, trembling hand holding mine.

I woke from my swoon hearing Selma saying quietly, "Come, my beloved, let us discuss the horrible future before it comes. My father has just left the house to see the man who is going to be my companion until death. My father, whom God chose for the purpose of my existence, will meet the man whom the world has selected to be my master for the rest of my life. In the heart of this city, the old man who accompanied me during my youth will meet the young man who will be my companion for the coming years. Tonight the two families will set the marriage date. What a strange and impressive hour! Last week at this time, under this jasmine tree, Love embraced my soul for the first time, while Destiny was writing the first word of my life's story at the Bishop's mansion. Now, while my father and my suitor are planning the day of marriage, I see your spirit quivering around me as a thirsty bird flickers above a spring of water guarded by a hungry serpent. Oh, how great this night is! And how deep is its mystery!"

Hearing these words, I felt that the dark ghost of complete despondency was seizing our love to choke it in its infancy, and I answered her, "That bird will remain flickering over that spring until thirst destroys him or falls into the grasp of a serpent and becomes its prey."

She responded, "No, my beloved, this nightingale should remain alive and sing until dark comes, until spring passes, until the end of the world, and keep on singing eternally. His voice should not be silenced, because he brings life to my heart, his wings should not be broken, because their motion removes the cloud from my heart."

Then I whispered, "Selma, my beloved, thirst will exhaust him; and fear will kill him."

She replied immediately with trembling lips, "The thirst of soul is sweeter than the wine of material things, and the fear of spirit is dearer than the security of the body. But listen, my beloved, listen carefully, I am standing today at the door of a new life which I know nothing about. I am like a blind man who feels his way so that he will not fall. My father's wealth has placed me in the slave market, and this man has bought me. I neither know nor love him, but I shall learn to love him, and I shall obey him, serve him, and make him happy. I shall give him all that a weak woman can give a strong man.

"But you, my beloved, are still in the prime of life. You can walk freely upon life's spacious path, carpeted with flowers. You are free to traverse the world, making of your heart a torch to light your way. You can think, talk, and act freely; you can write your name on the face of life because you are a man; you can live as a master because your father's wealth will not place you in the slave market to be bought and sold; you can marry the woman of your choice and, before she lives in your home, you can let her reside in your heart and can exchange confidences without hindrance."

Silence prevailed for a moment, and Selma continued, "But, is it now that Life will tear us apart so that you may attain the glory of a man and I the duty of a woman? Is it for this that the valley swallows the song of the nightingale in its depths, and the wind scatters the petals of the rose, and the feet tread upon the wine cup? Were all those nights we spent in the moonlight by the jasmine tree, where our souls united, in vain? Did we fly swiftly toward the stars until our wings tired, and are we descending now into the abyss? Or was Love asleep when he came to us, and did he, when he woke, become angry and decide to punish us? Or did our spirits turn the night's breeze into a wind that tore us to pieces and blew us like dust to the depth of the valley? We disobeyed no commandment, nor did we taste of forbidden fruit, so what is making us leave this paradise? We never conspired or practised mutiny, then why are we descending to hell? No, no, the moments which united us are greater than centuries, and the light that illuminated our spirits is stronger than the dark; and if the tempest separates us on this rough ocean, the waves will unite us on the calm shore; and if this life kills us, death will unite us. A woman's heart will not change with time or season; even if it dies eternally, it will never perish. A woman's heart is like a field turned into a battleground; after the trees are uprooted and the grass is burned and the rocks are reddened with blood and the earth is planted with bones and skulls, it is calm and silent as if nothing has happened; for the spring and autumn come at their intervals and resume their work.

"And now, my beloved, what shall we do? How shall we part and when shall we meet? Shall we consider love a strange visitor who came in the evening and left us in the morning? Or shall we suppose this affection a dream that came in our sleep and departed when we awoke?

"Shall we consider this week an hour of intoxication to be replaced by soberness? Raise your head and let me look at you, my beloved; open your lips and let me hear your voice. Speak to me! Will you remember me after this tempest has sunk the ship of our love? Will you hear the whispering of my wings in the silence of the night? Will you hear my spirit fluttering over you? Will you listen to my sighs? Will you see my shadow approach with the shadows of dusk and disappear with the flush of dawn? Tell me, my beloved, what will you be after having been magic ray to my eyes, sweet song to my ears, and wings to my soul? What will you be?"

Hearing these words, my heart melted, and I answered her, "I will be as you want me to be, my beloved."

Then she said, "I want you to love me as a poet loves his sorrowful thoughts. I want you to remember me as a traveler remembers a calm pool in which his image was reflected as he drank its water. I want you to remember me as a mother remembers her child that died before it saw the light, and I want you to remember me as a merciful king remembers a prisoner who died before his pardon reached him. I want you to be my companion, and I want you to visit my father and console him in his solitude because I shall be leaving him soon and shall be a stranger to him."

I answered her, saying, "I will do all you have said and will make my soul an envelope for your soul, and my heart a residence for your beauty and my breast a grave for your sorrows. I shall love you, Selma, as the prairies love the spring, and I shall live in you the life of a flower under the sun's rays. I shall sing your name as the valley sings the echo of the bells of the village churches; I shall listen to the language of your soul as the shore listens to the story of the waves. I shall remember you as a stranger remembers his beloved country, and as a hungry man remembers a banquet, and as a dethroned king remembers the days of his glory, and as a prisoner remembers the hours of ease and freedom. I shall remember you as a sower remembers the bundles of wheat on his threshing floor, and as a shepherd remembers the green prairies and sweet brooks."

Selma listened to my words with palpitating heart, and said, "Tomorrow the truth will become ghostly and the awakening will be like a dream. Will a lover be satisfied embracing a ghost, or will a thirsty man quench his thirst from the spring of a dream?"

I answered her, "Tomorrow, destiny will put you in the midst of a peaceful family, but it will send me into the world of struggle and warfare. You will be in the home of a person whom chance has made most fortunate through your beauty and virtue, while I shall be living a life of suffering and fear. You will enter the gate of life, while I shall enter the gate of death. You will be received hospitably, while I shall exist in solitude, but I shall erect a statue of love and worship it in the valley of death. Love will be my sole comforter, and I shall drink love like wine and wear it like a garment. At dawn, Love will wake me from slumber and take me to the distant field, and at noon will lead me to the shadows of trees, where I will find shelter with the birds from the heat of the sun. In the evening, it will cause me to pause before sunset to hear nature's farewell song to the light of day and will show me ghostly clouds sailing in the sky. At night, Love will embrace me, and I shall sleep, dreaming of the heavenly world where the spirits of lovers and poets abide. In the Spring I shall walk side by side with Love among violets and jasmines and drink the remaining drops of winter in the lily cups. In Summer we shall make the bundles of hay our pillows and the grass our bed, and the blue sky will cover us as we gaze at the stars and moon.

"In Autumn, Love and I will go to the vineyard and sit by the wine press and watch the grapevines being denuded of their golden ornaments, and the migrating flocks of birds will wing over us. In Winter we shall sit by the fireside reciting stories of long ago and chronicles of far countries. During my youth, Love will be my teacher; in middle age, my help; and in old age, my delight. Love, my beloved Selma, will stay with me to the end of my life, and after death the hand of God will unite us again."

All these words came from the depths of my heart like flames of fire which leap raging from the hearth and then disappear in the ashes. Selma was weeping as if her eyes were lips answering me with tears.

Those whom love has not given wings cannot fly behind the cloud of appearances to see the magic world in which Selma's spirit and mine existed together in that sorrowfully happy hour. Those whom Love has not chosen as followers do not hear when Love calls. This story is not for them. Even if they should comprehend these pages, they would not be able to grasp the shadowy meanings which are not clothed in words and do not reside on paper, but what human being is he who has never sipped the wine from the cup of love, and what spirit is it that has never stood reverently before that lighted altar in the temple whose pavement is the hearts of men and women and whose ceiling is the secret canopy of dreams? What flower is that on whose leaves the dawn has never poured a drop of dew; what streamlet is that which lost its course without going to the sea?

Selma raised her face toward the sky and gazed at the heavenly stars which studded the firmament. She stretched out her hands; her eyes widened, and her lips trembled. On her pale face, I could see the signs of sorrow, oppression, hopelessness, and pain. Then she cried, "Oh, Lord, what has a woman done that hath offended Thee? What sin has she committed to deserve such a punishment? For what crime has she been awarded everlasting castigation? Oh, Lord, Thou art strong, and I am weak. Why hast Thou made me suffer pain? Thou art great and almighty, while I am nothing but a tiny creature crawling before Thy throne. Why hast Thou crushed me with Thy foot? Thou art a raging tempest, and I am like dust; why, my Lord, hast Thou flung me upon the cold earth? Thou art powerful, and I am helpless; why art Thou fighting me? Thou art considerate, and I am prudent; why art Thou destroying me? Thou hast created woman with love, and why, with love, dost Thou ruin her? With Thy right hand dost Thou lift her, and with Thy left hand dost Thou strike her into the abyss, and she knows not why. In her mouth Thou blowest the breath of life, and in her heart Thou sowest the seeds of death. Thou dost show her the path of happiness, but Thou leadest her in the road of misery; in her mouth Thou dost place a song of happiness, but then Thou dost close her lips with sorrow and dost fetter her tongue with agony. With Thy mysterious fingers dost Thou dress her wounds, and with Thine hands Thou drawest the dread of pain round her pleasures. In her bed Thou hidest pleasure and peace, but beside it Thou dost erect obstacles and fear. Thou dost excite her affection through Thy will, and from her affection does shame emanate. By Thy will Thou showest her the beauty of creation, but her love for beauty becomes a terrible famine. Thou dost make her drink life in the cup of death, and death in the cup of life. Thou purifiest her with tears, and in tears her life streams away. Oh, Lord, Thou hast opened my eyes with love, and with love Thou hast blinded me. Thou hast kissed me with Thy lips and struck me with Thy strong hand. Thou hast planted in my heart a white rose, but around the rose a barrier of thorns. Thou hast tied my present with the spirit of a young man whom I love, but my life with the body of an unknown man. So help me, my Lord, to be strong in this deadly struggle and assist me to be truthful and virtuous until death. Thy will be done, Oh, Lord God."

Silence continued. Selma looked down, pale and frail; her arms dropped, and her head bowed and it seemed to me as if a tempest had broken a branch from a tree and cast it down to dry and perish.

I took her cold hand and kissed it, but when I attempted to console her, it was I who needed consolation more than she did. I kept silent, thinking of our plight and listening to my heartbeats. Neither of us said more.

Extreme torture is mute, and so we sat silent, petrified, like columns of marble buried under the sand of an earthquake. Neither wished to listen to the other because our heart-threads had become weak and even breathing would have broken them.

It was midnight, and we could see the crescent moon

rising from behind Mt. Sunnin, and it looked, in the midst of the stars, like the face of a corpse, in a coffin surrounded by the dim lights of candles. And Lebanon looked like an old man whose back was bent with age and whose eyes were a haven for insomnia, watching the dark and waiting for dawn, like a king sitting on the ashes of his throne in the debris of his palace.

The mountains, trees, and rivers change their appearance with the vicissitudes of times and seasons, as a man changes with his experiences and emotions. The lofty poplar that resembles a bride in the daytime, will look like a column of smoke in the evening; the huge rock that stands impregnable at noon, will appear to be a miserable pauper at night, with earth for his bed and the sky for his cover; and the rivulet that we see glittering in the morning and hear singing the hymn of Eternity, will, in the evening, turn to a stream of tears wailing like a mother bereft of her child, and Lebanon, that had looked dignified a week before, when the moon was full and our spirits were happy, looked sorrowful and lonesome that night.

We stood up and bade each other farewell, but love and despair stood between us like two ghosts, one stretching his wings with his fingers over our throats, one weeping and the other laughing hideously.

As I took Selma's hand and put it to my lips, she came close to me and placed a kiss on my forehead, then dropped on the wooden bench. She shut her eyes and whispered softly, "Oh, Lord God, have mercy on me and mend my broken wings!"

As I left Selma in the garden, I felt as if my senses were covered with a thick veil, like a lake whose surface is concealed by fog.

The beauty of trees, the moonlight, the deep silence, everything about me looked ugly and horrible. The true light that had showed me the beauty and wonder of the universe was converted to a great flame of fire that seared my heart; and the Eternal music I used to hear became a clamor, more frightening than the roar of a lion.

I reached my room, and like a wounded bird shot down by a hunter, I fell on my bed, repeating the words of Selma: "Oh, Lord God, have mercy on me and mend my broken wings!"

7

Before the Throne of Death

MARRIAGE in these days is a mockery whose management is in the hands of young men and parents. In most countries the young men win while the parents lose. The woman is looked upon as a commodity, purchased and delivered from one house to another. In time her beauty fades and she becomes like an old piece of furniture left in a dark corner.

Modern civilization has made woman a little wiser, but it has increased her suffering because of man's covetousness. The woman of yesterday was a happy wife, but the woman of today is a miserable mistress. In the past she walked blindly in the light, but now she walks open-eyed in the dark. She was beautiful in her ignorance, virtuous in her simplicity, and strong in her weakness. Today she has become ugly in her ingenuity, superficial and heartless in her knowledge. Will the day ever come when beauty and knowledge, ingenuity and virtue, and weakness of body and strength of spirit will be united in a woman?

I am one of those who believe that spiritual progress is a rule of human life, but the approach to perfection is slow and painful. If a woman elevates herself in one respect and is retarded in another, it is because the rough trail that leads to the mountain peak is not free of ambushes of thieves and lairs of wolves.

This strange generation exists between sleeping and waking. It holds in its hands the soil of the past and the seeds of the future. However, we find in every city a woman who symbolizes the future.

In the city of Beirut, Selma Karamy was the symbol of the future Oriental woman, but, like many who live ahead of their time, she became the victim of the present; and like a flower snatched from its stem and carried away by the current of a river, she walked in the miserable procession of the defeated.

Mansour Bey Galib and Selma were married, and lived together in a beautiful house at Ras Beyrouth, where all the wealthy dignitaries resided. Farris Effandi Karamy was left in his solitary home in the midst of his garden and orchards like a lonely shepherd amid his flock.

The days and merry nights of the wedding passed, but the honeymoon left memories of times of bitter sorrow, as wars leave skulls and dead bones on the battlefield. The dignity of an Oriental wedding inspires the hearts of young men and women, but its termination may drop them like millstones to the bottom of the sea. Their exhilaration is like footprints on sand which remain only till they are washed away by the waves.

Spring departed, and so did summer and autumn, but my love for Selma increased day by day until it became a kind of mute worship, the feeling that an orphan has toward the soul of his mother in Heaven. My yearning was converted to blind sorrow that could see nothing but itself, and the passion that drew tears from my eyes was replaced by perplexity that sucked the blood from my heart, and my sighs of affection became a constant prayer for the happiness of Selma and her husband and peace for her father.

My hopes and prayers were in vain, because Selma's misery was an internal malady that nothing but death could cure.

Mansour Bey was a man to whom all the luxuries of life came easily; but, in spite of that, he was dissatisfied and rapacious. After marrying Selma, he neglected her father in his loneliness and prayed for his death so that he could inherit what was left of the old man's wealth.

Mansour Bey's character was similar to his uncle's; the only difference between the two was that the Bishop got everything he wanted secretly, under the protection of his ecclesiastical robe and the golden cross which he wore on his chest, while his nephew did everything publicly. The Bishop went to church in the morning and spent the rest of the day pilfering from the widows, orphans, and simple-minded people. But Mansour Bey spent his days in pursuit of sexual satisfaction. On Sunday, Bishop Bulos Galib preached his Gospel; but during weekdays he never practiced what he preached, occupying himself with the political intrigues of the locality. And, by means of his uncle's prestige and influence, Mansour Bey made it his business to secure political plums for those who could offer a sufficient bribe.

Bishop Bulos was a thief who hid himself under the cover of night, while his nephew, Mansour Bey, was a swindler who walked proudly in daylight. However, the people of Oriental nations place trust in such as they—wolves and butchers who ruin their country through covetousness and crush their neighbors with an iron hand.

Why do I occupy these pages with words about the betrayers of poor nations instead of reserving all the space for the story of a miserable woman with a broken heart? Why do I shed tears for oppressed peoples rather than keep all my tears for the memory of a weak woman whose life was snatched by the teeth of death?

But my dear readers, don't you think that such a woman is like a nation that is oppressed by priests and rulers? Don't you believe that thwarted love which leads a woman to the grave is like the despair which pervades the people of the earth? A woman is to a nation as light is to a lamp. Will not the light be dim if the oil in the lamp is low?

Autumn passed, and the wind blew the yellow leaves from the trees, making way for winter, which came howling and crying. I was still in the City of Beirut without a companion save my dreams, which would lift my spirit to the sky and then bury it deep in the bosom of the earth.

The sorrowful spirit finds relaxation in solitude. It abhors people, as a wounded deer deserts the herd and lives in a cave until it is healed or dead.

One day I heard that Farris Effandi was ill. I left my solitary abode and walked to his home, taking a new route, a lonely path between olive trees, avoiding the main road with its rattling carriage wheels.

Arriving at the old man's house, I entered and found Farris Effandi lying on his bed, weak and pale. His eyes were sunken and looked like two deep, dark valleys haunted by the ghosts of pain. The smile which had always enlivened his face was choked with pain and agony; and the bones of his gentle hands looked like naked branches trembling before the tempest. As I approached him and inquired as to his health, he turned his pale face toward me, and on his trembling lips appeared a smile, and he said in a weak voice, "Go—go, my son, to the other room and comfort Selma and bring her to sit by the side of my bed."

I entered the adjacent room and found Selma lying on a divan, covering her head with her arms and burying her face in a pillow so that her father would not hear her weeping. Approaching slowly, I pronounced her name in a voice that seemed more like sighing than whispering. She moved fearfully, as if she had been interrupted in a terrible dream, and sat up, looking at me with glazed eyes, doubting whether I was a ghost or a living being. After a deep silence which took us back on the wings of memory to that hour when we were intoxicated with the wine of love, Selma wiped away her tears and said, "See how time has changed us! See how time has changed the course of our lives and left us in these ruins. In this place spring united us in a bond of love, and in this place has brought us together before the throne of death. How beautiful was spring, and how terrible is this winter!"

Speaking thus, she covered her face again with her hands as if she were shielding her eyes from the spectre of the past standing before her. I put my hand on her head and said, "Come, Selma, come and let us be as strong towers before the tempest. Let us stand like brave soldiers before the enemy and face his weapons. If we are killed, we shall die as martyrs; and if we win, we shall live as heroes. Braving obstacles and hardships is nobler than retreat to tranquility. The butterfly that hovers around the lamp until it dies is more admirable than the mole that lives in a dark tunnel. Come, Selma, let us walk this rough path firmly, with our eyes toward the sun so that we may not see the skulls and serpents among the rocks and thorns. If fear should stop us in the middle of the road, we would hear only ridicule from the voices of the night, but if we reach the mountain peak bravely we shall join the heavenly spirits in songs of triumph and joy. Cheer up, Selma, wipe away your tears and remove the sorrow from your face. Rise, and let us sit by the bed of your father, because his life depends on your life, and your smile is his only cure."

Kindly and affectionately she looked at me and said, "Are you asking me to have patience, while you are in need of it yourself? Will a hungry man give his bread to another hungry man? Or will a sick man give medicine to another which he himself needs badly?"

She rose, her head bent slightly forward, and we walked to the old man's room and sat by the side of his bed. Selma forced a smile and pretended to be patient, and her father tried to make her believe that he was feeling better and getting stronger; but both father and daughter were aware of each other's sorrow and heard the unvoiced sighs. They were like two equal forces, wearing each other away silently. The father's heart was melting because of his daughter's plight. They were two pure souls, one departing and the other agonized with grief, embracing in love and death; and I was between the two with my own troubled heart. We were three people, gathered and crushed by the hands of destiny; an old man like a dwelling ruined by flood, a young woman whose symbol was a lily beheaded by the sharp edge of a sickle, and a young man who was a weak sapling, bent by a snowfall; and all of us were toys in the hands of fate.

Farris Effandi moved slowly and stretched his weak hand toward Selma, and in a loving and tender voice said, "Hold my hand, my beloved." Selma held his hand; then he said, "I have lived long enough, and I have enjoyed the fruits of life's seasons. I have experienced all its phases with equanimity. I lost your mother when you were three years of age, and she left you as a precious treasure in my lap. I watched you grow, and your face reproduced your mother's features as stars reflected in a calm pool of water. Your character, intelligence, and beauty are your mother's, even your manner of speaking and gestures. You have been my only consolation in this life because you were the image of your mother in every deed and word. Now, I grow old, and my only resting place is between the soft wings of death. Be comforted, my beloved daughter, because I have lived long enough to see you as a woman. Be happy because I shall live in you after my death. My departure today would be no different from my going to-morrow or the day after, for our days are perishing like the leaves of autumn. The hour of my death approaches rapidly, and my soul is desirous of being united with your mother's."

As he uttered these words sweetly and lovingly, his face was radiant. Then he put his hand under his pillow and pulled out a small picture in a gold frame. With his eyes on the little photograph, he said, "Come, Selma, come and see your mother in this picture."

Selma wiped away her tears, and after gazing long at the picture, she kissed it repeatedly and cried, "Oh, my be-loved mother! Oh, mother!" Then she placed her trem-bling lips on the picture as if she wished to pour her soul into that image.

The most beautiful word on the lips of mankind is the word "Mother," and the most beautiful call is the call of "My mother." It is a word full of hope and love, a sweet and kind word coming from the depths of the heart. The mother is every thing—she is our consolation in sorrow, our hope in misery, and our strength in weakness. She is the source of love, mercy, sympathy, and forgiveness. He who loses his mother loses a pure soul who blesses and guards him constantly.

Every thing in nature bespeaks the mother. The sun is the mother of earth and gives it its nourishment of heat;

it never leaves the universe at night until it has put the earth to sleep to the song of the sea and the hymn of birds and brooks. And this earth is the mother of trees and flowers. It produces them, nurses them, and weans them. The trees and flowers become kind mothers of their great fruits and seeds. And the mother, the prototype of all existence, is the eternal spirit, full of beauty and love.

Selma Karamy never knew her mother because she had died when Selma was an infant, but Selma wept when she saw the picture and cried, "Oh, mother!" The word mother is hidden in our hearts, and it comes upon our lips in hours of sorrow and happiness as the perfume comes from the heart of the rose and mingles with clear and cloudy air.

Selma stared at her mother's picture, kissing it repeatedly, until she collapsed by her father's bed.

The old man placed both hands on her head and said, "I have shown you, my dear child, a picture of your mother on paper. Now listen to me and I shall let you hear her words."

She lifted her head like a little bird in the nest that hears its mother's wing, and looked at him attentively.

Farris Effandi opened his mouth and said, "Your mother was nursing you when she lost her father; she cried and wept at his going, but she was wise and patient. She sat by me in this room as soon as the funeral was over and held my hand and said, 'Farris, my father is dead now and you are my only consolation in this world. The heart's affections are divided like the branches of the cedar tree; if the tree loses one strong branch, it will suffer but it does not die. It will pour all its vitality into the next branch so that it will grow and fill the empty place.' This is what your mother told me when her father died, and you should say the same thing when death takes my body to its resting place and my soul to God's care."

Selma answered him with falling tears and broken heart, "When Mother lost her father, you took his place; but who is going to take yours when you are gone? She was left in the care of a loving and truthful husband; she found consolation in her little daughter, and who will be my consolation when you pass away? You have been my father and mother and the companion of my youth."

Saying these words, she turned and looked at me, and, holding the side of my garment, said, "This is the only friend I shall have after you are gone, but how can he console me when he is suffering also? How can a broken heart find consolation in a disappointed soul? A sorrowful woman cannot be comforted by her neighbor's sorrow, nor can a bird fly with broken wings. He is the friend of my soul, but I have already placed a heavy burden of sorrow upon him and dimmed his eyes with my tears till he can see nothing but darkness. He is a brother whom I dearly love, but he is like all brothers who share my sorrow and help me shed tears which increase my bitterness and burn my heart."

Selma's words stabbed my heart, and I felt that I could bear no more. The old man listened to her with depressed spirit, trembling like the light of a lamp before the wind. Then he stretched out his hand and said, "Let me go peacefully, my child. I have broken the bars of this cage; let me fly and do not stop me, for your mother is calling me. The sky is clear and the sea is calm and the boat is ready to sail; do not delay its voyage. Let my body rest with those who are resting; let my dream end and my soul awaken with the dawn; let your soul embrace mine and give me the kiss of hope; let no drops of sorrow or bitterness fall upon my body lest the flowers and grass refuse their nourishment. Do not shed tears of misery upon my hand, for they may grow thorns upon my grave. Do not draw lines of agony upon my forehead, for the wind may pass and read them and refuse to carry the dust of my bones to the green prairies . . . I loved you, my child, while I lived, and I shall love you when I am dead, and my soul shall always watch over you and protect you."

Then Farris Effandi looked at me with his eyes half closed and said, "My son, be a real brother to Selma as your father was to me. Be her help and friend in need, and do not let her mourn, because mourning for the dead is a mistake. Repeat to her pleasant tales and sing for her the songs of life so that she may forget her sorrows. Remember me to your father; ask him to tell you the stories of our youth and tell him that I loved him in the person of his son in the last hour of my life."

Silence prevailed, and I could see the pallor of death on the old man's face. Then he rolled his eyes and looked at us and whispered, "Don't call the physician, for he might extend my sentence in this prison by his medicine. The days of slavery are gone, and my soul seeks the freedom of the skies. And do not call the priest to my bedside, because his incantations would not save me if I were a sinner, nor would it rush me to Heaven if I were innocent. The will of humanity cannot change the will of God, as an astrologer cannot change the course of the stars. But after my death let the doctors and priest do what they please, for my ship will continue sailing until it reaches its destination."

At midnight Farris Effandi opened his tired eyes for the last time and focused them on Selma, who was kneeling by his bedside. He tried to speak, but could not, for death had already choked his voice; but he finally managed to say, "The night has passed . . . Oh, Selma . . . Oh . . . Oh, Selma . . ." Then he bent his head, his face turned white, and I could see a smile on his lips as he breathed his last.

Selma felt her father's hand. It was cold. Then she raised her head and looked at his face. It was covered with the veil of death. Selma was so choked that she could not shed tears, nor sigh, nor even move. For a moment she stared at him with fixed eyes like those of a statue; then she bent down until her forehead touched the floor, and said, "Oh, Lord, have mercy and mend our broken wings."

Farris Effandi Karamy died; his soul was embraced by Eternity, and his body was returned to the earth. Mansour Bey Galib got possession of his wealth, and Selma became a prisoner for life—a life of grief and misery.

I was lost in sorrow and reverie. Days and nights preyed upon me as the eagle ravages its victim. Many a time I tried to forget my misfortune by occupying myself with books and scriptures of past generations, but it was like extinguishing fire with oil, for I could see nothing in the procession of the past but tragedy and could hear nothing but weeping and wailing. The Book of Job was more fascinating to me than the Psalms and I preferred the Elegies of Jeremiah to the Song of Solomon. *Hamlet* was closer to my heart than all other dramas of western writers. Thus despair weakens our sight and closes our ears. We can see nothing but spectres of doom, and can hear only the beating of our agitated hearts.

8

Between Christ and Ishtar

In the midst of the gardens and hills which connect the city of Beirut with Lebanon there is a small temple, very ancient, dug out of white rock, surrounded by olive, almond, and willow trees. Although this temple is a half mile from the main highway, at the time of my story very few people interested in relics and ancient ruins had visited it. It was one of many interesting places hidden and forgotten in Lebanon. Due to its seclusion, it had become a haven for worshipers and a shrine for lonely lovers.

As one enters this temple he sees on the wall at the east side an old Phoenician picture, carved in the rock, depicting Ishtar, goddess of love and beauty, sitting on her throne, surrounded by seven nude virgins standing in different poses. The first one carries a torch; the second, a guitar; the third, a censer; the fourth, a jug of wine; the fifth, a branch of roses; the sixth, a wreath of laurel; the seventh, a bow and arrow; and all of them look at Ishtar reverently.

On the second wall there is another picture, more modern than the first one, symbolizing Christ nailed to the cross,

49

and at His side stand His sorrowful mother and Mary Magdalene and two other women weeping. This Byzantine picture shows that it was carved in the fifteenth or sixteenth century.*

On the west side wall there are two round transits through which the sun's rays enter the temple and strike the pictures and make them look as if they were painted with gold water color. In the middle of the temple there is a square marble with old paintings on its sides, some of which can hardly be seen under the petrified lumps of blood which show that the ancient people offered sacrifices on this rock and poured perfume, wine, and oil upon it.

There is nothing else in that little temple except deep silence, revealing to the living the secrets of the goddess and speaking wordlessly of past generations and the evolution of religions. Such a sight carries the poet to a world far away from the one in which he dwells and convinces the philosopher that men were born religious; they felt a need for that which they could not see and drew symbols, the meaning of which divulged their hidden secrets and their desires in life and death.

In that unknown temple, I met Selma once every month and spent the hours with her, looking at those strange pictures, thinking of the crucified Christ and pondering upon the young Phoenician men and women who lived, loved and worshipped beauty in the person of Ishtar by burning incense before her statue and pouring perfume on her shrine, people for whom nothing is left to speak

* It is known by the students of relics that most of the Christian churches in the East were temples for the old Phoenician and Greek gods. In Damascus, Antioch and Constantinople, there are many edifices, the walls of which echoed heathen hymns; these places were converted into churches and then into mosques.

except the name, repeated by the march of time before the face of Eternity.

It is hard to write down in words the memories of those hours when I met Selma—those heavenly hours, filled with pain, happiness, sorrow, hope, and misery.

We met secretly in the old temple, remembering the old days, discussing our present, fearing our future, and gradually bringing out the hidden secrets in the depths of our hearts and complaining to each other of our misery and suffering, trying to console ourselves with imaginary hopes and sorrowful dreams. Every now and then we would become calm and wipe our tears and start smiling, forgetting everything except Love; we embraced each other until our hearts melted; then Selma would print a pure kiss on my forehead and fill my heart with ecstasy; I would return the kiss as she bent her ivory neck while her cheeks became gently red like the first ray of dawn on the forehead of hills. We silently looked at the distant horizon where the clouds were colored with the orange ray of sunset.

Our conversation was not limited to love; every now and then we drifted on to current topics and exchanged ideas. During the course of conversation Selma spoke of woman's place in society, the imprint that the past generation had left on her character, the relationship between husband and wife, and the spiritual diseases and corruption which threatened married life. I remember her saying: "The poets and writers are trying to understand the reality of woman, but up to this day they have not understood the hidden secrets of her heart, because they look upon her from behind the sexual veil and see nothing but externals; they look upon her through a magnifying glass of hatefulness and find nothing except weakness and submission."

On another occasion she said, pointing to the carved pictures on the walls of the temple, "In the heart of this rock there are two symbols depicting the essence of a woman's desires and revealing the hidden secrets of her soul, moving between love and sorrow—between affection and sacrifice, between Ishtar sitting on the throne and Mary standing by the cross. The man buys glory and reputation, but the woman pays the price."

No one knew about our secret meetings except God and the flock of birds which flew over the temple. Selma used to come in her carriage to a place named Pasha Park and from there she walked to the temple, where she found me anxiously waiting for her.

We feared not the observer's eyes, neither did our consciences bother us; the spirit which is purified by fire and washed by tears is higher than what the people call shame and disgrace; it is free from the laws of slavery and old customs against the affections of the human heart. That spirit can proudly stand unashamed before the throne of God.

Human society has yielded for seventy centuries to corrupted laws until it cannot understand the meaning of the superior and eternal laws. A man's eyes have become accustomed to the dim light of candles and cannot see the sunlight. Spiritual disease is inherited from one generation to another until it has become a part of the people, who look upon it, not as a disease, but as a natural gift, showered by God upon Adam. If those people found someone free from the germs of this disease, they would think of him with shame and disgrace.

Those who think evil of Selma Karamy because she left her husband's home and met me in the temple are the diseased and weak-minded kind who look upon the healthy and sound as rebels. They are like insects crawling in the dark for fear of being stepped upon by the passers-by.

The oppressed prisoner, who can break away from his jail and does not do so, is a coward. Selma, an innocent and oppressed prisoner, was unable to free herself from slavery. Was she to blame because she looked through the jail window upon the green fields and spacious sky? Will the people count her as being untruthful to her husband because she came from his home to sit by me between Christ and Ishtar? Let the people say what they please; Selma had passed the marshes which submerge other spirits and had landed in a world that could not be reached by the howling of wolves and rattling of snakes. People may say what they want about me, for the spirit who has seen the spectre of death cannot be scared by the faces of thieves; the soldier who has seen the swords glittering over his head and streams of blood under his feet does not care about rocks thrown at him by the children on the streets.

9

The Sacrifice

ONE DAY in the late part of June, as the people left the city for the mountain to avoid the heat of summer, I went as usual to the temple to meet Selma, carrying with me a little book of Andalusian poems. As I reached the temple I sat there waiting for Selma, glancing at intervals at the pages of my book, reciting those verses which filled my heart with ecstasy and brought to my soul the memory of the kings, poets, and knights who bade farewell to Granada, and left, with tears in their eyes and sorrow in their hearts, their palaces, institutions and hopes behind. In an hour I saw Selma walking in the midst of the gardens and approaching the temple, leaning on her parasol as if she were carrying all the worries of the world upon her shoulders. As she entered the temple and sat by me, I noticed some sort of change in her eyes and I was anxious to inquire about it.

Selma felt what was going on in my mind, and she put her hand on my head and said, "Come close to me, come my beloved, come and let me quench my thirst, for the hour of separation has come."

54

I asked her, "Did your husband find out about our meetings here?" She responded, "My husband does not care about me, neither does he know how I spend my time, for he is busy with those poor girls whom poverty has driven into the houses of ill fame; those girls who sell their bodies for bread, kneaded with blood and tears."

I inquired, "What prevents you from coming to this temple and sitting by me reverently before God? Is your soul requesting our separation?"

She answered with tears in her eyes, "No, my beloved, my spirit did not ask for separation, for you are a part of me. My eyes never get tired of looking at you, for you are their light; but if destiny ruled that I should walk the rough path of life loaded with shackles, would I be satisfied if your fate should be like mine?" Then she added, "I cannot say everything, because the tongue is mute with pain and cannot talk; the lips are sealed with misery and cannot move; all I can say to you is that I am afraid you may fall in the same trap I fell in."

Then I asked, "What do you mean, Selma, and of whom are you afraid?" She covered her face with her hands and said, "The Bishop has already found out that once a month I have been leaving the grave which he buried me in."

I inquired, "Did the Bishop find out about our meetings here?" She answered, "If he did, you would not see me here sitting by you; but he is getting suspicious and he informed all his servants and guards to watch me closely. I am feeling that the house I live in and the path I walk on are all eyes watching me, and fingers pointing at me, and ears listening to the whisper of my thoughts."

She was silent for a while, and then she added, with tears pouring down her cheeks, "I am not afraid of the Bishop, for wetness does not scare the drowned, but I am afraid you might fall into the trap and become his prey; you are still young and free as the sunlight. I am not frightened of fate which has shot all its arrows in my breast, but I am afraid the serpent might bite your feet and detain you from climbing the mountain peak where the future awaits you with its pleasure and glory."

I said, "He who has not been bitten by the serpents of light and snapped at by the wolves of darkness will always be deceived by the days and nights. But listen, Selma, listen carefully; is separation the only means of avoiding people's evils and meanness? Has the path of love and freedom been closed and is nothing left except submission to the will of the slaves of death?"

She responded, "Nothing is left save separation and bidding each other farewell."

With rebellious spirit I took her hand and said excitedly, "We have yielded to the people's will for a long time; since the time we met until this hour we have been led by the blind and have worshipped with them before their idols. Since the time I met you we have been in the hands of the Bishop like two balls which he has thrown around as he pleased. Are we going to submit to his will until death takes us away? Did God give us the breath of life to place it under death's feet? Did He give us liberty to make it a shadow for slavery? He who extinguishes his spirit's fire with his own hands is an infidel in the eyes of Heaven, for Heaven set the fire that burns in our spirits. He who does not rebel against oppression is doing himself injustice. I love you, Selma, and you love me, too; and Love is a precious treasure, it is God's gift to sensitive and great spirits. Shall we throw this treasure away and let the pigs scatter it and trample on it? This world is full of wonder and beauty. Why are we living in this narrow tunnel which the Bishop and his assistants have dug out for us? Life is full of happiness and freedom; why don't we take this heavy yoke off our shoulders and break the chains tied to our feet, and walk freely toward peace? Get up and let us leave this small temple for God's great temple. Let us leave this country and all its slavery and ignorance for another country far away and unreached by the hands of the thieves. Let us go to the coast under the cover of night and catch a boat that will take us across the oceans, where we can find a new life full of happiness and understanding. Do not hesitate, Selma, for these minutes are more precious to us than the crowns of kings and more sublime than the thrones of angels. Let us follow the column of light that leads us from this arid desert into the green fields where flowers and aromatic plants grow."

She shook her head and gazed at something invisible on the ceiling of the temple; a sorrowful smile appeared on her lips; then she said, "No, no my beloved. Heaven placed in my hand a cup, full of vinegar and gall; I forced myself to drink it in order to know the full bitterness at the bottom until nothing was left save a few drops, which I shall drink patiently. I am not worthy of a new life of love and peace; I am not strong enough for life's pleasure and sweetness, because a bird with broken wings cannot fly in the spacious sky. The eyes that are accustomed to the dim light of a candle are not strong enough to stare at the sun. Do not talk to me of happiness; its memory makes me suffer. Mention not peace to me; its shadow frightens me; but look at me and I will show you the holy torch which Heaven has lighted in the ashes of my heart—you know that I love you as a mother loves her only child, and Love only taught me to protect you even from myself. It is Love, purified with fire, that stops me from following you to the farthest land. Love kills my desires so that you may live freely and virtuously. Limited love asks for possession of the beloved, but the unlimited asks only for itself. Love that comes between the naïveté and awakening of youth satisfies itself with possessing, and grows with embraces. But Love which is born in the firmament's lap and has descended with the night's secrets is not contented with anything but Eternity and immortality; it does not stand reverently before anything except deity.

"When I knew that the Bishop wanted to stop me from leaving his nephew's house and to take my only pleasure away from me, I stood before the window of my room and looked toward the sea, thinking of the vast countries beyond it and the real freedom and personal independence which can be found there. I felt that I was living close to you, surrounded by the shadow of your spirit, submerged in the ocean of your affection. But all these thoughts which illuminate a woman's heart and make her rebel against old customs and live in the shadow of freedom and justice, made me believe that I am weak and that our love is limited and feeble, unable to stand before the sun's face. I cried like a king whose kingdom and treasures have been usurped, but immediately I saw your face through my tears and your eyes gazing at me and I remembered what you said to me once (*Come, Selma, come and let us be strong towers before the tempest. Let us stand like brave soldiers before the enemy and face his weapons. If we are killed, we shall die as martyrs; and if we win, we shall live as heroes. Braving obstacles and hardships is nobler than retreat to tranquility.*) These words, my beloved, you uttered when the wings of death were hovering around my father's bed; I remembered them yesterday when the wings of despair were hovering above my head. I strengthened myself and felt, while in the darkness of my prison, some sort of precious freedom easing our difficulties and diminishing our sorrows. I found out that our love was as deep as the ocean and as high as the stars and as spacious as the sky. I came here to see you, and in my weak spirit there is a new strength, and this strength is the ability to sacrifice a great thing in order to obtain a greater one; it is the sacrifice of my happiness so that you may remain virtuous and honorable in the eyes of the people and be far away from their treachery and persecution . . .

"In the past, when I came to this place I felt as if heavy chains were pulling down on me, but today I came here with a new determination that laughs at the shackles and shortens the way. I used to come to this temple like a scared phantom, but today I came like a brave woman who feels the urgency of sacrifice and knows the value of suffering, a woman who likes to protect the one she loves from the ignorant people and from her hungry spirit. I used to sit by you like a trembling shadow, but today I came here to show you my true self before Ishtar and Christ.

"I am a tree, grown in the shade, and today I stretched my branches to tremble for a while in the daylight. I came here to tell you good-bye, my beloved, and it is my hope that our farewell will be great and awful like our love. Let our farewell be like fire that bends the gold and makes it more resplendent."

Selma did not allow me to speak or protest, but she looked at me, her eyes glittering, her face retaining its dignity, seeming like an angel worthy of silence and respect. Then she flung herself upon me, something which she had never done before, and put her smooth arms around me and printed a long, deep, fiery kiss on my lips.

As the sun went down, withdrawing its rays from those gardens and orchards, Selma moved to the middle of the temple and gazed long at its walls and corners as if she wanted to pour the light of her eyes on its pictures and symbols. Then she walked forward and reverently knelt before the picture of Christ and kissed His feet, and she whispered, "Oh, Christ, I have chosen Thy Cross and deserted Ishtar's world of pleasure and happiness; I have worn the wreath of thorns and discarded the wreath of laurel and washed myself with blood and tears instead of perfume and scent; I have drunk vinegar and gall from a cup which was meant for wine and nectar; accept me, my Lord, among Thy followers and lead me toward Galilee with those who have chosen Thee, contented with their sufferings and delighted with their sorrows."

Then she rose and looked at me and said, "Now I shall return happily to my dark cave, where horrible ghosts reside. Do not sympathize with me, my beloved, and do not feel sorry for me, because the soul that sees the shadow of God once will never be frightened, thereafter, of the ghosts of devils. And the eye that looks on Heaven once will not be closed by the pains of the world."

Uttering these words, Selma left the place of worship; and I remained there lost in a deep sea of thoughts, absorbed in the world of revelation where God sits on the throne and the angels write down the acts of human beings, and the souls recite the tragedy of life, and the brides of Heaven sing the hymns of love, sorrow and immortality.

Night had already come when I awakened from my swoon and found myself bewildered in the midst of the gardens, repeating the echo of every word uttered by Selma and remembering her silence, her actions, her movements, her expressions and the touch of her hands, until I realized the meaning of farewell and the pain of lonesomeness. I was depressed and heartbroken. It was my first discovery of the fact that men, even if they are born free, will remain slaves of strict laws enacted by their forefathers; and that the firmament, which we imagine as unchanging, is the yielding of today to the will of tomorrow and submission of yesterday to the will of today—Many a time, since that night, I have thought of the spiritual law which made Selma prefer death to life, and many a time I have made a comparison between nobility of sacrifice and happiness of rebellion to find out which one is nobler and more beautiful; but until now I have distilled only one truth out of the whole matter, and this truth is *sincerity*, which makes all our deeds beautiful and honorable. And this *sincerity* was in Selma Karamy.

10

The Rescuer

FIVE YEARS of Selma's marriage passed without bringing children to strengthen the ties of spiritual relation between her and her husband and bind their repugnant souls together.

A barren woman is looked upon with disdain everywhere because of most men's desire to perpetuate themselves through posterity.

The substantial man considers his childless wife as an enemy; he detests her and deserts her and wishes her death. Mansour Bey Galib was that kind of man; materially, he was like earth, and hard like steel and greedy like a grave. His desire of having a child to carry on his name and reputation made him hate Selma in spite of her beauty and sweetness.

A tree grown in a cave does not bear fruit; and Selma, who lived in the shade of life, did not bear children. . . .

The nightingale does not make his nest in a cage lest slavery be the lot of its chicks. . . . Selma was a prisoner of misery and it was Heaven's will that she would not have another prisoner to share her life. The flowers of the field are the children of sun's affection and nature's love; and the children of men are the flowers of love and compassion. . . .

The spirit of love and compassion never dominated Selma's beautiful home at Ras Beyrouth; nevertheless, she knelt down on her knees every night before Heaven and asked God for a child in whom she would find comfort and consolation. . . . She prayed successively until Heaven answered her prayers. . . .

The tree of the cave blossomed to bear fruit at last. The nightingale in the cage commenced making its nest with the feathers of its wings.

Selma stretched her chained arms toward Heaven to receive God's precious gift and nothing in the world could have made her happier than becoming a potential mother. . . .

She waited anxiously, counting the days and looking forward to the time when Heaven's sweetest melody, the voice of her child, should ring in her ears. . . .

She commenced to see the dawn of a brighter future through her tears. . . .

It was in the month of Nisan when Selma was stretched on the bed of pain and labor, where life and death were wrestling. The doctor and the midwife were ready to deliver to the world a new guest. Late at night Selma started her successive cry . . . a cry of life's partition from life . . . a cry of continuance in the firmament of nothingness . . . a cry of a weak force before the stillness of great forces . . . the cry of poor Selma who was lying down in despair under the feet of life and death.

At dawn Selma gave birth to a baby boy. When she opened her eyes she saw smiling faces all over the room, then she looked again and saw life and death still wrestling by her bed. She closed her eyes and cried, saying for the first time, "Oh, my son." The midwife wrapped the infant with silk swaddles and placed him by his mother, but the doctor kept looking at Selma and sorrowfully shaking his head.

The voices of joy woke the neighbors, who rushed into the house to felicitate the father upon the birth of his heir, but the doctor still gazed at Selma and her infant and shook his head. . . .

The servants hurried to spread the good news to Mansour Bey, but the doctor stared at Selma and her child with a disappointed look on his face.

As the sun came out, Selma took the infant to her breast; he opened his eyes for the first time and looked at his mother; then he quivered and closed them for the last time. The doctor took the child from Selma's arms, and on his cheeks fell tears; then he whispered to himself, "He is a departing guest."

The child passed away while the neighbors were celebrating with the father in the big hall at the house and drinking to the health of the heir; and Selma looked at the doctor, and pleaded, "Give me my child and let me embrace him."

Though the child was dead, the sounds of the drinking cups increased in the hall. . . .

He was born at dawn and died at sunrise. . . .

He was born like a thought and died like a sigh and disappeared like a shadow.

He did not live to console and comfort his mother.

His life began at the end of the night and ended at the beginning of the day, like a drop of dew poured by the eyes of the dark and dried by the touch of the light.

A pearl brought by the tide to the coast and returned by the ebb into the depth of the sea. . . .

A lily that has just blossomed from the bud of life and is mashed under the feet of death.

A dear guest whose appearance illuminated Selma's heart and whose departure killed her soul.

This is the life of men, the life of nations, the life of suns, moons and stars.

And Selma focused her eyes upon the doctor and cried, "Give me my child and let me embrace him; give me my child and let me nurse him."

Then the doctor bent his head. His voice choked and he said, "Your child is dead, Madame, be patient."

Upon hearing the doctor's announcement, Selma uttered a terrible cry. Then she was quiet for a moment and smiled happily. Her face brightened as if she had discovered something, and quietly she said, "Give me my child; bring him close to me and let me see him dead."

The doctor carried the dead child to Selma and placed him between her arms. She embraced him, then turned her face toward the wall and addressed the dead infant saying, "You have come to take me away, my child; you have come to show me the way that leads to the coast. Here I am, my child; lead me and let us leave this dark cave."

And in a minute the sun's ray penetrated the window curtains and fell upon two calm bodies lying on a bed, guarded by the profound dignity of silence and shaded by the wings of death. The doctor left the room with tears in his eyes, and as he reached the big hall the celebration was converted into a funeral, but Mansour Bey Galib never uttered a word or shed a tear. He remained standing motionless like a statue, holding a drinking cup with his right hand.

· · · · ·

The second day Selma was shrouded with her white wedding dress and laid in a coffin; the child's shroud was his swaddle; his coffin was his mother's arms; his grave was her calm breast. Two corpses were carried in one coffin, and I walked reverently with the crowd accompanying Selma and her infant to their resting place.

Arriving at the cemetery, Bishop Galib commenced chanting while the other priests prayed, and on their gloomy faces appeared a veil of ignorance and emptiness.

As the coffin went down, one of the bystanders whispered, "This is the first time in my life I have seen two corpses in one coffin." Another one said, "It seems as if the child had come to rescue his mother from her pitiless husband."

A third one said, "Look at Mansour Bey: he is gazing at the sky as if his eyes were made of glass. He does not look like he has lost his wife and child in one day." A fourth one added, "His uncle, the Bishop, will marry him again tomorrow to a wealthier and stronger woman."

The Bishop and the priests kept on singing and chanting until the grave digger was through filling the ditch. Then, the people, individually, approached the Bishop and his nephew and offered their respects to them with sweet words of sympathy, but I stood lonely aside without a soul to console me, as if Selma and her child meant nothing to me.

The farewell-bidders left the cemetery; the grave digger stood by the new grave holding a shovel with his hand.

As I approached him, I inquired, "Do you remember where Farris Effandi Karamy was buried?"

He looked at me for a moment, then pointed at Selma's grave and said, "Right here; I placed his daughter upon him and upon his daughter's breast rests her child, and upon all I put the earth back with this shovel."

Then I said, "In this ditch you have also buried my heart."

As the grave digger disappeared behind the poplar trees, I could not resist any more; I dropped down on Selma's grave and wept.

book 2

the voice
of the
master

Contents

71

CONTENTS

I came to say a word and I shall say it now. But if death prevents me, it will be said by Tomorrow, for Tomorrow never leaves a secret in the book of Eternity.

I came to live in the glory of Love and the light of Beauty, which are the reflections of God. I am here, living, and I cannot be exiled from the domain of life, for through my living word I will live in death.

I came here to be for all and with all, and what I do today in my solitude will be echoed Tomorrow by the multitude.

What I say now with one heart will be said Tomorrow by thousands of hearts.

Kahlil Gibran

THE VOICE OF THE MASTER

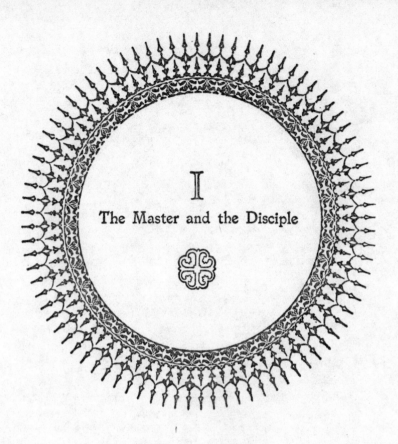

I

The Master and the Disciple

1

The Master's Journey to Venice

AND IT CAME TO PASS that the Disciple saw the Master walking silently to and fro in the garden, and signs of deep sorrow showed upon his pale face. The Disciple greeted the Master in the name of Allah, and inquired after the cause of his grief. The Master motioned with his staff, and bade the Disciple seat himself on the rock by the fish pond. The Disciple did so, and made ready to listen to the Master's story.

Said the Master:

"You desire me to tell you of the tragedy which Memory reenacts every day and night upon the stage of my heart. You are weary of my long silence and my unspoken secret, and you are troubled by my sighs and lamentations. To yourself you say, 'If the Master will not admit me into the temple of his sorrows, how shall I ever enter into the house of his affections?'

"Hearken to my story . . . Listen, but do not pity me; for pity is intended for the weak—and I am still strong in my affliction.

"From the days of my youth, I have been haunted, waking and sleeping, by the phantom of a strange woman. I see her when I am alone at night, sitting by my bedside. In the midnight silence I hear her heavenly voice. Often, when I close my eyes, I feel the touch of her gentle fingers upon my lips; and when I open my eyes, I am overcome with dread, and suddenly begin listening intently to the whispered sounds of Nothingness. . . .

"Often I wonder, saying to myself, 'Is it my fancy that sets me spinning until I seem to lose myself in the clouds? Have I fashioned from the sinews of my dreams a new divinity with a melodious voice and a gentle touch? Have I lost my senses, and in my madness have I created this dearly loved companion? Have I withdrawn myself from the society of men and the clamor of the city so that I might be alone with the object of my adoration? Have I shut my eyes and ears to Life's forms and accents so that I might the better see her and hear her divine voice?'

"Often I wonder: 'Am I a madman who is content to be alone, and from the phantoms of his loneliness fashions a companion and spouse for his soul?'

"I speak of a *Spouse*, and you marvel at that word. But how often are we puzzled by some strange experience, which we reject as impossible, but whose reality we cannot efface from our minds, try as we will?

"This visionary woman has indeed been my spouse, sharing with me all the joys and sorrows of life. When I awake in the morning, I see her bending over my pillow, gazing at me with eyes glowing with kindness and maternal love. She is with me when I plan some undertaking, and she helps me bring it to fulfilment. When I sit down to my repast, she sits with me, and we exchange thoughts and words. In the evening, she is with me again, saying, 'We have tarried too long in this place. Let us walk in the fields and meadows.' Then I leave my work, and follow her into the fields, and we sit on a high rock and gaze at the distant horizon. She points to the golden cloud; and makes me aware of the song the birds sing before they retire for the night, thanking the Lord for the gift of freedom and peace.

"Many a time she comes to my room when I am anxious and troubled. But no sooner do I spy her, than all care and worry are turned to joy and calm. When my spirit rebels against man's injustice to man, and I see her face amidst those other faces I would flee from, the tempest in my heart subsides and is replaced by the heavenly voice of peace. When I am alone, and the bitter darts of life stab at my heart, and I am chained to the earth by life's shackles, I behold my companion gazing at me with love in her eyes, and sorrow turns to joy, and Life seems an Eden of happiness.

"You may ask, how can I be content with such a strange existence, and how can a man, like myself, in the springtime of life, find joy in phantoms and dreams? But I say to you, the years I have spent in this state are the cornerstone of all that I have come to know about Life, Beauty, Happiness, and Peace.

"For the companion of my imagination and I have been like thoughts freely hovering before the face of the sun, or floating on the surface of the waters, singing a song in the moonlight—a song of peace that soothes the spirit and leads it toward ineffable beauty.

"Life is that which we see and experience through the spirit; but the world around us we come to know through our understanding and reason. And such knowledge brings us great joy or sorrow. It was sorrow I was destined to experience before I reached the age of thirty. Would that I had died before I attained the years that drained my heart's blood and my life's sap, and left me a withered tree with branches that no longer move in the frolicsome breeze, and where birds no longer build their nests."

The Master paused, and then, seating himself by his Disciple, continued:

"Twenty years ago, the Governor of Mount Lebanon sent me to Venice on a scholarly mission, with a letter of recommendation to the Mayor of the city, whom he had met in Constantinople. I left Lebanon on an Italian vessel in the month of Nisan. The spring air was fragrant, and the white clouds hung above the horizon like so many lovely paintings. How shall I describe to you the exultation I felt during the journey? Words are too poor and too scant to express the inmost feeling in the heart of man.

"The years I spent with my ethereal companion were filled with contentment, joy, and peace. I never suspected that Pain lay in wait for me, or that Bitterness lurked at the bottom of my cup of Joy.

"As the carriage bore me away from my native hills and valleys, and toward the coast, my companion sat by my side. She was with me during the three joyful days I spent in Beirut, roaming the city with me, stopping where I stopped, smiling when a friend accosted me.

"When I sat on the balcony of the inn, overlooking the city, she joined me in my reveries.

"But when I was about to embark, a great change swept over me. I felt a strange hand seizing hold of me and pulling me back; and I heard a voice within me whispering, 'Turn back! Do not go! Turn back to the shore before the ship sets sail!'

"I did not heed that voice. But when the ship hoisted sail, I felt like a tiny bird that had suddenly been snatched between the claws of a hawk and was being borne aloft into the sky.

"In the evening, as the mountains and hills of Lebanon receded on the horizon, I found myself alone at the prow of the ship. I looked around for the woman of my dreams, the woman my heart loved, the spouse of my days, but she was no longer at my side. The beautiful maiden whose face I saw whenever I gazed at the sky, whose voice I heard in the stillness of the night, whose hand I held whenever I walked the streets of Beirut—was no longer with me.

"For the first time in my life I found myself utterly alone on a boat sailing the deep ocean. I paced the deck, calling to her in my heart, gazing on the waves in the hope of seeing her face. But all in vain. At midnight, when all the other passengers had retired, I remained on deck, alone, troubled, and anxious.

"Suddenly I looked up, and I saw her, the companion of my life, above me, in a cloud, a short distance from the prow. I leaped with joy, opened my arms wide, and cried out, 'Why have you forsaken me, my beloved! Where have you gone? Where have you been? Be near me now, and never leave me alone again!'

"She did not move. On her face I descried signs of sorrow and pain, something I had never seen before. Speaking softly and in sad tones she said, 'I have come from the depths of the ocean to see you once more. Now go down to your cabin, and give yourself over to sleep and dreams.'

"And having uttered these words, she became one with the clouds, and vanished. Like a hungry child I called to her frantically. I opened my arms in all directions, but all they embraced was the night air, heavy with dew.

"I went down to my berth, feeling within me the ebb and flow of the raging elements. It was as if I were on another boat altogether, being tossed on the rough seas of Bewilderment and Despair.

"Strangely enough, as soon as I touched my pillow, I fell fast asleep.

"I dreamt, and in my dream I saw an apple tree shaped like a cross, and hanging from it, as if crucified, was the companion of my life. Drops of blood fell from her hands and feet upon the falling blossoms of the tree.

"The ship sailed on, day and night, but I was as though lost in a trance, not certain whether I was a human being sailing to a distant clime or a ghost moving across a cloudy sky. In vain I implored Providence for the sound of her voice, or a glimpse of her shadow, or the soft touch of her fingers on my lips.

"Fourteen days passed and I was still alone. On the fifteenth day, at noon, we sighted the coast of Italy at a distance, and at dusk we entered the harbor. A throng of people in gaily decorated gondolas came to greet the ship and convey the passengers to the city.

"The City of Venice is situated on many small islands, close to one another. Its streets are canals and its numerous palaces and residences are built on water. Gondolas are the only means of transportation.

"My gondolier asked where I was going, and when I told him to the Mayor of Venice, he looked at me with awe. As we moved through the canals, night was spreading her black cloak over the city. Lights gleamed from the open windows of palaces and churches, and their reflection in the water gave the city the appearance of something seen in a poet's dream, at once charming and enchanting.

"When the gondola reached the junction of two canals, I suddenly heard the mournful ringing of church bells. Though I was in a spiritual trance, and far removed from all reality, the sounds penetrated my heart and depressed my spirits.

"The gondola docked, and tied up at the foot of marble

steps that led to a paved street. The gondolier pointed to a magnificent palace set in the middle of a garden and said: 'Here is your destination.' Slowly I climbed the steps leading to the palace, followed by the gondolier carrying my belongings. When I reached the gate, I paid him and dismissed him with my thanks.

"I rang, and the door was opened. As I entered I was greeted by sounds of wailing and weeping. I was startled and amazed. An elderly servant came toward me, and in a sorrowful voice asked what was my pleasure. 'Is this the palace of the Mayor?' I inquired. He bowed and nodded, and I handed him the missive given me by the Governor of Lebanon. He looked at it and solemnly walked toward the door leading to the reception room.

"I turned to a young servant and asked the cause of the sorrow that pervaded the room. He said that the Mayor's daughter had died that day, and as he spoke, he covered his face and wept bitterly.

"Imagine the feelings of a man who has crossed an ocean, all the while hovering between hope and despair, and at the end of his journey stands at the gate of a palace inhabited by the cruel phantoms of grief and lamentation. Imagine the feelings of a stranger seeking entertainment and hospitality in a palace, only to find himself welcomed by white-winged Death.

"Soon the old servant returned, and bowing, said, 'The Mayor awaits you.'

"He led me to a door at the extreme end of a corridor, and motioned to me to enter. In the reception room I found a throng of priests and other dignitaries, all sunk in deep silence. In the center of the room, I was greeted by an elderly man with a long white beard, who shook my hand and said, 'It is our unhappy lot to welcome you, who come from a distant land, on a day that finds us bereft of our dearest daughter. Yet I trust our bereavement will not interfere with your mission, which, rest assured, I shall do all in my power to advance.'

"I thanked him for his kindness and expressed my deepest grief. Whereupon he led me to a seat, and I joined the rest of the silent throng.

"As I gazed at the sorrowful faces of the mourners, and listened to their painful sighs, I felt my heart contracting with grief and misery.

"Soon one after the other of the mourners took his departure, and only the grief-stricken father and I remained. When I, too, made a movement to leave, he held me back, and said, 'I beg you, my friend, do not go. Be our guest, if you can bear with us in our sorrow.'

"His words touched me deeply, and I bowed in acquiescence, and he continued, 'You men of Lebanon are most open-handed toward the stranger in your land. We should be seriously remiss in our duties were we to be less kind and courteous to our guest from Lebanon.' He rang, and in response to his summons a chamberlain appeared, attired in a magnificent uniform.

" 'Show our guest to the room in the east wing,' he said, 'and take good care of him while he is with us.'

"The chamberlain conducted me to a spacious and lavishly appointed room. As soon as he was gone, I sank down on the couch, and began reflecting on my situation in this foreign land. I reviewed the first few hours I had spent here, so far away from the land of my birth.

"Within a few minutes, the chamberlain returned, bringing my supper on a silver tray. After I had eaten, I began pacing the room, stopping now and then at the window to look out upon the Venetian sky, and to listen to the shouts of the gondoliers and the rhythmic beat of their oars. Before long I became drowsy, and dropping my wearied body on the bed, I gave myself over to an oblivion, in which was mingled the intoxication of sleep and the sobriety of wakefulness.

"I do not know how many hours I spent in this state, for there are vast spaces of life which the spirit traverses, and which we are unable to measure with time, the invention of man. All that I felt then, and feel now, is the wretched condition in which I found myself.

"Suddenly I became aware of a phantom hovering above me, of some ethereal spirit calling to me, but without any sensible signs. I stood up, and made my way toward the hall, as though prompted and drawn by some divine force. I walked, will-less, as if in a dream, feeling as though I were journeying in a world that was beyond time and space.

"When I reached the end of the hall, I threw open a door and found myself in a vast chamber, in the center of which stood a coffin surrounded by flickering candles and wreaths of white flowers. I knelt by the side of the bier and looked upon the departed. There before me, veiled by death, was the face of my beloved, my life-long companion. It was the woman I worshipped, now cold in death, white-shrouded, surrounded by white flowers, and guarded by the silence of the ages.

"O Lord of Love, of Life, and of Death! Thou art the creator of our souls. Thou leadest our spirits toward light and darkness. Thou calmest our hearts and makest them to quicken with hope and pain. Now Thou hast shown me the companion of my youth in this cold and lifeless form.

"Lord, Thou hast plucked me from my land and hast placed me in another, and revealed to me the power of Death over Life, and of Sorrow over Joy. Thou hast planted a white lily in the desert of my broken heart, and hast removed me to a distant valley to show me a withered one.

"Oh friends of my loneliness and exile: God has willed

that I must drink the bitter cup of life. His will be done. We are naught but frail atoms in the heaven of the infinite; and we cannot but obey and surrender to the will of Providence.

"If we love, our love is neither from us, nor is it for us. If we rejoice, our joy is not in us, but in Life itself. If we suffer, our pain lies not in our wounds, but in the very heart of Nature.

"I do not complain, as I tell this tale; for he who complains doubts Life, and I am a firm believer. I believe in the worth of the bitterness mingled in each potion that I drink from the cup of Life. I believe in the beauty of the sorrow that penetrates my heart. I believe in the ultimate mercy of these steel fingers that crush my soul.

"This is my story. How can I end it, when in truth it has no ending?

"I remained on my knees before that coffin, lost in silence, and I stared at that angelic face until dawn came. Then I stood up and returned to my room, bowed under the heavy weight of Eternity, and sustained by the pain of suffering humanity.

"Three weeks later I left Venice and returned to Lebanon. It was as though I had spent aeons of years in the vast and silent depths of the past.

"But the vision remained. Though I had found her again only in death, in me she was still alive. In her shadow I have labored and learned. What those labors were, you, my disciple, know well.

"The knowledge and wisdom I have acquired I strove to bring to my people and their rulers. I brought to Al-Haris, Governor of Lebanon, the cry of the oppressed, who were being crushed under the injustices and evils of his State and Church officials.

"I counseled him to follow the path of his forefathers

and to treat his subjects as they had done, with clemency, charity, and understanding. And I said to him, 'The people are the glory of our kingdom and the source of its wealth.' And I said further, 'There are four things a ruler should banish from his realm: Wrath, Avarice, Falsehood, and Violence.'

"For this and other teachings I was chastised, sent into exile, and excommunicated by the Church.

"There came a night when Al-Haris, troubled in heart, was unable to sleep. Standing at his window, he contemplated the firmament. Such marvels! So many heavenly bodies lost in the infinite! Who created this mysterious and admirable world? Who directs these stars in their courses? What relation have these distant planets to ours? Who am I and why am I here? All these things Al-Haris said to himself.

"Then he remembered my banishment and repented of the harsh treatment he had meted out to me. At once he sent for me, imploring my pardon. He honored me with an official robe and proclaimed me before all the people as his advisor, placing a golden key in my hand.

"For my years in exile I regret nothing. He who would seek Truth and proclaim it to mankind is bound to suffer. My sorrows have taught me to understand the sorrows of my fellow men; neither persecution nor exile have dimmed the vision within me.

"And now I am tired . . ."

Having finished his story, the Master dismissed his Disciple, whose name was Almuhtada, which means "the Convert," and went up to his retreat to rest body and soul from the fatigues of ancient memories.

2

The Death of the Master

Two weeks later, the Master fell ill, and a multitude of admirers came to the hermitage to inquire after his health. When they reached the gate of the garden, they saw coming out of the Master's quarters a priest, a nun, a doctor, and Almuhtada. The beloved Disciple announced the death of the Master. The crowd began to wail and lament, but Almuhtada neither wept nor spoke a word.

For a time the Disciple pondered within himself, then he stood upon the rock by the fish pond, and spoke:

"Brothers and countrymen: You have just heard the news of the Master's death. The immortal Prophet of Lebanon has given himself over to eternal sleep, and his blessed soul is hovering over us in the heavens of the spirit, high beyond all sorrow and mourning. His soul has cast off the servitude of the body and the fever and burdens of this earthly life.

"The Master has left this world of matter, attired in the garments of glory, and has gone to another world free of hardships and afflictions. He is now where our eyes cannot see him and our ears cannot hear him. He dwells in the world of the spirit, whose inhabitants sorely need him. He is now gathering knowledge in a new cosmos, whose history and beauty have always fascinated him and whose speech he has always striven to learn.

"His life on this earth was one long chain of great deeds. It was a life of constant thought; for the Master knew no rest except in work. He loved work, which he defined as *Visible Love.*

"His was a thirsty soul that could not rest except in the lap of wakefulness. His was a loving heart that overflowed with kindness and zeal.

"Such was the life he led on this earth. . . .

"He was a spring of knowledge that issued from the bosom of Eternity, a pure stream of wisdom that waters and refreshes the mind of Man.

"And now that river has reached the shores of Eternal Life. Let no intruder lament for him or shed tears at his departure!

"Remember, only those who have stood before the Temple of Life, and never fructified the earth with one drop of the sweat of their brow are deserving your tears and lamentations when they leave it.

"But as for the Master—did he not spend all the days of his life laboring for the benefit of Mankind? Is there any among you who has not drunk from the pure fountain of his wisdom? And so, if you wish to honor him, offer his blessed soul a hymn of praise and thanksgiving, and not your mournful dirges and laments. If you wish to pay him due reverence, assert your claim to a portion of the knowledge in the books of wisdom he has left as a legacy to the world.

"Do not *give* to genius, but *take* from him! Thus only shall you be honoring him. Do not mourn for him, but be merry, and drink deeply of his wisdom. Only thus will you be paying him the tribute rightly his."

After hearing the words of the Disciple, the multitude returned to their homes, with smiles upon their lips, and songs of thanksgiving in their hearts.

Almuhtada was left alone in this world; but loneliness never possessed his heart, for the voice of the Master always resounded in his ears, urging him to carry on his work and sow the words of the Prophet in the hearts and minds of all who would listen of their own free will. He spent many hours alone in the garden meditating upon the scrolls which the Master had bequeathed to him, and in which he had set down his words of wisdom.

After forty days of meditation, Almuhtada left his Master's retreat and began his wanderings through the hamlets, villages, and cities of Ancient Phoenicia.

One day, as he was crossing the market place of the city of Beirut, a multitude followed him. He stopped at a public walk, and the throng gathered around him, and he spoke to them with the voice of the Master, saying:

"The tree of my heart is heavy with fruit; come, ye hungry ones, and gather it. Eat and be satisfied. . . . Come and receive from the bounty of my heart and lighten my burden. My soul is weary under the weight of gold and silver. Come, ye seekers after hidden treasures, fill your purses and relieve me of my burden. . . .

"My heart overflows with the wine of the ages. Come, all ye thirsty ones, drink and quench your thirst.

"The other day I saw a rich man standing at the temple door, stretching out his hands, which were full of precious stones, toward all passers-by, and calling to them, saying: 'Have pity on me. Take these jewels from me. For they have made my soul sick and hardened my heart. Pity me, take them, and make me whole again.'

"But none of the passers-by paid heed to his pleas.

"And I looked at the man, and I said to myself, 'Surely it were better for him to be a pauper, roaming the streets of Beirut, stretching out a trembling hand for alms, and returning home at eventide empty-handed.'

"I have seen a wealthy and open-handed sheik of Damascus, pitching his tents in the wilderness of the Arabian desert, and by the sides of the mountains. In the evening he sent his slaves out to waylay travelers and bring them to his tents to be sheltered and entertained. But the rough roads were deserted, and the servants brought him no guests.

"And I pondered the plight of the lonely sheik, and my heart spoke to me, saying: 'Surely it is better for him to be a straggler, with a staff in his hand and an empty bucket hanging from his arm, sharing at noontide the bread of friendship with his companions by the refuse heaps at the edge of the city. . . .'

"In Lebanon I saw the Governor's daughter rising from her slumber, attired in a precious gown. Her hair was sprinkled with musk and her body was anointed with perfume. She walked into the garden of her father's palace, seeking a lover. The dewdrops upon the carpeted grass moistened the hem of her garment. But alas! Among all her father's subjects there was no one who loved her.

"As I meditated upon the wretched state of the Governor's daughter, my soul admonished me, saying, 'Were it not better for her to be the daughter of a simple peasant, leading her father's flocks to pasture and bringing them back to the fold in the evening, with the fragrance of the earth and of the vineyards in her coarse shepherd's gown? At the very least, she could steal away from her father's hut, and in the silence of the night walk toward her beloved, waiting for her by the murmuring brook!'

"The tree of my heart is heavy with fruit. Come, ye hungry souls, gather it, eat and be satisfied. My spirit overflows with aged wine. Come, oh ye thirsty hearts, drink and quench your thirst. . . .

"Would that I were a tree that neither blossoms nor bears fruit; for the pain of fertility is harsher than the bitterness of barrenness; and the ache of the open-handed rich is more terrible than the misery of the wretched poor. . . .

"Would that I were a dry well, so people might throw stones into my depths. For it is better to be an empty well than a spring of pure water untouched by thirsty lips.

"Would I were a broken reed, trampled by the foot of man, for that is better than to be a lyre in the house of one whose fingers are blistered and whose household is deaf to sound.

"Hear me, Oh ye sons and daughters of my motherland; meditate upon these words that come to you through the voice of the Prophet. Make room for them in the precincts of your heart, and let wisdom's seed blossom in the garden of your soul. For that is the precious gift of the Lord."

And the fame of Almuhtada spread all over the land, and many people came to him from other countries to do him reverence and to listen to the spokesman of the Master.

Physicians, men-of-law, poets, philosophers overwhelmed him with questions whenever they would meet him, whether in the street, in the church, in the mosque, or in the synagogue, or any other place where men foregather. Their minds were enriched by his beautiful words, which passed from lips to lips.

He spoke to them of Life and the Reality of Life, saying:

"Man is like the foam of the sea, that floats upon the surface of the water. When the wind blows, it vanishes, as if it had never been. Thus are our lives blown away by Death. . . .

"The Reality of Life is Life itself, whose beginning is not in the womb, and whose ending is not in the grave. For the years that pass are naught but a moment in eternal life; and the world of matter and all in it is but a dream compared to the awakening which we call the terror of Death.

"The ether carries every sound of laughter, every sigh that comes from our hearts, and preserves their echo, which responds to every kiss whose source is joy.

"The angels keep count of every tear shed by Sorrow; and they bring to the ears of the spirits hovering in the heavens of the Infinite each song of Joy wrought from our affections.

"There, in the world to come, we shall see and feel all the vibrations of our feelings and the motions of our hearts. We shall understand the meaning of the divinity within us, whom we contemn because we are prompted by Despair.

"That deed which in our guilt we today call weakness, will appear tomorrow as an essential link in the complete chain of Man.

"The cruel tasks for which we received no reward will live with us, and show forth in splendor, and declare our glory; and the hardships we have sustained shall be as a wreath of laurel on our honored heads . . ."

Having uttered these words, the Disciple was about to withdraw from the crowds and repose his body from the labors of the day, when he spied a young man gazing at a lovely girl, with eyes that reflected bewilderment.

And the Disciple addressed him, saying:

"Are you troubled by the many faiths that Mankind professes? Are you lost in the valley of conflicting beliefs? Do you think that the freedom of heresy is less burdensome than the yoke of submission, and the liberty of dissent safer than the stronghold of acquiescence?

"If such be the case, then make Beauty your religion, and worship her as your godhead; for she is the visible, manifest and perfect handiwork of God. Cast off those who have toyed with godliness as if it were a sham, joining together greed and arrogance; but believe instead in the divinity of beauty that is at once the beginning of your worship of Life, and the source of your hunger for Happiness.

"Do penance before Beauty, and atone for your sins, for Beauty brings your heart closer to the throne of woman, who is the mirror of your affections and the teacher of your heart in the ways of Nature, which is your life's home."

And before dismissing the assembled throng, he added:

"In this world there are two sorts of men: the men of yesterday and the men of tomorrow. To which of these do you belong, my brethren? Come, let me gaze at you, and learn whether you are of those entering into the world of light, or of those going forth into the land of darkness. Come, tell me who you are and what you are.

"Are you a politician who says to himself: 'I will use my country for my own benefit'? If so, you are naught but a parasite living on the flesh of others. Or are you a devoted patriot, who whispers into the ear of his inner self: 'I love to serve my country as a faithful servant.' If so, you are an oasis in the desert, ready to quench the thirst of the way-farer.

"Or are you a merchant, drawing advantage from the needs of the people, engrossing goods so as to resell them at an exorbitant price? If so, you are a reprobate; and it matters naught whether your home is a palace or a prison.

"Or are you an honest man, who enables farmer and weaver to exchange their products, who mediates between buyer and seller, and through his just ways profits both himself and others?

"If so, you are a righteous man; and it matters not whether you are praised or blamed.

"Are you a leader of religion, who weaves out of the simplicity of the faithful a scarlet robe for his body; and of their kindness a golden crown for his head; and while living on Satan's plenty, spews forth his hatred of Satan? If so, you are a heretic; and it matters not that you fast all day and pray all night.

"Or are you the faithful one who finds in the goodness of people a groundwork for the betterment of the whole nation; and in whose soul is the ladder of perfection leading to the Holy Spirit? If you are such, you are like a lily in the garden of Truth; and it matters not if your fragrance is lost upon men, or dispersed into the air, where it will be eternally preserved.

"Or are you a journalist who sells his principles in the markets of slaves and who fattens on gossip and misfortune and crime? If so, you are like a ravenous vulture preying upon rotting carrion.

"Or are you a teacher standing upon the raised stage of history, who, inspired by the glories of the past, preaches to mankind and acts as he preaches? If so, you are a restorative to ailing humanity and a balm for the wounded heart.

"Are you a governor looking down on those you govern,

never stirring abroad except to rifle their pockets or to exploit them for your own profit? If so, you are like tares upon the threshing floor of the nation.

"Are you a devoted servant who loves the people and is ever watchful over their welfare, and zealous for their success? If so, you are as a blessing in the granaries of the land.

"Or are you a husband who regards the wrongs he has committed as lawful, but those of his wife as unlawful? If so, you are like those extinct savages who lived in caves and covered their nakedness with hides.

"Or are you a faithful companion, whose wife is ever at his side, sharing his every thought, rapture, and victory? If so, you are as one who at dawn walks at the head of a nation toward the high noon of justice, reason and wisdom.

"Are you a writer who holds his head high above the crowd, while his brain is deep in the abyss of the past, that is filled with the tatters and useless cast-offs of the ages? If so, you are like a stagnant pool of water.

"Or are you the keen thinker, who scrutinizes his inner self, discarding that which is useless, outworn and evil, but preserving that which is useful and good? If so, you are as manna to the hungry, and as cool, clear water to the thirsty.

"Are you a poet full of noise and empty sounds? If so, you are like one of those mountebanks that make us laugh when they are weeping, and make us weep, when they laugh.

"Or are you one of those gifted souls in whose hands God has placed a viol to soothe the spirit with heavenly music, and bring his fellow men close to Life and the Beauty of Life? If so, you are a torch to light us on our way, a sweet longing in our hearts, and a revelation of the divine in our dreams.

"Thus is mankind divided into two long columns, one composed of the aged and bent, who support themselves on crooked staves, and as they walk on the path of Life, they pant as if they were climbing toward a mountaintop, while they are actually descending into the abyss.

"And the second column is composed of youth, running as with winged feet, singing as if their throats were strung with silver strings, and climbing toward the mountaintop as though drawn by some irresistible, magic power.

"In which of these two processions do you belong, my brethren? Ask yourselves this question, when you are alone in the silence of the night.

"Judge for yourselves whether you belong with the Slaves of Yesterday or the Free Men of Tomorrow."

And Almuhtada returned to his retreat, and kept himself in seclusion for many months, while he read and pondered the words of wisdom the Master had set down in the scrolls bequeathed to him. He learned much; but there were many things he found he had not learned, nor ever heard from the lips of the Master. He vowed that he would not leave the hermitage until he had thoroughly studied and mastered all that the Master had left behind, so that he might deliver it to his countrymen. In this way Almuhtada became engrossed in the perusal of his Master's words, oblivious of himself and all around him, and forgetting all those who had hearkened to him in the market places and streets of Beirut.

In vain his admirers tried to reach him, having become concerned about him. Even when the Governor of Mount Lebanon summoned him with a request that he address the officials of the state, he declined, saying, "I shall come back to you soon, with a special message for all the people."

The Governor decreed that on the day Almuhtada was to appear all citizens should receive and welcome him with honor in their homes, and in the churches, mosques, synagogues, and houses of learning, and they should hearken with reverence to his words, for his was the voice of the Prophet.

The day when Almuhtada finally emerged from his retreat to begin his mission became a day of rejoicing and festivity for all. Almuhtada spoke freely and without hindrance; he preached the gospel of love and brotherhood. No one dared threaten him with exile from the country or excommunication from the Church. How unlike the fate of his Master, whose portion had been banishment and excommunication, before eventual pardon and recall!

Almuhtada's words were heard all over Lebanon. Later they were printed in a book, in the form of epistles, and distributed in Ancient Phoenicia and other Arabic lands. Some of the epistles are in the Master's own words; others were culled by Master and Disciple from ancient books of wisdom and lore.

II

The Words of the Master

1

Of Life

LIFE IS AN ISLAND in an ocean of loneliness, an island whose rocks are hopes, whose trees are dreams, whose flowers are solitude, and whose brooks are thirst.

Your life, my fellow men, is an island separated from all other islands and regions. No matter how many are the ships that leave your shores for other climes, no matter how many are the fleets that touch your coast, you remain a solitary island, suffering the pangs of loneliness and yearning for happiness. You are unknown to your fellow men and far removed from their sympathy and understanding.

My brother, I have seen you sitting on your hillock of gold rejoicing over your riches—proud of your treasures and secure in your belief that each handful of gold you have amassed is an invisible link that joins other men's desires and thoughts with yours.

I have seen you in my mind's eye as a great conqueror leading your troops, intent on the destruction of your enemies' strongholds. But when I looked again, I saw naught but a solitary heart pining behind your coffers of gold, a thirsty bird in a golden cage, with its water tray empty.

I have seen you, my brother, sitting upon the throne of glory, and around you stood your people acclaiming your majesty, and singing praises of your great deeds, extolling your wisdom, and gazing upon you as though in the presence of a prophet, their spirits exulting even to the canopy of heaven.

And as you gazed upon your subjects, I saw in your face the marks of happiness and power and triumph, as if you were the soul of their body.

But when I looked again, behold I found you alone in your loneliness, standing by the side of your throne, an exile stretching his hand in every direction, as if pleading for mercy and kindness from invisible ghosts—begging for shelter, even such as has naught in it but warmth and friendliness.

I have seen you, my brother, enamoured of a beautiful woman, laying down your heart at the altar of her loveliness. When I saw her gazing upon you with tenderness and maternal love, I said to myself, "Long live Love that has done away with this man's loneliness and joined his heart with another's."

Yet, when I looked again, I saw within your loving heart another solitary heart, crying out in vain to reveal its secrets to a woman; and behind your love-filled soul, another lonely soul that was like a wandering cloud, wishing in vain that it might turn into teardrops in the eyes of your beloved. . . .

Your life, my brother, is a solitary habitation separated from other men's dwellings. It is a house into whose interior no neighbor's gaze can penetrate. If it were plunged into darkness, your neighbor's lamp could not illumine it. If it were emptied of provisions, the stores of your neighbors could not fill it. If it stood in a desert, you could not move it into other men's gardens, tilled and planted by other hands. If it stood on a mountaintop, you could not bring it down into the valley trod by other men's feet.

Your spirit's life, my brother, is encompassed by loneliness, and were it not for that loneliness and solitude, you would not be *you*, nor would I be *I*. Were it not for this loneliness and solitude, I would come to believe on hearing your voice that it was my voice speaking; or seeing your face, that it was myself looking into a mirror.

2

Of the Martyrs to Man's Law

ARE YOU ONE who was born in the cradle of sorrow, and reared in the lap of misfortune and in the house of oppression? Are you eating a dry crust, moistened with tears? Are you drinking the turbid water in which are mingled blood and tears?

Are you a soldier compelled by the harsh law of man to forsake wife and children, and go forth into the field of battle for the sake of *Greed*, which your leaders mis-call *Duty*?

Are you a poet content with your crumbs of life, happy in the possession of parchment and ink, and sojourning in your land as a stranger, unknown to your fellow men?

Are you a prisoner, pent up in a dark dungeon for some petty offence and condemned by those who seek to reform man by corrupting him?

Are you a young woman on whom God has bestowed beauty, but who has fallen prey to the base lust of the rich, who deceived you and bought your body but not your heart, and abandoned you to misery and distress?

If you are one of these, you are a martyr to man's law.

You are wretched, and your wretchedness is the fruit of the iniquity of the strong and the injustice of the tyrant, the brutality of the rich, and the selfishness of the lewd and the covetous.

Comfort ye, my beloved weak ones, for there is a Great Power behind and beyond this world of Matter, a Power that is all Justice, Mercy, Pity and Love.

You are like a flower that grows in the shade; the gentle breeze comes and bears your seed into the sunlight, where you will live again in beauty.

You are like the bare tree bowed with winter's snow; Spring shall come and spread her garments of green over you; and Truth shall rend the veil of tears that hides your laughter. I take you unto me, my afflicted brothers, I love you, and I contemn your oppressors.

3

Thoughts and Meditations

LIFE TAKES US UP and bears us from one place to another; Fate moves us from one point to another. And we, caught up between these twain, hear dreadful voices and see only that which stands as a hindrance and obstacle in our path.

Beauty reveals herself to us as she sits on the throne of glory; but we approach her in the name of Lust, snatch off her crown of purity, and pollute her garment with our evil-doing.

Love passes by us, robed in meekness; but we flee from her in fear, or hide in the darkness; or else pursue her, to do evil in her name.

Even the wisest among us bows under the heavy weight of Love; but in truth she is as light as the frolicsome breeze of Lebanon.

Freedom bids us to her table where we may partake of her savory food and rich wine; but when we sit down at her board, we eat ravenously and glut ourselves.

Nature reaches out to us with welcoming arms, and bids us enjoy her beauty; but we dread her silence and rush into the crowded cities, there to huddle like sheep fleeing from a ferocious wolf.

Truth calls to us, drawn by the innocent laughter of a child, or the kiss of a loved one; but we close the doors of affection in her face and deal with her as with an enemy.

The human heart cries out for help; the human soul implores us for deliverance; but we do not heed their cries, for we neither hear nor understand. But the man who hears and understands we call mad, and flee from him.

Thus the nights pass, and we live in unawareness; and the days greet us and embrace us. But we live in constant dread of day and night.

We cling to the earth, while the gate of the Heart of the Lord stands wide open. We trample upon the bread of Life, while hunger gnaws at our hearts. How good is Life to Man; yet how far removed is Man from Life!

4

Of the First Look

IT IS THAT MOMENT that divides the intoxication of Life from the awakening. It is the first flame that lights up the inner domain of the heart. It is the first magic note plucked on the silver string of the heart. It is that brief moment that unfolds before the soul the chronicles of time, and reveals to the eyes the deeds of the night, and the works of conscience. It opens Eternity's secrets of the future. It is the seed cast by Ishtar, goddess of Love, and sown by the eyes of the beloved in the field of Love, brought forth by affection, and reaped by the Soul.

The first glance from the eyes of the beloved is like the spirit that moved upon the face of the waters, giving birth to heaven and earth, when the Lord spoke and said, "Let there be."

Of the First Kiss

IT IS THE FIRST SIP from the cup filled by the goddess with the nectar of Life. It is the dividing line between Doubt that beguiles the spirit and saddens the heart, and Certi-

tude that floods the inner self with joy. It is the beginning
of the song of Life and the first act in the drama of the
Ideal Man. It is the bond that unites the strangeness of
the past with the brightness of the future; the link between the silence of the feelings and their song. It is a word
uttered by four lips proclaiming the heart a throne, Love a
king, and fidelity a crown. It is the gentle touch of the delicate fingers of the breeze on the lips of the rose—uttering
a long sigh of relief and a sweet moan.

It is the beginning of that magic vibration that carries
the lovers from the world of weights and measures into
the world of dreams and revelations.

It is the union of two fragrant flowers; and the mingling
of their fragrance toward the creation of a third soul.

As the first glance is like a seed sown by the goddess in
the field of the human heart, so the first kiss is the first
flower at the tip of the branch of the Tree of Life.

Of Marriage

HERE LOVE BEGINS to render the prose of Life into hymns
and canticles of praise, with music that is set by night, to
be sung in the day. Here Love's longing draws back the
veil, and illumines the recesses of the heart, creating a happiness that no other happiness can surpass but that of the
Soul when she embraces God.

Marriage is the union of two divinities that a third might
be born on earth. It is the union of two souls in a strong
love for the abolishment of separateness. It is that higher
unity which fuses the separate unities within the two spirits. It is the golden ring in a chain whose beginning is a
glance, and whose ending is Eternity. It is the pure rain
that falls from an unblemished sky to fructify and bless
the fields of divine Nature.

As the first glance from the eyes of the beloved is like a seed sown in the human heart, and the first kiss of her lips like a flower upon the branch of the Tree of Life, so the union of two lovers in marriage is like the first fruit of the first flower of that seed.

5

Of the Divinity of Man

SPRING CAME, and Nature began speaking in the murmur of brooks and rivulets and in the smiles of the flowers; and the soul of Man was made happy and content.

Then suddenly Nature waxed furious and laid waste the beautiful city. And man forgot her laughter, her sweetness, and her kindness.

In one hour a frightful, blind force had destroyed what it had taken generations to build. Terrifying death seized man and beast in his claws and crushed them.

Ravaging fires consumed man and his goods; a deep and terrifying night hid the beauty of life under a shroud of ashes. The fearful elements raged and destroyed man, his habitations, and all his handiwork.

Amidst this frightful thunder of Destruction from the bowels of the Earth, amidst all this misery and ruin, stood the poor Soul, gazing upon all this from a distance, and meditating sorrowfully upon the weakness of Man and the omnipotence of God. She reflected upon the enemy of Man hidden deep beneath the layers of the earth and among the atoms of the ether. She heard the wailing of the mothers and of the hungry children and she shared their suffering. She pondered the savagery of the elements and the smallness of Man. And she recalled how only yesterday the children of Man had slept safely in their homes —but today they were homeless fugitives, bewailing their beautiful city as they gazed upon it from a distance, their hope turned to despair, their joy to sorrow, their life of peace to warfare. She suffered with the brokenhearted, who were caught in the iron claws of Sorrow, Pain, and Despair.

And as the Soul stood there pondering, suffering, doubting the justice of the Divine Law that binds all of the world's forces, she whispered into the ear of Silence:

"Behind all this creation there is eternal Wisdom that brings forth wrath and destruction, but which will yet bring forth unpredictable beauty.

"For fire, thunder, and tempests are to the Earth what hatred, envy and evil are to the human heart. While the afflicted nation was filling the firmament with groans and lamentations, Memory brought to my mind all the warnings and calamities and tragedies that have been enacted on the stage of Time.

"I saw Man, throughout history, erecting towers, palaces, cities, temples on the face of the earth; and I saw the earth turn in her fury upon them and snatch them back into her bosom.

"I saw strong men building impregnable castles and I observed artists embellishing their walls with paintings; then I saw the earth gape, open wide her mouth, and swallow all that the skilful hand and the luminous mind of genius had shaped.

"And I knew that the earth is like a beautiful bride who needs no man-made jewels to heighten her loveliness but is content with the green verdure of her fields, and the golden sands of her seashores, and the precious stones on her mountains.

"But man in his Divinity I saw standing like a giant in the midst of Wrath and Destruction, mocking the anger of the earth and the raging of the elements.

"Like a pillar of light Man stood amidst the ruins of Babylon, Nineveh, Palmyra and Pompeii, and as he stood he sang the song of Immortality:

> *Let the Earth take*
> *That which is hers,*
> *For I, Man, have no ending.*"

6

Of Reason and Knowledge

WHEN REASON SPEAKS TO YOU, hearken to what she says, and you shall be saved. Make good use of her utterances, and you shall be as one armed. For the Lord has given you no better guide than Reason, no stronger arm than Reason. When Reason speaks to your inmost self, you are proof against Desire. For Reason is a prudent minister, a loyal guide, and a wise counsellor. Reason is light in darkness, as anger is darkness amidst light. Be wise—let Reason, not Impulse, be your guide.

Yet be mindful that even if Reason be at your side, she is helpless without the aid of Knowledge. Without her blood-sister, Knowledge, Reason is like houseless poverty; and Knowledge without Reason is like a house unguarded. And even Love, Justice, and Goodness avail little if Reason be not there too.

The learned man who has not judgment is like an unarmed soldier proceeding into battle. His wrath will poison the pure spring of the life of his community and he will be like the grain of aloes in a pitcher of pure water.

Reason and learning are like body and soul. Without the

body, the soul is nothing but empty wind. Without the soul, the body is but a senseless frame.

Reason without learning is like the untilled soil, or like the human body that lacks nourishment.

Reason is not like the goods sold in the market places—the more plentiful they are, the less they are worth. Reason's worth waxes with her abundance. But were she sold in the market, it is only the wise man who would understand her true value.

The fool sees naught but folly; and the madman only madness. Yesterday I asked a foolish man to count the fools among us. He laughed and said, "This is too hard a thing to do, and it will take too long. Were it not better to count only the wise?"

Know your own true worth, and you shall not perish. Reason is your light and your beacon of Truth. Reason is the source of Life. God has given you Knowledge, so that by its light you may not only worship him, but also see yourself in your weakness and strength.

If you do not descry the mote in your own eye, surely you will not see it in your neighbor's.

Each day look into your conscience and amend your faults; if you fail in this duty you will be untrue to the Knowledge and Reason that are within you.

Keep a watchful eye over yourself as if you were your own enemy; for you cannot learn to govern yourself, unless you first learn to govern your own passions and obey the dictates of your conscience.

I once heard a learned man say, "Every evil has its remedy, except folly. To reprimand an obstinate fool or to preach to a dolt is like writing upon the water. Christ healed the blind, the halt, the palsied, and the leprous. But the fool He could not cure.

"Study a question from all sides, and you will be sure to discover where error has crept in.

"When the portal of your house is wide, see to it that the postern-gate be not too narrow.

"He who tries to seize an opportunity after it has passed him by is like one who sees it approach but will not go to meet it."

God does not work evil. He gives us Reason and Learning so that we may ever be on our guard against the pitfalls of Error and Destruction.

Blessed are they on whom God has conferred the gift of Reason.

7

Of Music

I sat by one whom my heart loves, and I listened to her words. My soul began to wander in the infinite spaces where the universe appeared like a dream, and the body like a narrow prison.

The enchanting voice of my Beloved entered my heart.

This is Music, oh friends, for I heard her through the sighs of the one I loved, and through the words, half-uttered between her lips.

With the eyes of my hearing I saw my Beloved's heart.

My friends: Music is the language of spirits. Its melody is like the frolicsome breeze that makes the strings quiver with love. When the gentle fingers of Music knock at the door of our feelings, they awaken memories that have long lain hidden in the depths of the Past. The sad strains of Music bring us mournful recollections; and her quiet strains bring us joyful memories. The sound of strings makes us weep at the departure of a dear one, or makes us smile at the peace God has bestowed upon us.

The soul of Music is of the Spirit, and her mind is of the Heart.

When God created Man, he gave him Music as a language different from all other languages. And early man sang her glory in the wilderness; and she drew the hearts of kings and moved them from their thrones.

Our souls are like tender flowers at the mercy of the winds of Destiny. They tremble in the morning breeze, and bend their heads under the falling dews of heaven.

The song of the bird awakens Man from his slumber, and invites him to join in the psalms of glory to Eternal Wisdom that has created the song of the bird.

Such music makes us ask ourselves the meaning of the mysteries contained in ancient books.

When the birds sing, do they call to the flowers in the fields, or are they speaking to the trees, or are they echoing the murmur of the brooks? For Man with his understanding cannot know what the bird is saying, nor what the brook is murmuring, nor what the waves whisper when they touch the beaches slowly and gently.

Man with his understanding cannot know what the rain is saying when it falls upon the leaves of the trees or when it taps at the window panes. He cannot know what the breeze is saying to the flowers in the fields.

But the Heart of Man can feel and grasp the meaning of these sounds that play upon his feelings. Eternal Wisdom often speaks to him in a mysterious language; Soul and Nature converse together, while Man stands speechless and bewildered.

Yet has not Man wept at the sounds? And are not his tears eloquent understanding?

Divine Music!
Daughter of the Soul of Love

Vase of bitterness and of
Love

Dream of the human heart, fruit
of sorrow

Flower of joy, fragrance and
bloom of feeling

Tongue of lovers, revealer of
secrets

Mother of the tears of hidden love

Inspirer of poets, composers,
architects

Unity of thoughts within fragments
of words

Designer of love out of beauty
Wine of the exulting heart in
a world of dreams

Heartener of warriors, and strengthener
of souls
Ocean of mercy and sea of tenderness

O Music
In your depths we deposit our hearts
and souls
Thou hast taught us to see with our
ears
And hear with our hearts.

8

Of Wisdom

THE WISE MAN is he who loves and reveres God. A man's merit lies in his knowledge and in his deeds, not in his color, faith, race, or descent. For remember, my friend, the son of a shepherd who possesses knowledge is of greater worth to a nation than the heir to the throne, if he be ignorant. Knowledge is your true patent of nobility, no matter who your father or what your race may be.

Learning is the only wealth tyrants cannot despoil. Only death can dim the lamp of knowledge that is within you. The true wealth of a nation lies not in its gold or silver but in its learning, wisdom, and in the uprightness of its sons.

The riches of the spirit beautify the face of man and give birth to sympathy and respect. The spirit in every being is made manifest in the eyes, the countenance, and in all bodily movements and gestures. Our appearance, our words, our actions are never greater than ourselves. For the soul is our house; our eyes its windows; and our words its messengers.

Knowledge and understanding are life's faithful companions who will never prove untrue to you. For knowledge is your crown, and understanding your staff; and when they are with you, you can possess no greater treasures.

He who understands you is greater kin to you than your own brother. For even your own kindred may neither understand you nor know your true worth.

Friendship with the ignorant is as foolish as arguing with a drunkard.

God has bestowed upon you intelligence and knowledge. Do not extinguish the lamp of Divine Grace and do not let the candle of wisdom die out in the darkness of lust and error. For a wise man approaches with his torch to light up the path of mankind.

Remember, one just man causes the Devil greater affliction than a million blind believers.

A little knowledge that *acts* is worth infinitely more than much knowledge that is idle.

If your knowledge teaches you not the value of things, and frees you not from the bondage to matter, you shall never come near the throne of Truth.

If your knowledge teaches you not to rise above human weakness and misery and lead your fellow man on the right path, you are indeed a man of little worth and will remain such till Judgment Day.

Learn the words of wisdom uttered by the wise and apply them in your own life. Live them—but do not make a show of reciting them, for he who repeats what he does not understand is no better than an ass that is loaded with books.

9

Of Love and Equality

MY POOR FRIEND, if you only knew that the Poverty which causes you so much wretchedness is the very thing that reveals the knowledge of Justice and the understanding of Life, you would be contented with your lot.

I say knowledge of Justice: for the rich man is too busy amassing wealth to seek this knowledge.

And I say understanding of Life: for the strong man is too eager in his pursuit of power and glory to keep to the straight path of truth.

Rejoice then, my poor friend, for you are the mouth of Justice and the book of Life. Be content, for you are the source of virtue in those who rule over you and the pillar of integrity of those who guide you.

If you could see, my sorrowful friend, that the misfortune which has defeated you in life is the very power that illumines your heart and raises your soul from the pit of derision to the throne of reverence, you would be content with your share and you would look upon it as a legacy to instruct you and make you wise.

For Life is a chain made up of many diverse links. Sorrow is one golden link between submission to the present and the promised hope of the future.

It is the dawn between slumber and awakening.

My fellow poor, Poverty sets off the nobility of the spirit, while wealth discloses its evil. Sorrow softens the feelings, and Joy heals the wounded heart. Were Sorrow and Poverty abolished, the spirit of man would be like an empty tablet, with naught inscribed save the signs of selfishness and greed.

Remember that Divinity is the true self of Man. It cannot be sold for gold; neither can it be heaped up as are the riches of the world today. The rich man has cast off his Divinity, and has clung to his gold. And the young today have forsaken their Divinity and pursue self-indulgence and pleasure.

My beloved poor, the hour you spend with your wife and your children when you return home from the field is the earnest of all human families to come; it is the emblem of the happiness that will be the lot of all coming generations.

But the life that the rich man spends in heaping up gold is in truth like the life of the worms in the grave. It is a sign of fear.

The tears you shed, my sorrowful friend, are purer than the laughter of him that seeks to forget and sweeter than the mockery of the scoffer. These tears cleanse the heart of the blight of hatred, and teach man to share the pain of the brokenhearted. They are the tears of the Nazarene.

The strength you sow for the rich you shall reap in time to come, for all things return to their source, according to the Law of Nature.

And the sorrow you have borne shall be turned to gladness by the will of Heaven.

And generations to come shall learn of Sorrow and Poverty a lesson of Love and Equality.

10

Further Sayings of the Master

I HAVE BEEN HERE since the beginning, and I shall be until the end of days; for there is no ending to my existence. The human soul is but a part of a burning torch which God separated from Himself at Creation.

My brothers, seek counsel of one another, for therein lies the way out of error and futile repentance. The wisdom of the many is your shield against tyranny. For when we turn to one another for counsel we reduce the number of our enemies.

He who does not seek advice is a fool. His folly blinds him to Truth and makes him evil, stubborn, and a danger to his fellow man.

When you have grasped a problem clearly, face it with resolution, for that is the way of the strong.

Seek ye counsel of the aged, for their eyes have looked on the faces of the years and their ears have hearkened to the voices of Life. Even if their counsel is displeasing to you, pay heed to them.

Do not expect good counsel from a tyrant, or a wrong-doer, or a presumptuous man, or a deserter from honor. Woe to him who conspires with the wrongdoer who comes seeking advice. For to agree with the wrongdoer is infamy, and to hearken to that which is false is treachery.

Unless I be endowed with wide knowledge, keen judg-ment and great experience, I cannot account myself a counsellor of men.

Make haste slowly, and do not be slothful when oppor-tunity beckons. Thus you will avoid grave errors.

My friend, be not like him who sits by his fireside and watches the fire go out, then blows vainly upon the dead ashes. Do not give up hope or yield to despair because of that which is past, for to bewail the irretrievable is the worst of human frailties.

Yesterday I repented of my deed, and today I understand my error and the evil I brought upon myself when I broke my bow and destroyed my quiver.

I love you, my brother, whoever you are—whether you worship in your church, kneel in your temple, or pray in your mosque. You and I are all children of one faith, for the divers paths of religion are fingers of the loving hand of one Supreme Being, a hand extended to all, offering completeness of spirit to all, eager to receive all.

God has given you a spirit with wings on which to soar

into the spacious firmament of Love and Freedom. Is it not pitiful then that you cut your wings with your own hands and suffer your soul to crawl like an insect upon the earth?

My soul, living is like a courser of the night; the swifter its flight, the nearer the dawn.

11

The Listener

OH WIND, you who pass by us, now singing sweetly and softly, now sighing and lamenting: we hear you, but we cannot see you. We feel your touch, but we cannot descry your shape. You are like an ocean of love that engulfs our spirits, but does not drown them.

You ascend with the hills, and descend with the valleys, diffusing yourself over field and meadow. There is strength in your ascent and gentleness in your descent; and grace in your dispersion. You are like a merciful king, gracious toward the oppressed, but stern toward the arrogant and strong.

In Autumn you moan through the valleys, and the trees echo your wailing. In Winter you break your chains, and all Nature rebels with you.

In Spring you stir from your slumbers, still weak and infirm, and through your faint stirrings the fields begin to awake.

In Summer you hide behind the veil of Silence as if you had died, smitten by the shafts of the sun and the spears of heat.

Were you indeed lamenting in the late Autumn days, or were you laughing at the blushes of the naked trees? Were you angry in Winter, or were you dancing around the snow-decked tomb of Night?

Were you indeed languishing in the Spring, or were you grieving for the loss of your beloved, the Youth of all Seasons?

Were you perchance dead in those Summer days, or were you only asleep in the heart of the fruits, in the eyes of the vineyards, or in the ears of the wheat upon the threshing floors?

From the streets of the cities you raise up and bear the seeds of plagues; and from the hills you waft the fragrant breath of flowers. Thus the great Soul sustains the sorrow of Life and silently meets its joys.

Into the ears of the rose you whisper a secret whose meaning she grasps; often she is troubled—then she rejoices. Such is the way of God with the soul of Man.

Now you tarry. Now you hasten here and yonder, moving ceaselessly. Such too is the mind of Man, who lives when he acts and dies when he is idle.

You write your songs on the face of the waters; then you erase them. So does the poet when he is creating.

From the South you come as warm as Love; and from the North as cold as Death. From the East as gentle as the touch of the Soul; and from the West as fierce as Wrath and Fury. Are you as fickle as Age, or are you the courier of weighty tidings from the four points of the compass?

You rage through the desert, you trample the innocent caravans underfoot and bury them in mountains of sand. Are you that same frolicsome breeze that trembles with the dawn among the leaves and branches and flits like a dream through the windings of the valleys where the flowers bow in greeting and where the grass droops heavy-lidded with the intoxication of your breath?

You rise from the oceans and shake their silent depths from your tresses, and in your rage you lay waste ships and crews. Are you that selfsame gentle breeze that caresses the locks of children as they play around their homes?

Whither do you carry our hearts, our sighs, our breaths, our smiles? What do you do with the flying torches of our souls? Do you bear them beyond the horizon of Life? Do you drag them like sacrificial victims to distant and horrible caves to destroy them?

In the still night, hearts reveal their secrets to you. And at dawn, eyes open at your gentle touch. Are you mindful of what the heart has felt or the eyes have seen?

Between your wings the anguished lays the echo of his mournful songs, the orphan the fragments of his broken heart, and the oppressed his painful sighs. Within the folds of your mantle the stranger lays his longing, the forsaken his burden, and the fallen woman her despair.

Do you preserve all these in safekeeping for the humble? Or are you like Mother Earth, who entombs all that she brings forth?

Do you hear these cries and lamentations? Do you hear these moans and sighs? Or are you like the proud and mighty who do not see the outstretched hand or hear the cries of the poor?

O Life of all Listeners, do you hear?

12

Love and Youth

A YOUTH in the dawn of life sat at his desk in a solitary house. Now he looked through the window at the sky that was studded with glittering stars, now he turned his gaze toward a maiden's picture, which he held in his hand. Its lines and colors were worthy of a master; they became reflected in the youth's mind, and opened to him the secrets of the World and the mystery of Eternity.

The picture of the woman called to the youth, and at that moment turned his eyes into ears, so that he understood the language of the spirits that hovered over the room, and his heart became seared with love.

Thus the hours passed as if they were only a moment of some beautiful dream, or only a year in a life of Eternity.

Then the youth set the picture before him, took up his pen, and poured out his heart's feelings upon the parchment:

"Beloved: Great truth that transcends Nature does not pass from one being to another by way of human speech. Truth chooses Silence to convey her meaning to loving souls.

"I know that the silence of the night is the worthiest messenger between our two hearts, for she bears Love's message and recites the psalms of our hearts. Just as God has made our souls prisoners of our bodies, so Love has made me a prisoner of words and speech.

"They say, O Beloved, that Love is a devouring flame in the heart of man. I knew at our first meeting that I had known you for ages, and I knew at the time of parting that nothing was strong enough to keep us apart.

"My first glimpse of you was not in truth the first. The hour in which our hearts met confirmed in me the belief in Eternity and in the immortality of the Soul.

"At such a moment Nature lifts the veil from him who believes himself oppressed, and reveals her everlasting justice.

"Do you recall the brook by which we sat and gazed at each other, Beloved? Do you know your eyes told me at that moment that your love was not born of pity but of justice? And now I can proclaim to myself and to the world that the gifts which derive from justice are greater than those that spring from charity.

"And I can say too that Love which is the child of chance is like the stagnant waters of the marshes.

"Beloved, before me stretches a life which I can fashion into greatness and beauty—a life that began with our first meeting, and which will last to eternity.

"For I know that it is within you to bring forth the power that God has bestowed upon me, to be embodied in great words and deeds, even as the sun brings to life the fragrant flowers of the field.

"And thus, my love for you shall endure for ever."

The youth rose and walked slowly and reverently across the room. He looked through the window and saw the moon rising above the horizon and filling the spacious sky with her gentle radiance.

Then he returned to his desk and wrote:

"Forgive me, my Beloved, for speaking to you in the second person. For you are my other, beautiful, half, which I have lacked ever since we emerged from the sacred hand of God. Forgive me, my Beloved!"

13

Wisdom and I

IN THE SILENCE of the night, Wisdom came into my chamber and stood by my bed. She gazed upon me like a loving mother, dried my tears, and said:

"I have heard the cries of your soul, and have come here to comfort you. Open your heart to me and I shall fill it with light. Ask, and I shall show you the path of Truth."

I complied with her bidding, and asked:

"Who am I, Wisdom, and how came I to this place of horrors? What are these mighty hopes, these mountains of books, and these strange figures? What are these thoughts that come and go like a flock of doves? What are these words we compose with desire and write down in joy? What are these sorrowful and joyous conclusions that embrace my soul and envelope my heart? Whose are these eyes that stare at me and pierce the very inmost recesses of my soul, and yet are oblivious of my grief? What are these voices that lament the passing of my days and chant the praises of my childhood? Who is this youth that toys with my desires and mocks my feelings, forgetting the deeds of yesterday, contenting himself with the littleness of today, and arming himself against the slow approach of tomorrow?

"What is this dreadful world that moves me and to what unknown land?

"What is this earth that opens wide her jaws to swallow our bodies and prepares an everlasting shelter for greed? Who is this Man who contents himself with the favors of Fortune and craves a kiss from the lips of Life while Death smites him in the face? Who is this Man who buys a moment of pleasure with a year of repentance and gives himself over to sleep, while dreams call to him? Who is this Man who swims on the waves of Ignorance toward the gulf of Darkness?

"Tell me, Wisdom, what are all these things?"

And Wisdom opened her lips and spoke:
"You, Man, would see the world with the eyes of God, and would grasp the secrets of the hereafter by means of human thought. Such is the fruit of ignorance.

"Go into the field, and see how the bee hovers over the sweet flowers and the eagle swoops down on its prey. Go into your neighbor's house and see the infant child bewitched by the firelight, while the mother is busied at her tasks. Be like the bee, and do not waste your spring days gazing on the doings of the eagle. Be like the child rejoicing at the firelight and let the mother be. All that you see was, and still is, yours.

"The many books and strange figures and the lovely thoughts around you are ghosts of the spirits that have been before you. The words your lips utter are the links in the chain that binds you and your fellow men. The sorrowful and joyful conclusions are the seeds sown by the past in the field of your soul to be reaped by the future.

"The youth that toys with your desires is he who will

open the gate of your heart for Light to enter. The earth that opens wide her mouth to swallow man and his works is the redeemer of our souls from bondage to our bodies.

"The world that moves with you is your heart, which is the world itself. And Man, whom you deem so small and ignorant, is God's messenger who has come to learn the joy of life through sorrow and gain knowledge from ignorance."

Thus spoke Wisdom, and laid a hand upon my burning brow, saying:

"March on. Do not tarry. To go forward is to move toward perfection. March on, and fear not the thorns or the sharp stones on Life's path."

14

The Two Cities

LIFE TOOK ME up on her wings and bore me to the top of Mount Youth. Then she beckoned and pointed behind her. I looked back and saw a strange city, from which rose dark smoke of many hues moving slowly like phantoms. A thin cloud almost hid the city from my gaze.

After a moment of silence, I exclaimed: "What is this I see, Life?"

And Life answered: "This is the City of the Past. Look upon it and ponder."

And I gazed upon this wonderful scene and I saw many objects and sights: halls built for action, standing giant-like beneath the wings of Slumber; temples of talk around which hovered spirits at once crying in despair, and singing songs of hope. I saw churches built by Faith and destroyed by Doubt. I spied minarets of Thought, lifting their spires like the upraised arms of beggars; I saw avenues of Desire stretching like rivers through valleys; storehouses of secrets guarded by sentinels of Concealment and pillaged by thieves of Disclosure; towers of strength raised by Valor and demolished by Fear; shrines of Dreams, embellished by Slumber and destroyed by Wakefulness; slight huts inhabited by Weakness; mosques of Solitude and Self-Denial; institutions of learning lighted by Intelligence and darkened by Ignorance; taverns of Love, where lovers became drunk and Emptiness mocked at them; theatres upon whose boards Life acted out its play, and Death rounded out Life's tragedies.

Such is the City of the Past—in appearance far away, though in reality nearby—visible, though barely, through the dark clouds.

Then Life beckoned to me and said, "Follow me. We have tarried here too long." And I replied, "Whither are we going, Life?"

And Life said, "We are going to the City of the Future."

And I said, "Have pity on me, Life. I am weary, and my feet are bruised and the strength is gone out of me."

But Life replied, "March on, my friend. Tarrying is cowardice. To remain forever gazing upon the City of the Past is Folly. Behold, the City of the Future beckons. . . ."

15

Nature and Man

AT DAYBREAK I sat in a field, holding converse with Nature, while Man rested peacefully under coverlets of slumber. I lay in the green grass and meditated upon these questions: "Is Truth Beauty? Is Beauty Truth?"

And in my thoughts I found myself carried far from mankind, and my imagination lifted the veil of matter that hid my inner self. My soul expanded and I was brought closer to Nature and her secrets, and my ears were opened to the language of her wonders.

As I sat thus deep in thought, I felt a breeze passing through the branches of the trees, and I heard a sighing like that of a strayed orphan.

"Why do you sigh, gentle breeze?" I asked.

And the breeze replied, "Because I have come from the city that is aglow with the heat of the sun, and the seeds of plagues and contaminations cling to my pure garments. Can you blame me for grieving?"

Then I looked at the tear-stained faces of the flowers, and heard their soft lament. And I asked, "Why do you weep, my lovely flowers?"

One of the flowers raised her gentle head and whispered, "We weep because Man will come and cut us down, and offer us for sale in the markets of the city."

And another flower added, "In the evening, when we are wilted, he will throw us on the refuse heap. We weep because the cruel hand of Man snatches us from our native haunts."

And I heard the brook lamenting like a widow mourning her dead child and I asked, "Why do you weep, my pure brook?"

And the brook replied, "Because I am compelled to go to the city where Man contemns me and spurns me for stronger drinks and makes of me a scavenger for his offal, pollutes my purity, and turns my goodness to filth."

And I heard the birds grieving, and I asked, "Why do you cry, my beautiful birds?" And one of them flew near, and perched at the tip of a branch and said, "The sons of Adam will soon come into this field with their deadly weapons and make war upon us as if we were their mortal enemies. We are now taking leave of one another, for we know not which of us will escape the wrath of Man. Death follows us wherever we go."

Now the sun rose from behind the mountain peaks, and gilded the treetops with coronals. I looked upon this beauty and asked myself, "Why must Man destroy what Nature has built?"

16

The Enchantress

THE WOMAN whom my heart has loved sat yesterday in this lonely room and rested her lovely body upon this velvet couch. From these crystal goblets she sipped the aged wine.

This is yesterday's dream; for the woman my heart has loved is gone to a distant place—the Land of Oblivion and Emptiness.

The print of her fingers is yet upon my mirror; and the fragrance of her breathing is still within the folds of my garments; and the echo of her sweet voice can be heard in this room.

But the woman my heart has loved is gone to a distant place called the Valley of Exile and Forgetfulness.

By my bed hangs a portrait of this woman. The love-letters she wrote to me I have kept in a silver case, studded with emeralds and coral. And all these things will remain with me till tomorrow, when the wind will blow them away into oblivion, where only mute silence reigns.

The woman I have loved is like the women to whom you have given your hearts. She is strangely beautiful, as if fashioned by a god; as meek as the dove, as wily as the serpent, as proudly graceful as the peacock, as fierce as the wolf, as lovely as the white swan, and as fearful as the black night. She is compounded of a handful of earth and a beakerful of sea-foam.

I have known this woman since childhood. I have followed her into the fields and laid hold of the hem of her garments as she walked in the streets of the city. I have known her since the days of my youth, and I have seen the shadow of her face in the pages of the books I have read. I have heard her heavenly voice in the murmur of the brook.

To her I opened my heart's discontents and the secrets of my soul.

The woman whom my heart has loved is gone to a cold, desolate and distant place—the Land of Emptiness and Oblivion.

The woman my heart has loved is called *Life*. She is beautiful, and draws all hearts to herself. She takes our lives in pawn and buries our yearnings in promises.

Life is a woman bathing in the tears of her lovers and anointing herself with the blood of her victims. Her raiments are white days, lined with the darkness of night. She takes the human heart to lover, but denies herself in marriage.

> *Life is an enchantress*
> *Who seduces us with her beauty—*
> *But he who knows her wiles*
> *Will flee her enchantments.*

17

Youth and Hope

YOUTH WALKED before me and I followed him until we came to a distant field. There he stopped, and gazed at the clouds that drifted over the horizon like a flock of white lambs. Then he looked at the trees whose naked branches pointed toward the sky as if praying to Heaven for the return of their foliage.

And I said, "Where are we now, Youth?"

And he replied, "We are in the field of Bewilderment. Take heed."

And I said, "Let us go back at once, for this desolate place affrights me, and the sight of the clouds and the naked trees saddens my heart."

And he replied, "Be patient. Perplexity is the beginning of knowledge."

Then I looked around me and saw a form moving gracefully toward us and I asked, "Who is this woman?"

And Youth replied, "This is Melpomene, daughter of Zeus, and Muse of Tragedy."

"Oh, happy Youth!" I exclaimed, "what does Tragedy want of me, while you are at my side?"

And he answered, "She has come to show you the earth and its sorrows; for he who has not looked on Sorrow will never see Joy."

Then the spirit laid a hand upon my eyes. When she withdrew it, Youth was gone, and I was alone, divested of my earthly garments, and I cried, "Daughter of Zeus, where is Youth?"

Melpomene did not answer; but took me up under her wings, and carried me to the summit of a high mountain. Below me I saw the earth and all in it, spread out like the pages of a book, upon which were inscribed the secrets of the universe. I stood in awe beside the maiden, pondered the mystery of Man, and struggled to decipher Life's symbols.

And I saw woeful things: The Angels of Happiness warring with the Devils of Misery, and standing between them was Man, now drawn one way by Hope and now another by Despair.

I saw Love and Hate dallying with the human heart; Love concealing Man's guilt and besotting him with the wine of submission, praise and flattery; while Hatred provoked him, and sealed his ears and blinded his eyes to Truth.

And I beheld the city crouching like a child of its slums and snatching at the garment of the son of Adam. From afar I saw the lovely fields weeping over man's sorrow.

I beheld priests foaming like sly foxes; and false messiahs contriving and conspiring against Man's happiness.

And I saw Man calling upon Wisdom for deliverance; but Wisdom did not hearken to his cries, for he had contemned her when she spoke to him in the streets of the city.

And I saw preachers gazing in adoration toward the heavens, while their hearts were interred in the pits of Greed.

I saw a youth winning a maiden's heart with sweet speech; but their true feelings were asleep, and their divinity was far away.

I saw the lawmakers chattering idly, selling their wares in the market places of Deceit and Hypocrisy.

I saw physicians toying with the souls of the simple-hearted and trustful. I saw the ignorant sitting with the wise, exalting their past to the throne of glory, adorning their present with the robes of plenty, and preparing a couch of luxury for the future.

I saw the wretched poor sowing the seed, and the strong reaping; and oppression, miscalled Law, standing guard.

I saw the thieves of Ignorance despoiling the treasures of Knowledge, while the sentinels of Light lay drowned in the deep sleep of inaction.

And I saw two lovers; but the woman was like a lute in the hand of a man who cannot play, but understands only harsh sounds.

And I beheld the forces of Knowledge laying siege to the city of Inherited Privilege; but they were few in number and were soon dispersed.

And I saw Freedom walking alone, knocking at doors, and asking for shelter, but no one heeded her pleas. Then I saw Prodigality striding in splendor, and the multitude acclaiming her as Liberty.

I saw Religion buried in books, and Doubt stood in her place.

And I saw Man wearing the garments of Patience as a cloak for Cowardice and calling Sloth Tolerance, and Fear Courtesy.

I saw the intruder sitting at the board of Knowledge, uttering folly, but the guests were silent.

I saw gold in the hands of the wasteful, a means of evil-doing; and in the hands of the miserly as a bait for hatred. But in the hands of the wise I saw no gold.

When I beheld all these things, I cried out in pain, "Oh Daughter of Zeus, is this indeed the Earth? Is this Man?"

In a soft and anguished voice she replied, "What you see is the Soul's path, and it is paved with sharp stones and carpeted with thorns. This is only the shadow of Man. This is Night. But wait! Morning will soon be here!"

Then she laid a gentle hand upon my eyes, and when she withdrew it, behold! there was Youth walking slowly by my side, and ahead of us, leading the way, marched Hope.

18

Resurrection

YESTERDAY, MY BELOVED, I was almost alone in the world, and my solitude was as pitiless as death. I was like a flower that grows in the shadow of a huge rock, of whose existence Life is not aware, and which is not aware of Life.

But today my soul awakened, and I beheld you standing by my side. I rose to my feet and rejoiced; then I knelt in reverence and worshipped before you.

Yesterday the touch of the frolicsome breeze seemed harsh, my beloved, and the sun's beams seemed weak, a mist hid the face of the earth, and the waves of the ocean roared like a tempest.

I looked all about me, but saw naught but my own suffering self standing by my side, while the phantoms of darkness rose and fell around me like ravenous vultures.

But today Nature is bathed in light, and the roaring waves are calm and the fogs are dispersed. Wherever I look I see Life's secrets lying open before me.

Yesterday I was a soundless word in the heart of the Night; today I am a song on the lips of Time.

And all this has come to pass in a moment, and was fashioned by a glance, a word, a sigh, and a kiss.

That moment, my beloved, has blended my soul's past readiness with my heart's hopes of the future. It was like a white rose that bursts from the bosom of the earth into the light of day.

That moment was to my life what the birth of Christ has been to the ages of Man, for it was filled with love and goodness. It turned darkness into light, sorrow into joy, and despair to bliss.

Beloved, the fires of Love descend from heaven in many shapes and forms, but their impress on the world is one. The tiny flame that lights up the human heart is like a blazing torch that comes down from heaven to light up the paths of mankind.

For in one soul are contained the hopes and feelings of all Mankind.

The Jews, my beloved, awaited the coming of a Messiah, who had been promised them, and who was to deliver them from bondage.

And the Great Soul of the World sensed that the worship of Jupiter and Minerva no longer availed, for the thirsty hearts of men could not be quenched with that wine.

In Rome men pondered the divinity of Apollo, a god without pity, and the beauty of Venus already fallen into decay.

For deep in their hearts, though they did not understand it, these nations hungered and thirsted for the supreme teaching that would transcend any to be found on the earth. They yearned for the spirit's freedom that would teach man to rejoice with his neighbor at the light of the sun and the wonder of living. For it is this cherished freedom that brings man close to the Unseen, which he can approach without fear or shame.

All this took place two thousand years ago, my beloved, when the heart's desires hovered around visible things, fearful of approaching the eternal spirit—while Pan, Lord of Forests, filled the hearts of shepherds with terror, and Baal, Lord of the Sun, pressed with the merciless hands of priests upon the souls of the poor and lowly.

And in one night, in one hour, in one moment of time, the lips of the spirit parted and spoke the sacred word, "Life"; and it became flesh in an infant lying asleep in the lap of a virgin, in a stable where shepherds guarded their flocks against the assault of wild beasts of the night and looked with wonder upon that humble infant, asleep in the manger.

The Infant King, swaddled in his mother's wretched garments, sat upon a throne of burdened hearts and hungry souls, and through his humility wrested the sceptre of power from the hands of Jove and gave it to the poor shepherd watching over his flock.

And from Minerva he took Wisdom, and set it in the heart of a poor fisherman who was mending his fishing net.

From Apollo he drew Joy through his own sorrows and bestowed it upon the brokenhearted beggar by the wayside.

From Venus he took Beauty and poured it into the soul of the fallen woman trembling before her cruel oppressor.

He dethroned Baal and set in his place the humble plowman, who sowed his seed and tilled the soil by the sweat of his brow.

Beloved, was not my soul yesterday like unto the tribes of Israel? Did I not wait in the silence of the night for the coming of my Savior to deliver me from the bondage and evils of Time? Did I not feel the great thirst and the spirit's hunger as did those nations of the past? Did I not walk the road of Life like a child lost in some wilderness, and was not my life like a seed cast upon a stone, that no bird would seek, nor the elements split and bring to life?

All this came to pass yesterday, my beloved, when my dreams crouched in the dark, and feared the approach of the day.

All this came to pass when Sorrow tore my heart, and Hope strove to mend it.

In one night, in one hour, in one moment of time, the Spirit descended from the center of the circle of divine light and looked at me with your heart's eyes. From that glance Love was born, and found a dwelling in my heart.

This great Love, swaddled in the robes of my feelings, has turned sorrow to joy, despair to bliss, aloneness to paradise.

Love, the great King, has restored life to my dead self; returned light to my tear-blinded eyes; raised me up from the pit of despair to the celestial kingdom of Hope.

For all my days were as nights, my beloved. But behold! the dawn has come; soon the sun will rise. For the breath of the Infant Jesus has filled the firmament and is mingled with the ether. Life, once full of woe, is now overflowing with joy, for the arms of the Infant are around me and embrace my soul.

book 3

thoughts
and
meditations

Contents

CONTENTS

Preface

In his youth, the author of *The Prophet* conceived the universe as perfect and devoid of evil. He pictured a joyous world free of suffering, a world of enlightenment unflawed by ignorance, a world whose great minds rejected superstitions, a world of progress that abhorred corruption. Justice and wisdom lived side by side in this paradise of his conception, and unity and good will prevailed among men. But after finding out that the haven he fashioned was different from mundane reality, he felt disappointed and embittered.

Gibran had looked upon the heads of state and the hierarchs of the religions as truly the pillars of society. He expected them to provide examples of justice and wisdom. He assumed that the privileges and the plenty they enjoyed were their due for the noble services they rendered to their people. He imagined that it was on this account that the people yielded them honor, trust, and obedience. They would not have obtained these, he assumed, were they not worthy.

It was in this light that he looked upon the rulers and

their luxurious life and failed to see how they exploited the people. When he began to perceive the realities of life, he saw the rich abusing the poor who lived under the yoke of slavery and despotism. That which Gibran called "tyranny" masked itself under the name of "politics." And the prophet from Lebanon began to express his feelings through scorching articles in Arabic newspapers, books, and magazines. I have included a selection of these in the present volume.

The world that Gibran was seeking was a world of understanding, a world of logic, and of positive thinking. The people of such a world are not beguiled by impostors and do not cling to superstitions. For them the mind is the only lamp that illuminates the dark path of ignorance, and this lamp should be kept eternally lit.

Gibran's life was an example of the belief in the authority of the great mind. His keen mind led him to open a new road for himself. The world that Gibran imagined is a place illumined by reason and understanding. In it superstitions and fantasies melt like ice under the rays of the sun. But alas, what is in the actual world we live in? Every kind of ruler has won power except the ruler with a mind. The honest man is forced into deceit, the impostor holds sway, and the people are chained by custom and tradition. Their religion bows to hardened custom. The people live in the ruts trodden by their ancestors; they do not follow the light of their own minds or the dictates of their own hearts. This has led the people into narrow, separated faiths and suspicious, unfriendly, separated nations, instead of a universal faith and a world nation. Thus they remained the victims of superstitions. And in the world so conditioned, success is gained by the sacrifice of conscience and honor. The man of integrity sinks into the jaws of poverty. The honest man is reviled and the liar admired and rewarded with possessions.

Gibran lamented such a world. His sorrowing songs became a beautiful and soothing melody. In his poetry, this beloved son of Lebanon projected a bewildered person, a convert, a skeptic, or a believer according to the vicissitudes in his inner self. This diversity reflects the wealth and philosophic depths of his knowledge, expressed in both his Arabic and English writings.

Gibran came to this world to say his word and to benefit his fellow men. It is my sincerest hope that *Thoughts and Meditations*, the words of wisdom which the Prophet of Lebanon wrote and uttered, will foster love and peace, and enlarge understanding throughout the world.

ANTHONY R. FERRIS

THOUGHTS AND MEDITATIONS

The Poet from Baalbek

*Sarkis Effandi, one of Gibran's closest friends, was highly
regarded among the intelligentsia of Lebanon. He owned
a publishing house and a daily Arabic newspaper called
Lisan-Ul-Hal. In the year 1912, the Arab League of
Progress, organized for the promotion of Arab unity and
culture, decided to honor the great Lebanese poet Khalil
Effandi Mutran.*

*Since Sarkis was the head of the committee honoring
the poet, he extended an invitation to his friend Gibran,
now settled in New York, to join them in Beirut on
that occasion. Gibran could not make the trip, but he
sent Sarkis a story with instructions to read it in his
behalf before the poet. In the story, which eulogises the
poet, Gibran expresses his belief in the transmigration of
souls and praises the great soul reincarnated in the honored poet.*

IN THE CITY OF BAALBEK, THE YEAR 112 B. C.

THE EMIR sat on his golden throne surrounded by glittering lamps and gilded censers. The aromatic scent of the
latter filled the palace. At his right and left sides were the
high priests and the chiefs; the slaves and guards stood
immobile before him like statues of bronze erected before
the face of the sun.

After the cantors had chanted echoing hymns, an elderly vizier stood before the Emir, and in a voice modulated in the serenity of age, said, "Oh great and merciful Prince, yesterday there arrived in our city a sage from India who believes in a diversity of religions and speaks of strange things difficult to understand. He preaches the doctrine of the transmigration of souls and the incarnation of spirits which move from one generation to another seeking more and more perfect avatars until they become godlike. This sage seeks an audience with you to explain his dogma."

The Emir shook his head, smiled, and said, "From India come many strange and wonderful things. Call in the sage that we may hear his words of wisdom."

As soon as he uttered these words, a dark-hued, aged man walked in with dignity and stood before the Emir. His large brown eyes spoke, without words, of deep secrets. He bowed, raised his head, his eyes glittered, and he commenced to speak.

He explained how the spirits pass from one body to another, elevated by the good acts of the medium which they choose, and influenced by their experience in each existence; aspiring toward a splendor that exalts them and strengthens their growth by Love that makes them both happy and miserable. . . .

Then the philosopher dwelt on the manner in which the spirits move from place to place in their quest for perfection, atoning in the present for sins committed in the past, and reaping in one existence what they had sown in another.

Observing signs of restlessness and weariness on the Emir's countenance, the old vizier whispered to the sage, "You have preached enough at present; please postpone the rest of your discourse until our next meeting."

Thereupon the sage withdrew from the Emir's presence

and sat among the priests and chiefs, closing his eyes as if weary of gazing into the deeps of Existence.

After a profound silence, similar to the trance of a prophet, the Emir looked to the right and to the left and inquired, "Where is our poet, we have not seen him for many days. What became of him? He always attended our meeting."

A priest responded, saying, "A week ago I saw him sitting in the portico of Ishtar's temple, staring with glazed and sorrowful eyes at the distant evening twilight as if one of his poems had strayed among the clouds."

And a chief added, "I saw him yesterday standing beneath the shade of the willow and cypress trees. I greeted him but he gave no heed to my greeting, and remained submerged in the deep sea of his thoughts and meditations."

Then the Grand Eunuch said, "I saw him today in the palace garden, with pale and haggard face, sighing, and his eyes full of tears."

"Go seek out this unhappy soul, for his absence from our midst troubles us," ordered the Emir.

At this command, the slaves and the guards left the hall to seek the poet, while the Emir and his priests and chiefs remained in the assembly hall awaiting their return. It seemed as if their spirits had felt his invisible presence among them.

Soon the Grand Eunuch returned and prostrated himself at the feet of the Emir like a bird shot by the arrow of an archer. Whereupon the Emir shouted at him saying, "What happened . . . what have you to say?" The slave raised his head and said in a trembling voice, "We found the poet dead in the palace garden."

Then the Emir rose and hastened sorrowfully to the palace garden, preceded by his torchbearers and followed by the priests and the chiefs. At the end of the garden close by the almond and pomegranate trees, the yellow light of the torches brought the dead youth into their sight. His corpse lay upon the green grass like a withered rose.

"Look how he embraced his viol as if the two were lovers pledged to die together!" said one of the Emir's aides.

Another one said, "He still stares, as in life, at the heart of space; he still seems to be watching the invisible movements of an unknown god among the planets."

And the high priest addressed the Emir, saying, "Tomorrow let us bury him, as a great poet, in the shade of Ishtar's temple, and let the townspeople march in his funeral procession, while youths sing his poems and virgins strew flowers over his sepulchre. Let it be a commemoration worthy of his genius."

The Emir nodded his head without diverting his eyes from the young poet's face, pale with the veil of Death. "We have neglected this pure soul when he was alive, filling the Universe with the fruit of his brilliant intellect and spreading throughout space the aromatic scent of his soul. If we do not honor him now, we will be mocked and reviled by the gods and the nymphs of the prairies and valleys.

"Bury him in this spot where he breathed his last and let his viol remain between his arms. If you wish to honor him and pay him tribute, tell your children that the Emir had neglected him and was the cause of his miserable and lonely death." Then the monarch asked, "Where is the sage from India?" And the sage walked forth and said, "Here, oh great Prince."

And the Emir inquired, saying, "Tell us, oh sage, will the gods ever restore me to this world as a prince and bring back the deceased poet to life? Will my spirit become incarnated in a body of a great king's son, and will the poet's soul transmigrate into the body of another genius? Will the sacred Law make him stand before the face of Eternity that he may compose poems of Life? Will he be restored that I may honor him and pay him tribute by showering upon him precious gifts and rewards that will enliven his heart and inspire his soul?"

And the sage answered the Emir, saying, "*Whatever the soul longs for, will be attained by the spirit.* Remember, oh great Prince, that the sacred Law which restores the sublimity of Spring after the passing of Winter will reinstate you a prince and him a genius poet."

The Emir's hopes were revived and signs of joy appeared on his face. He walked toward his palace thinking and meditating upon the words of the sage: "*Whatever the soul longs for, will be attained by the spirit.*"

In Cairo, Egypt, the Year 1912 A. D.

The full moon appeared and spread her silver garment upon the city. The Prince of the land stood at the balcony of his palace gazing at the clear sky and pondering upon the ages that have passed along the bank of the Nile. He seemed to be reviewing the processions of the nations that marched, together with Time, from the Pyramid to the palace of Abedine.

As the circle of the Prince's thoughts widened and extended into the domain of his dreams, he looked at his boon companion sitting by his side and said, "My soul is thirsty; recite a poem for me tonight."

And the boon companion bowed his head and began a pre-Islamic poem. But before he had recited many stanzas, the Prince interrupted him saying, "Let us hear a modern poem . . . a more recent one."

And, bowing, the boon companion began to recite verses composed by a Hadramout poet. The Prince stopped him again, saying, "More recent . . . a more recent poem."

The singer raised his hand and touched his forehead as if trying to recall to memory all the poems composed by contemporary poets. Then his eyes glittered, his face brightened, and he began to sing lovely verses in soothing rhythm, full of enchantment.

Intoxicated and seeming to feel the movement of hidden hands beckoning him from his palace to a distant land, the Prince fervently inquired, "Who composed these verses?" And the singer answered, "The Poet from Baalbek."

The Poet from Baalbek is an ancient name and it brought into the Prince's memory images of forgotten days. It awakened in the depth of his heart phantoms of remembrance, and drew before his eyes, with lines formed by the mist, a picture of a dead youth embracing his viol and surrounded by priests, chiefs, and ministers.

Like dreams dissipated by the light of Morn, the vision soon left the Prince's eyes. He stood up and walked toward his palace with crossed arms repeating the words of Mohammed, "*You were dead and He brought you back to life, and He will return you to the dead and then restore you to life. Whereupon you shall go back to Him.*"

Then he looked at his boon companion and said, "We are fortunate to have the Poet from Baalbek in our land, and shall make it our paramount duty to honor and befriend him." After a few moments worthy of silence and respect, the Prince added in a low voice, "The poet is a bird of strange moods. He descends from his lofty domain to tarry among us, singing; if we do not honor him he will unfold his wings and fly back to his dwelling place."

The night was over, and the skies doffed their garments studded with stars, and put on raiment woven from the sinews of the rays of Morn. And the Prince's soul swayed between the wonders and strangeness of Existence and the concealed mysteries of Life.

The Return of the Beloved

By NIGHTFALL the enemy fled with slashes of the sword and wounds of lance tips scarring their backs. Our heroes waved banners of triumph and chanted songs of victory to the cadence of their horses' hoofs that drummed upon the stones of the valley.

The moon had already risen from behind Fam El Mizab. The mighty and lofty rocks seemed to ascend with the spirits of the people, and the forest of cedars to lie like a medal of honor upon the bosom of Lebanon.

They continued their march, and the moon shone upon their weapons. The distant caves echoed their songs of praise and victory, until they reached the foot of a slope. There they were arrested by the neighing of a horse standing among gray rocks as though carved from them.

Near the horse they found a corpse, and the earth on which he lay was stained with his blood. The leader of the troop shouted, "Show me the man's sword and I will tell you who the owner is."

Some of the horsemen dismounted and surrounded the dead man and then one said to the chief, "His fingers have taken too strong a hold on the hilt. It would be a shame to undo them."

Another said, "The sword has been sheathed with escaping life that hides its metal."

A third one added, "The blood has congealed on both the hand and the hilt and made them one piece."

Whereupon the chief dismounted and walked to the corpse and said, "Raise his head and let the moon shine on his face so we may identify him." The men did as ordered, and the face of the slain man appeared from behind the veil of Death showing the marks of valor and nobility. It was the face of a strong horseman, and it bespoke manhood. It was the face of a sorrowing and rejoicing man; the face of one who had met the enemy courageously and faced death smilingly; the face of a Lebanese hero who, on that day, had witnessed the triumph but had not lived to march and sing and celebrate the victory with his comrades.

As they removed the silk head-wrapper and cleaned the dust of battle from his pale face, the chief cried out, in agony, "This is the son of Assaaby, what a great loss!" And the men repeated that name, sighing. Then silence fell upon them, and their hearts, intoxicated with the wine of victory, sobered. For they had seen something greater than the glory of triumph, in the loss of a hero.

Like statues of marble they stood in that scene of dread, and their taut tongues were mute and voiceless. This is what death does to the souls of heroes. Weeping and lamentation are for women; and moans and cries for children. Nothing befits the sorrow of men of the sword save silence which grips the strong heart as the eagle's talons grip the throat of its prey. It is that silence which rises above tears and wailing which, in its majesty, adds more awe and anguish to the misfortune; that silence which causes the soul to descend from the mountain-top into the abyss. It is the silence which proclaims the coming tempest. And when the tempest makes not its appearance, it is because the silence is stronger than the tempest.

They removed the raiment of the young hero to see where death had placed its iron claws. And the wounds appeared in his breast like speaking lips proclaiming, in the calmness of the night, the bravery of men.

The chief approached the corpse and dropped on his knees. Taking a closer look at the slain warrior, he found a scarf embroidered with gold threads tied around the arm. He recognized the hand that had spun its silk and the fingers that had woven its thread. He hid it under his raiment and withdrew slowly, hiding his stricken face with a trembling hand. Yet this trembling hand, with its might, had disjoined the heads of the enemy. Now it trembled because it had touched the edge of a scarf tied by loving fingers around the arm of a slain hero, who would return to her lifeless, borne upon the shoulders of his comrades.

While the leader's spirit wavered, considering both the tyranny of death and the secrets of love, one of the men suggested, "Let us dig a grave for him under that oak tree so that its roots may drink from his blood and its branches may receive nourishment from his remains. It will gain strength and become immortal and stand as a sign declaring to the hills and valleys his bravery and his might."

Another man said, "Let us carry him to the forest of the cedars and bury him by the church. There his bones will be eternally guarded by the shadow of the Cross."

And another said, "Bury him here where his blood is mingled with the earth. And let his sword remain in his right hand; plant his lance by his side and slay his horse over his grave and let his weapons be his cheer in his solitude."

But another objected, "Do not bury a sword stained with the enemy blood, nor slay a steed that has withstood death in the battlefield. Do not leave in the wilderness weapons accustomed to action and strength, but carry them to his relatives as a great and good inheritance."

"Let us kneel down by his side and pray the Nazarene's prayers that God might forgive him and bless our victory," said another.

"Let us raise him upon our shoulders and make our shields and lances a bier for him and circle again this valley of our victory singing the songs of triumph so that the lips of his wounds will smile before they are muffled by the earth of the grave," said a comrade.

And another: "Let us mount him upon his charger and support him with the skulls of the dead enemy and gird him with his lance and bring him to the village a victor. He never yielded to death until he burdened it with the enemy's souls."

Another one said, "Come, let us bury him at the foot of this mountain. The echo of the caves shall be his companion and the murmur of the brook his minstrel. His bones shall rest in a wilderness where the tread of the silenced night is light and gentle."

Another objected, "No. Do not leave him in this place, for here dwells tedium and solitude. But let us carry him to the burial-ground of the village. The spirits of our forefathers will be his comrades and will speak to him in the silenced night and relate to him tales of their wars and sagas of their glory."

Then the chief walked to the center and motioned them to silence. He sighed and said, "Do not annoy him with memories of war or repeat to the ears of his soul, that hovers over us, the tales of swords and lances. Rather come and let us carry him calmly and silently to his birthplace, where a loving soul awaits his homecoming . . . a soul of a maiden awaiting his return from the battlefield. Let us return him to her so she may not be denied the sight of his face and the printing of a last kiss upon his forehead."

So they carried him upon their shoulders and walked silently with bent heads and downcast eyes. His sorrowful horse plodded behind them dragging its reins on the ground, uttering from time to time a desolate neighing echoed by the caves as if those caves had hearts and shared their grief.

Through the thorny path of the valley illuminated by a full moon, the procession of victory walked behind the cavalcade of Death and the spirit of Love led the way dragging his broken wings.

Union

In this poem the prophet of Lebanon appears to have previsioned the union of Egypt and Syria.

WHEN THE NIGHT had embellished heaven's garment with the stars' gems, there rose a houri from the Valley of the Nile and hovered in the sky on invisible wings. She sat upon a throne of mist hung between heaven and the sea. Before her passed a host of angels chanting in unison, "Holy, holy, holy the daughter of Egypt whose grandeur fills the globe."

Then on the summit of Fam el Mizab, girdled by the forest of the cedars, a phantom youth was raised by the hands of the seraphim, and he sat upon the throne beside the houri. The spirits circled them singing, "Holy, holy, holy the youth of Lebanon, whose magnificence fills the ages."

And when the suitor held the hands of his beloved and gazed into her eyes, the wave and wind carried their communion to all the universe:

How faultless is your radiance, Oh daughter of Isis, and how great my adoration for you!

How graceful you are among the youths, Oh son of Astarte, and how great my yearning for you!

My love is as strong as your Pyramids, and the ages shall not destroy it.

My love is as staunch as your Holy Cedars, and the elements shall not prevail over it.

The wise men of all the nations come from East and West to discern your wisdom and to interpret your signs.

The scholars of the world come from all the kingdoms to intoxicate themselves with the nectar of your beauty and the magic of your voice.

Your palms are fountains of abundance.

Your arms are springs of pure water, and your breath is a refreshing breeze.

The palaces and temples of the Nile announce your glory, and the Sphinx narrates your greatness.

The cedars upon your bosom are like a medal of honor, and the towers about you speak your bravery and might.

Oh how sweet is your love and how wonderful is the hope that you foster.

Oh what a generous partner you are, and how faithful a spouse you have proved to be. How sublime are your gifts, and how precious your sacrifice!

You sent to me young men who were as an awakening after deep slumber. You gave me men of daring to conquer the weakness of my people, and scholars to exalt them, and geniuses to enrich their powers.

From the seeds I sent you you wrought flowers; from saplings you raised trees. For you are a virgin meadow on which roses and lilies grow and the cypresses and the cedar trees rise.

I see sorrow in your eyes, my beloved; do you grieve while you are at my side?

I have sons and daughters who emigrated beyond the seas and left me weeping and longing for their return.

Are you afraid, oh daughter of the Nile, and dearest of all nations?

I fear a tyrant approaching me with a sweet voice so that he may later rule me with the strength of his arms.

The life of the nations, my love, is like the life of individuals; a life cheered by Hope and married to Fear, beset by desires and frowned upon by Despair.

And the lovers embraced and kissed and drank from the cups of love the scented wine of the ages; and the host of spirits chanted, "Holy, holy, holy, Love's glory fills heaven and earth."

My Soul Preached to Me

My soul preached to me and taught me to love that which the people abhor and befriend him whom they revile.

My soul showed me that Love prides itself not only in the one who loves, but also in the beloved.

Ere my soul preached to me, Love was in my heart as a tiny thread fastened between two pegs.

But now Love has become a halo whose beginning is its end, and whose end is its beginning. It surrounds every being and extends slowly to embrace all that shall be.

My soul advised me and taught me to perceive the hidden beauty of the skin, figure, and hue. She instructed me to meditate upon that which the people call ugly until its true charm and delight appear.

Ere my soul counselled me, I saw Beauty like a trembling torch between columns of smoke. Now since the smoke has vanished, I see naught save the flame.

My soul preached to me and taught me to listen to the

voices which the tongue and the larynx and the lips do not utter.

Ere my soul preached to me, I heard naught but clamor and wailing. But now I eagerly attend Silence and hear its choirs singing the hymns of the ages and the songs of the firmament announcing the secrets of the Unseen.

My soul preached to me and instructed me to drink the wine that cannot be pressed and cannot be poured from cups that hands can lift or lips can touch.

Ere my soul preached to me, my thirst was like a dim spark hidden under the ashes that can be extinguished by a swallow of water.

But now my longing has become my cup, my affections my wine, and my loneliness my intoxication; yet, in this unquenchable thirst there is eternal joy.

My soul preached to me and taught me to touch that which has not become incarnate; my soul revealed to me that whatever we touch is part of our desire.

But now my fingers have turned into mist penetrating that which is seen in the universe and mingling with the Unseen.

My soul instructed me to inhale the scent that no myrtle or incense emits. Ere my soul preached to me, I craved the scent of perfume in the gardens or in flasks or in censers.

But now I can savor the incense that is not burnt for offering or sacrifice. And I fill my heart with a fragrance that has never been wafted by the frolicsome breeze of space.

My soul preached to me and taught me to say, "I am ready" when the Unknown and Danger call on me.

Ere my soul preached to me, I answered no voice save

the voice of the crier whom I knew, and walked not save upon the easy and smooth path.

Now the Unknown has become a steed that I can mount in order to reach the Unknown; and the plain has turned into a ladder on whose steps I climb to the summit.

My soul spoke to me and said, "Do not measure Time by saying, 'There was yesterday, and there shall be to-morrow.'"

And ere my soul spoke to me, I imagined the Past as an epoch that never returned, and the Future as one that could never be reached.

Now I realize that the present moment contains all time and within it is all that can be hoped for, done and realized.

My soul preached to me exhorting me not to limit space by saying, "Here, there, and yonder."

Ere my soul preached to me, I felt that wherever I walked was far from any other space.

Now I realize that wherever I am contains all places; and the distance that I walk embraces all distances.

My soul instructed me and advised me to stay awake while others sleep. And to surrender to slumber when others are astir.

Ere my soul preached to me, I saw not their dreams in my sleep, neither did they observe my vision.

Now I never sail the vessel of my dreams unless they watch me, and they never soar into the sky of their vision unless I rejoice in their freedom.

My soul preached to me and said, "Do not be delighted because of praise, and do not be distressed because of blame."

Ere my soul counselled me, I doubted the worth of my work.

Now I realize that the trees blossom in Spring and bear fruit in Summer without seeking praise; and they drop their leaves in Autumn and become naked in Winter without fearing blame.

My soul preached to me and showed me that I am neither more than the pygmy, nor less than the giant.

Ere my soul preached to me, I looked upon humanity as two men: one weak, whom I pitied, and the other strong, whom I followed or resisted in defiance.

But now I have learned that I was as both are and made from the same elements. My origin is their origin, my conscience is their conscience, my contention is their contention, and my pilgrimage is their pilgrimage.

If they sin, I am also a sinner. If they do well, I take pride in their well-doing. If they rise, I rise with them. If they stay inert, I share their slothfulness.

My soul spoke to me and said, "The lantern which you carry is not yours, and the song that you sing was not composed within your heart, for even if you bear the light, you are not the light, and even if you are a lute fastened with strings, you are not the lute player."

My soul preached to me, my brother, and taught me much. And your soul has preached and taught as much to you. For you and I are one, and there is no variance between us save that I urgently declare that which is in my inner self, while you keep as a secret that which is within you. But in your secrecy there is a sort of virtue.

The Sons of the Goddess
And the Sons of the Monkeys

HOW STRANGE Time is, and how queer we are! Time has really changed, and lo, it has changed us too. It walked one step forward, unveiled its face, alarmed us and then elated us.

Yesterday we complained about Time and trembled at its terrors. But today we have learned to love it and revere it, for we now understand its intents, its natural disposition, its secrets, and its mysteries.

Yesterday we crawled in fright like shuddering ghosts between the fears of the night and the menaces of the day. But today we walk joyously towards the mountain peak, the dwelling place of the raging tempest and the birthplace of thunder.

Yesterday we ate our bread kneaded with blood, and we drank our water mixed with tears. But today we began to receive the manna from the hands of the morning brides and drank the aged wine scented with the sweet breath of Spring.

Yesterday we were a toy in the hands of Destiny. But today Destiny has awakened from her intoxication to play and laugh and walk with us. We do not follow her but she follows us.

Yesterday we burned incense before the idols and offered sacrifices to the angry gods. But today we burn incense and offer sacrifices to our own being, for the greatest and most beautiful of all gods has raised his temple in our hearts.

Yesterday we bowed to the kings and bent our necks to the sultans. But today we do not pay reverence save to Right and we follow no one except Beauty and Love.

Yesterday we honored false prophets and sorcerers. But today Time has changed, and lo, it has changed us too. We can now stare at the face of the sun and listen to the songs of the sea, and nothing can shake us except a cyclone.

Yesterday we tore down the temples of our souls and from their debris we built tombs for our forefathers. But today our souls have turned into sacred altars that the ghosts of the Past cannot approach, that the fleshless fingers of the dead cannot touch.

We were a silent thought hidden in the corners of Oblivion. Today we are a strong voice that can make the firmament reverberate.

We were a tiny spark buried under the ashes. Today we are a raging fire burning at the head of the valley.

We spent many a night awake, with the earth as our pillow and the snow as our blanket.

Like sheep without a shepherd we flocked together many nights grazing on our thoughts, and chewing the cud of our emotions; yet we remained hungry and athirst.

Oftentime we stood between a passing day and a coming night lamenting our withering youth and longing for someone unknown, and gazing at the void and dark sky listening to the moaning of Silence and the shrieking of nothingness.

Those ages passed like wolves among the graves. But today the skies are clear, and we can rest peacefully upon divine beds and welcome our thoughts and dreams, and embrace our desires. Grasping with untrembling fingers the torches that sway around us, we can talk to the genii with explicit meaning. As the choirs of angels pass us, they become intoxicated with the longing of our hearts and the hymns of our souls.

Yesterday we were, and today we are! This is the will of the goddess among the sons of the goddess. What is your will, oh sons of the monkeys? Have you walked a single step forward since you came forth from the crevices of the earth? Have you gazed toward heaven since Satan opened your eyes? Have you uttered a word from the book of Right since the lips of vipers kissed your lips? Or have you listened a moment to the song of Life since Death closed your ears?

Seventy thousand years ago I passed by and saw you moving like insects inside the caves; and seven minutes ago I glanced at you through the crystal glass of my window and saw you walking through the alleys fettered by slavery while the wings of Death hovered over you. You look the same today as you looked yesterday; and tomorrow, and the day after it, you shall look as I saw you in the beginning.

Yesterday we were, and today we are! This is the will of the goddess among the sons of the goddess; what is your will, oh sons of the monkeys?

Decayed Teeth

I HAD a decayed tooth in my mouth that troubled me. It stayed dormant during the day. But in the tranquility of the night, when the dentists were asleep and drug stores closed, it began to ache.

One day, as I grew impatient, I went to the dentist and told him to extract that damned tooth that dealt me misery and denied me the joy of slumber by converting the silence of my night into moaning and uproar.

The dentist shook his head and said, "It is foolish to have your tooth extracted if we can cure it."

Then he started to drill its sides and clean its cavities and used every means to restore it and free it from decay. Having finished drilling, he filled it with pure gold and said boastfully, "Your bad tooth now is stronger and more solid than your good ones." I believed him and paid him and departed from the place.

But before the week was over, the cursed tooth returned to its diseased condition and the torture it inflicted converted the beautiful songs of my soul into wailing and agony.

So I went to another dentist and said to him, "Extract this damned tooth without asking me any question, for the person who receives the blows is not like the one who counts them."

Obeying my command, he extracted the tooth. Looking at it he said, "You have done well to have this rotten tooth extracted."

In the mouth of Society are many diseased teeth, decayed to the bones of the jaws. But Society makes no efforts to have them extracted and be rid of the affliction. It contents itself with gold fillings. Many are the dentists who treat the decayed teeth of Society with glittering gold.

Numerous are those who yield to the enticements of such reformers, and pain, sickness, and death are their lot.

In the mouth of the Syrian nation are many rotten, black, and dirty teeth that fester and stink. The doctors have attempted cures with gold fillings instead of extraction. And the disease remains.

A nation with rotten teeth is doomed to have a sick stomach. Many are the nations afflicted with such indigestion.

If you wish to take a look at the decayed teeth of Syria, visit its schools where the sons and daughters of today are preparing to become the men and women of tomorrow.

Visit the courts and witness the acts of the crooked and corrupted purveyors of justice. See how they play with the thoughts and minds of the simple people as a cat plays with a mouse.

Visit the homes of the rich where conceit, falsehood, and hypocrisy reign.

But don't neglect to go through the huts of the poor as well, where dwell fear, ignorance, and cowardice.

Then visit the nimble-fingered dentists, possessors of

delicate instruments, dental plasters and tranquilizers, who spend their days filling the cavities in the rotten teeth of the nation to mask the decay.

Talk to those reformers who pose as the intelligentsia of the Syrian nation and organize societies, hold conferences, and deliver public speeches. When you talk to them you will hear tunes that perhaps sound more sublime than the grinding of a millstone, and nobler than the croaking of frogs on a June night.

When you tell them the Syrian nation gnaws its bread with decayed teeth and each morsel it chews is mixed with poisoned saliva that spreads diseases in the nation's stomach, they answer, "Yes, but we are seeking better tooth fillings and tranquilizers."

And if you suggest "extraction" to them, they will laugh at you because you have not yet learned the noble art of dentistry that conceals disease.

If you were to insist, they would go off and shun you, saying to themselves:

"Many are the idealists in this world, and weak are their dreams."

Mister Gabber

I AM BORED with gabbers and their gab; my soul abhors them.

When I wake up in the morning to peruse the letters and magazines placed by my bedside, I find them full of gab; all I see is loose talk empty of meaning but stuffed with hypocrisy.

When I sit by the window to lower the veil of slumber from my eyes and sip my Turkish coffee, Mister Gabber appears before me, hopping, crying, and grumbling. He condescends to sip my coffee and smoke my cigarettes.

When I go to work Mister Gabber follows, whispering in my ears and tickling my sensitive brain. When I try to get rid of him he giggles and is soon midstream again, in his flood of meaningless talk.

When I go to the market, Mister Gabber stands at the door of every shop passing judgment on people. I see him even upon the faces of the silent for he accompanies them too. They are unaware of his presence, yet he disturbs them.

If I sit down with a friend Mister Gabber, uninvited,

makes a third. If I elude him, he manages to remain so close that the echo of his voice irritates me and upsets my stomach like spoiled meat.

When I visit the courts and the institutions of learning, I find him and his father and mother dressing Falsehood in silky garments and Hypocrisy in a magnificent cloak and a beautiful turban.

When I call at factory offices, there too, to my surprise, I find Mister Gabber, in the midst of his mother, aunt, and grandfather chattering and flapping his thick lips. And his kinfolks applaud him and mock me.

On my visit to the temples and other places of worship, there he is, seated on a throne, his head crowned and a gleaming sceptre in his hand.

Returning home at eventide, I find him there, too. From the ceiling he hangs like a snake; or crawls like a boa in the four corners of my house.

In short, Mister Gabber is found everywhere; within and beyond the skies, on land and underground, on the wings of the ether and upon the waves of the sea, in the forests, in the caves, and on the mountaintops.

Where can a lover of silence and tranquility find rest from him? Will God ever have mercy on my soul and grant me the grace of dumbness so I may reside in the paradise of Silence?

Is there in this universe a nook where I can go and live happily by myself?

Is there any place where there is no traffic in empty talk?

Is there on this earth one who does not worship himself talking?

Is there any person among all persons whose mouth is not a hiding place for the knavish Mister Gabber?

If there were but one kind of gabber, I would be resigned. But gabbers are innumerable. They can be divided into clans and tribes:

There are those who live in marshes all day long, but when night comes, they move to the banks and raise their heads out of the water and the slime, and fill the silent night with horrible croaking that bursts the eardrums.

There are those who belong to the family of gnats. It is they who hover around our heads and make tiny devilish noises out of spite and hatred.

There is the clan whose members swill brandy and beer and stand at the street corners and fill the ether with a bellowing thicker than a buffalo's wallow.

We see also a queer tribe of people who pass their time at the tombs of Life converting silence into a sort of wailing more lugubrious than the screeching of the owl.

Then there is the gang of gabbers who imagine life as a piece of lumber from which they try to shape something for themselves, raising as they do so, a screeching sound uglier than the din of a sawmill.

Following this gang is a denomination of creatures who pound themselves with mallets to produce hollow tones more awful than the tomtoms of jungle savages.

Supporting these creatures is a sect whose members have nothing to do save to sit down, whenever a seat is available, and there chew words instead of uttering them.

Once in a while we find a party of gabbers who weave air from air, but remain without a garment.

Oftentime we run across a unique order of gabbers whose representatives are like starlings but deem themselves eagles when they soar in the currents of their words.

And what of those gabbers who are like ringing bells calling the people to worship but who never enter the church.

There are still more tribes and clans of gabbers, but they are too many to enumerate. Of these the strangest, in my opinion, is a sleeping denomination whose members trouble the universe with their snoring and awaken themselves, from time to time, to say, "How erudite we are!"

Having expressed my abhorrence of Mister Gabber and his comrades, I find myself like the doctor who cannot heal himself, or like a convict preaching to his cellmates. I have satirized Mister Gabber and his gabbing friends—with my own gabbing. I have fled from gabbers but I am one of them.

Will God ever forgive my sins before He blesses me and places me in the world of Thought, Truth, and Affection, where gabbers do not exist?

In the Dark Night

Written in World War I during the famine in Lebanon

IN THE DARK NIGHT we call to one another and cry for help, while the ghost of Death stands in our midst stretching his black wings over us and, with his iron hands, pushes our souls into the abyss.

In the dark night Death strides on and we follow him frightened and moaning. Not one of us is capable of halting the fateful procession or even nourishing a hope of its end.

In the dark night Death walks and we walk behind him. And when he looks backward, hundreds of souls fall down on both sides of the road. And he who falls, sleeps and never awakens. And he who keeps his footing marches on fearfully in the dread certainty of falling later and joining those who have yielded to Death and entered the eternal sleep. But Death marches on, gazing at the distant Evening Twilight.

In the dark night the brother calls his brother, the father

his son, and the mother her children; but the pangs and torments of hunger afflict us equally.

But Death does not hunger or thirst. He devours our souls and bodies, drinks our blood and tears and is never sated.

During the first part of the night the child calls his mother saying, "I am hungry, mother," and the mother replies, "Wait a while, my child."

In the second part of the night the child repeats, "I am hungry, mother, give me some bread," and the mother answers him, saying, "I have no bread, my beloved child."

In the third part of the night Death arrives and smites both the mother and the child with his wings and they both sleep eternally by the side of the road. And Death marches on, gazing at the distant Evening Twilight.

In the morn the husband goes to the field in search of nourishment, but he finds naught in it save dust and stones.

At noontide he returns to his wife and children pale, weak, and empty-handed.

And at eventide Death arrives and the husband, his wife, and children lie in eternal sleep. And he laughs and marches on toward the distant Evening Twilight.

In the morn the farmer leaves his hut for the city, carrying in his pocket his mother's and sisters' jewelry to exchange for bread. At eventide he returns without bread and without jewels, to find his mother and sisters sunk into eternal sleep, their eyes staring at nothingness. Whereupon he lifts his arms toward heaven and drops like a bird shot by a merciless hunter.

And Death, seeing the farmer, his mother and sisters beguiled to eternal sleep by the evil angel, laughs again and marches on toward the distant Evening Twilight.

Oh, you who walk in the light of the day, we call you

from the endless dark of the night. Do you hear our cries?

We have sent to you the spirits of our dead as our apostles. Have you heeded the apostles' word?

We have burdened the East Wind with our gasps. Has the Wind reached your distant shores to unload his burden in your hands? Are you aware of our misery? Have you thought of coming to our rescue? Or have you hugged to yourselves your peace and comfort, saying, "What can the sons of the light do for the sons of the dark? Let the dead bury their dead and God's will be done."

Yes, let God's will be done. But can you not raise yourselves above yourselves so that God may make you instruments of His will and use you for our aid?

In the dark night we call one another.

The brother calls his brother, the mother her daughter, the man his wife, and the lover his beloved.

And when our voices mingle together and reach the heart of heaven, Death pauses and laughs, then mocks us and marches on, gazing at the distant Evening Twilight.

The Silver-Plated Turd

SILMAN EFFANDI is a well-dressed man, tall and handsome, thirty-five years of age. He curls his mustaches and wears silk socks and patent-leather shoes. In his soft and delicate hand he carries a gold-headed and bejewelled walking stick. He eats in the most expensive restaurants where the fashionable forgather. In his magnificent carriage, drawn by thoroughbreds, he rides through the upper-class boulevards.

Silman Effandi's wealth was not inherited from his father, who (may his soul rest in peace) was a poor man. Neither did Silman Effandi amass wealth by shrewd and persevering business activities. He is lazy and hates to work, regarding any form of labor as degrading.

Once we heard him say, "My physique and temperament unfit me for work; work is meant for those with sluggish character and brutish body."

Then how did Silman attain his riches? By what magic was the dirt in his hands transformed into gold and silver? This is a secret hidden in a silver-plated turd which Azrael, the angel of Death, has revealed to us, and we in turn shall reveal it to you:

Five years ago Silman Effandi married the lady Faheema, widow of Betros Namaan, famous for his honesty, perseverence, and hard work.

Faheema was then forty-five years of age, but only sweet sixteen in her thoughts and behavior. She now dyes her hair and by the use of cosmetics deludes herself that she remains young and beautiful. She does not see Silman, her young husband, except after midnight when he vouchsafes her a scornful look and some vulgarities and abuse by way of conversation. This entitles him, he believes, to spend the money which her first husband earned by the sweat of his brow.

ADEEB EFFANDI is a young man, twenty-seven years of age, blessed with a big nose, small eyes, dirty face and ink-spotted hands with filth-encrusted fingernails. His clothes are frayed and adorned with oil, grease and coffee stains.

His ugly appearance is not due to Adeeb Effandi's poverty but to his preoccupation with spiritual and theological ideas. He often quotes Ameen El Jundy's saying that a scholar cannot be both clean and intelligent.

In his incessant talk Adeeb Effandi has nothing to say except to deliver judgment on others. On investigation, we found that Adeeb Effandi had spent two years in a school at Beirut studying rhetoric. He wrote poems, essays, and articles, which never saw print. His reasons for failing to achieve publication are the degeneration of the Arabic press and the ignorance of the Arabic reading public.

Recently Adeeb Effandi has been occupying himself with the study of the old and new philosophy. He admires Socrates and Nietzsche, and relishes the sayings of Saint Augustine as well as Voltaire and Rousseau. At a wedding

party we heard him discussing Hamlet; but his talk was
a soliloquy, for the others preferred to drink and sing.

On another occasion, at a funeral, the subjects of his
talk were the love poems of Ben Al Farid and the wine-
ism of Abi Nawaas. But the mourners ignored him, being
oppressed by grief.

Why, we often wonder, does Adeeb Effandi exist? What
use are his rotting books and his parchments falling into
dust? Would it not be better for him to buy himself an ass
and become a healthy and useful ass-driver?

This is a secret hidden in the silver-plated turd revealed
to us by Baal-Zabul and we in turn shall now reveal it to
you:

Three years ago Adeeb Effandi composed a poem in
praise of His Excellency, Bishop Joseph Shamoun. His
Excellency placed his hand on the shoulder of Adeeb
Effandi, smiled and said, "Bravo, my son, God bless you!
I have no doubt about your intelligence; some day you
will be among the great men of the East."

FAREED BEY DAVIS is a man in his late thirties, tall, with
a small head and large mouth, narrow forehead and a
bald pate. He walks with a pompous rolling gait, swelling
his chest and stretching his long neck like a camel.

From his loud voice and his haughty manner you might
imagine him (provided you had not met him before) the
minister of a great empire, absorbed in public affairs.

But Fareed has nothing to do aside from enumerating
and glorifying the deeds of his ancestors. He is fond of
citing exploits of famous men, and deeds of heroes such
as Napoleon and Antar. He is a collector of weapons of
which he has never learned the use.

One of his sayings is that God created two different
classes of people: the leaders and those who serve them.

Another is that the people are like stubborn asses who do not stir unless you whip them. Another, that the pen was meant for the weak and the sword for the strong.

What prompts Fareed to boast of his ancestry and behave as he does? This is a secret hidden in the silver-plated turd which Satanael has revealed to us, and we, in turn, reveal to you:

In the third decade of the nineteenth century when Emeer Basheer, the great Governor of Mount Lebanon, was passing with his retinue through the Lebanese valleys, they approached the village in which Mansour Davis, Fareed's grandfather lived. It was an exceedingly hot day, and the Emeer dismounted from his horse and ordered his men to rest in the shadow of an oak tree.

Mansour Davis, discovering the Emeer's presence, called the neighboring farmers, and the good news spread through the village. Led by Mansour the villagers brought baskets of grapes and figs, and jars of honey, wine and milk for the Emeer. When they reached the oak tree, Mansour kneeled before the Emeer and kissed the hem of his robe. Then he stood up and killed a sheep in the Emeer's honor, saying, "The sheep is from thy bounty, oh Prince and protector of our lives." The Emeer, pleased with such hospitality, said to him, "Henceforth you shall be the mayor of this village which I will exempt from taxes for this year."

That night, after the Emeer had left, the villagers met at the house of "Sheik" Mansour Davis and vowed loyalty to the newly appointed Sheik. May God have mercy on their souls.

There are too many secrets contained in the silver-plated turd to enumerate them all. The devils and satans reveal some to us every day and night, which we shall share with you before the angel of death wraps us under his wings and takes us into the Great Beyond.

Since it is now midnight and our eyes are getting heavy, permit us to surrender ourselves to Slumber and perhaps the beautiful bride of dreams will carry our souls into a world cleaner than this one.

Martha

I

HER FATHER DIED when she was in the cradle, and she lost her mother before reaching the age of ten. As an orphan, Martha was left in the care of a poor peasant whose servant she became. They lived in an obscure hamlet on a slope of the beautiful mountains of North Lebanon.

At his death, her father had left his family only his good name and a hut standing amidst willow and walnut trees. It was the death of her mother which truly orphaned her. It left an emptiness in her heart which could not be filled. She became a stranger in her birthplace. Every day she walked barefoot leading a cow to pasture. While the cow grazed she sat under a tree, singing with the birds, weeping with the stream, envying the cow her serenity, and gazing at the flowers over which the butterflies hovered.

At night she returned home to a simple dinner of bread, olives, and dried fruit. She slept in a bed of straw, with her arms for a pillow; and it was her prayer that her whole life might be uninterrupted slumber. At dawn her master would wake her so that she would get the housework done before she led the cow to pasture. She trembled and did as she was ordered.

Thus the gloomy and puzzling years passed, and Martha grew like a sapling. In her heart there developed a quiet affection of which she herself was unaware . . . like fragrance born in the heart of a flower. She followed her fancy as sheep follow a stream to quench their thirst. Her mind was like virgin land where knowledge had sown no seeds and upon which no feet had trod.

We who live amid the excitements of the city know nothing of the life of the mountain villagers. We are swept into the current of urban existence, until we forget the peaceful rhythms of simple country life, which smiles in the spring, toils in summer, reaps in autumn, rests in winter, imitating nature in all her cycles. We are wealthier than the villagers in silver or gold, but they are richer in spirit. What we sow we reap not; they reap what they sow. We are slaves of gain, and they the children of contentment. Our draught from the cup of life is mixed with bitterness and despair, fear and weariness; but they drink the pure nectar of life's fulfillment.

At sixteen, Martha's soul was like a clear mirror that reflects a beautiful landscape; her heart like a primeval valley that echoes all voices.

One day in autumn she sat by the spring, gazing at the falling yellow leaves, stripped from the trees by the breeze that moved between the branches as death moves into a man's soul. She looked at the withering flowers whose hearts were dry and whose seeds sought shelter in earth's bosom like refugees seeking a new life.

While thus engrossed, she heard hoofbeats upon the ground. Turning, she observed a horseman approaching. As he reached the spring he dismounted and greeted her with kind words, such as she had not heard from a man before. Then he went on to say, "Young lady, I have lost my way. Will you please direct me to the road to the coast?"

Looking like a tender branch, there by the spring, she replied, "I regret, sir, that I am unable to direct you, never having been away from home; but if you will ask my master I am sure he can help you." Her flushed face, as she spoke, made her look more gentle and beautiful. As she started away he stopped her. His expression became soft as he said, "Please do not go."

And a strange power in the man's voice held her immobile. When she stole a glance at his face she found him gazing at her steadily. She could not understand his silent adoration.

He eyed her lovely bare feet, her graceful arms and smooth neck and shining hair. Lovingly and wonderingly he regarded her sun-warmed cheeks and her chiseled features. She could not utter a single word or move a muscle.

The cow returned alone to the barn that evening. Martha's master searched all through the valley but could not find her. His wife wept all that night. She said the next morning, "I saw Martha in my dream last night, and she was between the paws of a wild beast who lured her; the beast was about to kill Martha, but she smiled."

II

In the autumn of 1900, after a vacation in North Lebanon, I returned to Beyrouth. Before re-entering school I spent a week roaming the city with my classmates. We were like birds whose cage-door is unlocked, and who come and go as they please.

Youth is a beautiful dream, on whose brightness books

shed a blinding dust. Will ever the day come when the wise link the joy of knowledge to youth's dream? Will ever the day come when Nature becomes the teacher of man, humanity his book and life his school? Youth's joyous purpose cannot be fulfilled until that day comes. Too slow is our march toward spiritual elevation, because we make so little use of youth's ardor.

One evening, as I was contemplating the jostling street crowds of Beyrouth, and feeling deafened by the shouts of the street vendors, I noticed a ragged boy of about five carrying some flowers on a tray. In a dispirited voice he asked me, "Will you buy some flowers, sir?" His mouth was half-open, resembling and echoing a deep wound in the soul. His arms were thin and bare, and his frail body was bent over his flower tray like a branch of withering roses.

In my reply I tried to keep from my voice any intrusive edge of charity.

I bought some of his flowers but my chief purpose was to converse with him. I felt that his heart was a stage upon which a continuous drama of misery was being enacted.

At my careful, tactful words he began to feel secure and a smile brightened his face. He was surprised to hear words of kindness, for like all the poor he was accustomed to harshness. I asked his name, which was Fu'ad, and then, "Whose son are you?" He replied, "I am the son of Martha." "And who is your father?" I inquired. He shook his head, puzzled, as if unaware of the meaning of the word. I continued, "Where is your mother now, Fu'ad?" He replied, weeping, "She is at home, sick."

Suddenly remembrance formed in my mind. Martha, whose unfinished story I had heard from an old villager, was ill nearby. That young woman who yesterday safely roamed the valley and enjoyed the beauty of nature was now suffering the anguish of destitution; that orphan who spent her early life in the haven of Nature was undergoing the tortures that city sophistication inflicts upon the innocent.

As the boy started to leave, I took hold of his hand saying, "Take me to your mother. I would like to see her." He led the way silently, looking back now and then to see if I followed.

Through narrow, dirty streets with an odor of death in the air, and between houses of ill-fame, raucous with the sounds of sin, I walked behind Fu'ad, admiring the courage in his stride. It took courage to walk in these slums, where violence, crime and plague mocked the glory of this city, called "The Bride of Syria" and "The Pearl of the Sultan's Crown."

As we entered a particularly squalid quarter, the boy pointed to a hovel whose walls appeared to be collapsing. My heartbeats quickened and I followed Fu'ad into a sunless, airless room, unfurnished except for an oil lamp and a hard bed upon which Martha was lying, her face to the wall as if to hide from the oppression of the city. Fu'ad touched her shoulder and said, "Mama." As she turned painfully, he pointed at me. She moved her weak body under the ragged quilt, and with a despairing voice said, "What brings you here, stranger? What do you want? Did you come here to buy the last remnant of my soul and pollute it with your desire? Go away from here; the streets are full of women who sell themselves. What is left of my broken soul death shall soon buy. Go away from me and my boy."

Those few words completed her tragic story. I said, "Fear me not, Martha; I come here not as a devourer, but as a fellow sufferer. I am a Lebanese who lived near your valley by the cedars of Lebanon. Do not be frightened."

Realizing then that my words came from a feeling soul, she shook like a thin branch before a strong wind, and placed her hands upon her face, trying to hide away the terrible and beautiful memory whose sweetness was ravaged by bitterness.

Then in a strangely strong yet hopeless voice she said, "You have come here as a benefactor, and may God reward you; but I beg you to leave, for your presence here will bring disgrace upon you. Avoid being recognized. Your merciful heart does not restore my virtue; it neither effaces my shame nor protects me from the hands of death. My own sin brought this misery upon me; do not let your mercy bring you into shame. I am like a leper who must be avoided. Go, lest you be polluted! Do not mention my name in North Lebanon. The lamb with the mange is destroyed by the shepherd for fear he will infect the other lambs. If you speak of me, say I am dead."

Then she embraced her little boy and said: "People will taunt my son, saying he is the fruit of sin; the son of Martha the adulteress; Martha the prostitute. For they are blind and do not see that his mother gave him life through misery. I shall die and leave him as an orphan among other children, and his remembrance of me will bring him shame. But when he becomes a man, he will help heaven to end that which brought sin upon me; and when he dies in the trap of time, he will find me waiting for him in Eternity, where light and peace abide."

With a desolate heart I said, "Martha, you are not a leper. You live in a grave yet you are clean. The filth of the body cannot reach a pure soul."

Hearing my heartfelt words, Martha's face brightened. But it was plain that her death was near. Yesterday she had roamed the valleys of Lebanon; today, weak and sorrowful, she awaited release from the shackles of life.

Gathering her last fragments of strength she whispered, "I am everything you say, although my own weakness brought my agony . . . the horseman came . . . he spoke politely and cleverly . . . he kissed me . . . I knew nothing and relied on his words. He took me away and his fine words and smiles masked his ugly desires. After accomplishing my disgrace, he abandoned me. He split my life in two parts—my helpless self, and my baby. We were cold . . . we suffered. . . . For the sake of my child I took gold from men who bought my body. Many times I was close to taking my life. Now, at last, the hour has come and beloved death has arrived to enfold me under his sheltering wings."

Suddenly in a strong but calm voice she said, "Oh Justice, hidden behind those terrible images, hear the shrieking of my departing soul and the call of my broken heart! Have mercy on me by saving my child and taking me away!"

Her breathing became weak. She looked sorrowfully and sweetly at her son and then whispered, "Our Father which art in heaven, hallowed be Thy name. Thy kingdom come, Thy will be done on earth as it is in heaven. . . . Forgive us our sins as we . . ."

Her voice gave out but her lips still moved. Then she breathed her last on earth. Her eyes remained open as if seeing the invisible.

As dawn came, the body of Martha was carried in a rough casket to a graveyard by two poor men. Far out from the City of Beyrouth they carried her. The priests refused to pray for her, and prohibited her interment in hallowed ground. And no one accompanied Martha to her resting place except her little son Fu'ad and a youth to whom life had taught mercy and kindness.

Vision

WHEN NIGHT CAME and Slumber spread its garment upon the face of the earth, I left my bed and walked toward the sea saying, "The sea never sleeps, and in its vigil there is consolation for a sleepless soul."

When I reached the shore, the mist from the mountains had engauzed the region as a veil adorns the face of a young woman. I gazed at the teeming waves and listened to their praise of God and meditated upon the eternal power hidden within them—that power which runs with the tempest and rises with the volcano and smiles through the lips of the roses and sings with the brooks.

Then I saw three phantoms sitting upon a rock. I stumbled toward them as if some power were pulling me against my will.

Within a few paces from the phantoms, I halted as though held still by a magic force. At that moment one of the phantoms stood up and in a voice that seemed to rise from the depth of the sea said:

"Life without Love is like a tree without blossom and fruit. And love without Beauty is like flowers without scent and fruits without seeds. . . . Life, Love, and Beauty are three persons in one, who cannot be separated or changed."

A second phantom spoke with a voice that roared like cascading water and said:

"Life without Rebellion is like seasons without Spring. And Rebellion without Right is like Spring in an arid desert. . . . Life, Rebellion, and Right are three-in-one who cannot be changed or separated."

Then the third phantom in a voice like a clap of thunder spoke:

"Life without Freedom is like a body without a soul, and Freedom without Thought is like a confused spirit. . . . Life, Freedom, and Thought are three-in-one, and are everlasting and never pass away."

Then the three phantoms stood up together, and with one tremendous voice said:

> "That which Love begets,
> That which Rebellion creates,
> That which Freedom rears,
> Are three manifestations of God.
> And God is the expression
> Of the intelligent Universe."

At that moment Silence mingled with the rustling of invisible wings and trembling of ethereal bodies; and it prevailed.

I closed my eyes and listened to the echoes of the sayings which I had just heard, and when I opened them I saw nothing but the sea wreathed in mist. I walked toward the rock where the three phantoms were sitting, but I saw naught save a column of incense spiralling toward heaven.

Communion of Spirits

Awake, my love, awake! For my spirit hails you from beyond the seas, and offers you her wings above the raging waves.

Awake, for silence has halted the clamor of the horses' hoofs and the tramp of the passers-by.

Slumber has embraced the spirits of men, while I alone remain awake; longing lifts me out of enveloping sleep.

Love brings me close to you but then, anxiety takes me far away.

I have left my bed, my love, for fear of the ghost of forgetfulness hiding in the quilts.

I have thrown my book aside, for my sighs silenced the words and left the pages blank before my eyes!

Awake, awake, my love, and hear me.

I hear you, my beloved! I heard your call from beyond the seas and felt the soft touch of your wings; I have left my bed and walked upon the grass and the night dew has wet my feet and the hem of my garment. Here I stand under the blossoms of the almond tree, heeding the call of your spirit.

Speak to me, my love, and let your breath mount the breeze that comes towards me from the valleys of Lebanon. Speak. No one hears but me. Night has taken all others to their resting places.

Heaven has woven a veil of moonlight and drawn it over all Lebanon, my beloved.

Heaven has fashioned from the shadows of night a thick cloak lined with the fumes of workshops and the breath of Death, and laid it over the frame of the city, my love.

The villagers have surrendered to Slumber in their huts in the midst of the willow and walnut trees. Their spirits have sped towards the land of dreams, my beloved.

Men are bent under the burden of gold, and the steep road of green weakens their knees. Their eyes are heavy with trouble and weariness, and they drop on their beds as a haven, my love, from the Ghosts of Fear and Despair.

The ghosts of past ages walk in the valleys, and the spirits of the kings and prophets hover over the knolls and the hills. And my thoughts, fashioned by memory, show me the might of the Chaldeans, the splendor of the Assyrians, and the nobility of the Arabs.

In the sinister alleys walk the grim spirits of the thieves; the heads of the vipers of lust appear from the crevices of the ramparts; and the ague of sickness, mingled with the agony of Death, shudders through the streets. Memory has removed the veil of forgetfulness from my eyes and shows me the loathsomeness of Sodom and the sins of Gomorrah.

The branches sway, my beloved, and their rustling joins the murmur of the rivulet in the valley, repeating to our ears the canticles of Solomon, the strains of David's harp, and the songs of Ishak al-Mausili.

The souls of the hungry children in the lodgings tremble; and the sighs of the mothers tossing upon the beds of misery and despair have reached the sky; and anxious dreams afflict the hearts of the infirm. I hear their bitter lamentations.

The fragrance of flowers has mingled with the pungent breath of the cedars. Brought by the frolicsome breeze over the hills, it fills the soul with affection and inspires longing for flight.

But the miasmas from the marshes also rise, steaming with disease. Like sharp secret arrows they have penetrated the senses and poisoned the air.

The morning has come, my beloved, and the soft fingers of wakefulness fondle the eyes of the dreamers. Rays of light force open the shutters and reveal Life's resolution and glory. The villages, reposing in peace and tranquility upon the shoulders of the valley, rise from their slumber; church bells fill the air with their pleasing summons to morning prayer. And from the caves echo the chimes as if all Nature joins in reverent prayer. The calves have left their stalls, and the sheep and the goats their sheds, to graze upon the glittering, dewy grass. The shepherds walk before them, piping on their reeds; and behind them walk the damsels singing like the birds welcoming the morn.

And now the heavy hand of the Day lies upon the city. The curtains have been drawn from the windows and the doors are open. The fatigued eyes and drawn faces of toilers appear in the workshops. They feel death encroaching upon their lives, and on their shrivelled countenances appear Fear and Despair. The streets are congested with hurrying greedy souls; and everywhere are heard the clanking of iron, the rattling of wheels, and whistling of steam. The city has turned into a battlefield where the strong wrestle down the weak and the rich exploit and tyrannize over the poor.

How beautiful is life, my beloved; it is like the poet's heart, filled with light and tenderness.

And how cruel is life, my love, it is like a criminal's heart, throbbing with vice and fear.

Under the Sun

I have seen all things that are done under the sun, and behold all is vanity and vexation of spirit.

ECCLESIASTES

O SPIRIT of Solomon that hovers in the ethereal realm; you, who cast aside the tattered garment of matter, have left behind you these words, born of weakness and misery, which deject those still imprisoned in bodies.

You know there is a meaning in this life which Death does not conceal. But how could humanity attain a knowledge which comes only when the soul is freed from earthly ties?

You realize now that life is not a vexation of spirit; that things done under the sun are not all vanity; that somehow everything has ever marched and shall ever march toward Truth. We miserable creatures have adhered to your earthly sayings as words of great wisdom. But they are shutters that darken the mind and obliterate hope.

You now understand that ignorance, evil, and despotism have their causes; and that Beauty is the revelation of wisdom, the product of virtue and the fruit of justice.

213

You now know that sorrow and poverty purify man's heart; though our weak minds see nothing worthy in the universe save ease and happiness.

You can see now that the spirit advances toward the light in spite of worldly hardships. Yet we repeat your words which teach that a man is but a toy in the hands of the unknown.

You have regretted your planting in our hearts a faintness toward life in the world and apprehension toward life in the hereafter. Yet we persist in heeding your earthly words.

O spirit of Solomon who now dwells in Eternity, reveal yourself to the lovers of wisdom and teach them not to walk the path of heresy and misery. Perchance this shall be an atonement for an unintended error.

A Glance at the Future

From behind the wall of the Present I heard the hymns of humanity. I heard the sounds of the bells announcing the beginning of the prayer in the temple of Beauty. Bells moulded in the metal of emotion and poised above the holy altar—the human heart.

From behind the Future I saw multitudes worshipping on the bosom of Nature, their faces turned toward the East and awaiting the inundation of the morning light—the morning of Truth.

I saw the city in ruins and nothing remaining to tell man of the defeat of Ignorance and the triumph of Light.

I saw the elders seated under the shade of cypress and willow trees, surrounded by youths listening to their tales of former times.

I saw the youths strumming their guitars and piping on their reeds and the loose-tressed damsels dancing under the jasmine trees.

I saw the husbandmen harvesting the wheat, and the wives gathering the sheaves and singing mirthful songs.

I saw woman adorning herself with a crown of lilies and a girdle of green leaves.

I saw Friendship strengthened between man and all creatures, and clans of birds and butterflies, confident and secure, winging toward the brooks.

I saw no poverty; neither did I encounter excess. I saw fraternity and equality prevailing among man.

I saw not one physician, for everyone had the means and knowledge to heal himself.

I found no priest, for conscience had become the High Priest. Neither did I see a lawyer, for Nature has taken the place of the courts, and treaties of amity and companionship were in force.

I saw that man knew that he is the cornerstone of creation, and that he has raised himself above littleness and baseness and cast off the veil of confusion from the eyes of the soul; this soul now reads what the clouds write on the face of heaven and what the breeze draws on the surface of the water; now understands the meaning of the flower's breath and the cadences of the nightingale.

From behind the wall of the Present, upon the stage of coming ages, I saw Beauty as a groom and Spirit as a bride, and Life as the ceremonial Night of the Kedre.*

* A night during the Moslem Lent when God is said to grant the wishes of the devout.

The Goddess of Fantasy

AND AFTER a wearying journey I reached the ruins of
Palmyra. There I dropped, exhausted, upon the grass that
grew among columns shattered and leveled by the ages.
They looked like the debris left by invading armies.

At nightfall, as the black mantle of silence enfolded all
creatures, I savored a strange scent in the air. It was as
fragrant as incense and as inebriating as wine. My spirit
opened her mouth to sip the ethereal nectar. Then a hidden hand seemed to press upon my senses and my eyelids
grew heavy, while my spirit felt freed of its shackles.

Then the earth swayed under me and the sky trembled
over me; whereupon I leaped up as though raised by a
magic power. And I found myself in a meadow the like of
which no human being has ever fancied. I found myself in
the midst of a host of virgins who wore no other raiment
than the beauty God gave them. They walked around me,
but their feet touched not the grass. They chanted hymns
expressing dreams of love. Each maiden played on a lute
framed with ivory and strung with gold.

I came upon a vast clearing in the center of which stood

a throne inlaid with precious stones and illuminated with the rays of the rainbow. The virgins stood at both sides, raised their voices and faced the direction whence came the scent of myrrh and frankincense. The trees were in bloom and from between the branches, laden with blossoms, a queen walked majestically to the throne. As she seated herself, a flock of doves, white as snow, descended and settled around her feet and formed a crescent, while the maidens chanted hymns of glory. I stood there watching what no man's eyes had seen, and hearing what no man's ears had heard.

Then the Queen motioned, and silence fell. And in a voice that caused my spirit to quiver like the strings of the lute under a player's fingers, she said, "I have called you, man, for I am the Goddess of Fantasy. I have bestowed upon you the honor of standing before me, the Queen of the prairies of dreams. Listen to my commandments, for I appoint you to preach them to the whole human race: explain to man that the city of dreams is a wedding feast at whose door a mighty giant stands on guard. No one may enter unless he wears a wedding garment. Let it be known that this city is a paradise whose sentinel is the angel of Love, and no human may glance at it save he on whose forehead the sign of Love is inscribed. Picture to them these beautiful fields whose streams flow with nectar and wine, whose birds sail in the skies and sing with the angels. Describe the aromatic scent of its flowers and let it be known that only the Son of Dream may tread its soft grass.

"Say that I gave man a cupful of joy; but he, in his ignorance, poured it out. Then the angels of Darkness filled the cup with the brew of Sorrow which he drank and became inebriated.

"Say that none can play the lyre of Life unless his fingers have been blessed by my touch and his eyes sanctified by the sight of my throne.

"Isaiah composed words of wisdom as a necklace of precious stones mounted on the golden chain of my love. Saint John recounted his vision in my behalf. And Dante could not explore the haven of souls save by my guidance. I am metaphor embracing reality, and reality revealing the singleness of the spirit; and a witness confirming the deeds of the gods.

"Truly I say to you that thoughts have a higher dwelling place than the visible world, and its skies are not clouded by sensuality. Imagination finds a road to the realm of the gods, and there man can glimpse that which is to be after the soul's liberation from the world of substance."

And the Goddess of Fantasy drew me toward her with her magic glance and imprinted a kiss upon my burning lips and said, "Tell them that he who passes not his days in the realm of dreams is the slave of the days."

Thereupon the voices of the virgins rose again and the column of incense ascended. Then the earth began to sway again and the sky to tremble; and suddenly I found myself again among Palmyra's sorrowful ruins.

The smiling Dawn had already made its appearance, and between my tongue and my lips were these words: "He who passes not his days in the realm of dreams is the slave of the days."

History and the Nation

By the side of a rivulet that meandered among the rocks at the foot of Lebanon's Mountain sat a shepherdess surrounded by her flock of lean sheep grazing upon dry grass. She looked into the distant twilight as if the future were passing before her. Tears had jewelled her eyes like dewdrops adorning flowers. Sorrow had caused her lips to open that it might enter and occupy her sighing heart.

After sunset, as the knolls and hills wrapped themselves in shadow, History stood before the maiden. He was an old man whose white hair fell like snow over his breast and shoulders, and in his right hand he held a sharp sickle. In a voice like the roaring sea he said, "Peace unto you, Syria."*

The virgin rose, trembling with fear. "What do you wish of me, History?" she asked. Then she pointed to her sheep. "This is the remnant of a healthy flock that once filled this valley. This is all that your covetousness has left me. Have you come now to sate your greed on that?

* At the writing of this story Lebanon and Syria were one country known as Syria.

"These plains that were once so fertile have been trodden to barren dust by your trampling feet. My cattle that once grazed upon flowers and produced rich milk, now gnaw thistles that leave them gaunt and dry.

"Fear God, oh History, and afflict me no more. The sight of you has made me detest life, and the cruelty of your sickle has caused me to love Death.

"Leave me in my solitude to drain the cup of sorrow—my best wine. Go, History, to the West where Life's wedding feast is being celebrated. Here let me lament the bereavement you have prepared for me."

Concealing his sickle under the folds of his garment, History looked upon her as a loving father looks upon his child, and said, "Oh Syria, what I have taken from you were my own gifts. Know that your sister-nations are entitled to a part of the glory which was yours. I must give to them what I gave you. Your plight is like that of Egypt, Persia, and Greece, for each one of them also has a lean flock and dry pasture. Oh Syria, that which you call degradation is an indispensable sleep from which you will draw strength. The flower does not return to life save through death, and love does not grow except after separation."

The old man came close to the maiden, stretched forth his hand and said, "Shake my hand, oh Daughter of the Prophets." And she shook his hand and looked at him from behind a screen of tears and said, "Farewell, History, farewell." And he responded, "Until we meet again, Syria, until we meet again."

And the old man disappeared like swift lightning, and the shepherdess called her sheep and started on her way, saying to herself, *"Shall there be another meeting?"*

The Speechless Animal

*In the glance of the speechless animal there is a discourse
that only the soul of the wise can really understand.*
AN INDIAN POET

IN THE TWILIGHT of a beautiful day, when fancy seized upon
my mind, I passed by the edge of the city and tarried before the wreck of an abandoned house of which only
rubble was left.

In the rubble I saw a dog lying upon dirt and ashes.
Sores covered his skin, and sickness racked his feeble body.
Staring now and then at the setting sun, his sorrowful eyes
expressed humiliation, despair, and misery.

I walked slowly toward him wishing that I knew animal
speech so that I might console him with my sympathy.
But my approach only terrified him, and he tried to rise
on his palsied legs. Falling, he turned a look on me in
which helpless wrath was mingled with supplication. In
that glance was speech more lucid than man's and more
moving than a woman's tears. This is what I understood
him to say:

222

"Man, I have suffered through illness caused by your brutality and persecution.

"I have run from your bruising foot and taken refuge here, for dust and ashes are gentler than man's heart, these ruins less melancholy than the soul of man. Begone, you intruder from the world of misrule and injustice.

"I am a miserable creature who served the son of Adam with faith and loyalty. I was man's faithful companion, I guarded him day and night. I grieved during his absence and welcomed him with joy upon his return. I was contented with the crumbs that fell from his board, and happy with the bones that his teeth had stripped. But when I grew old and ill, he drove me from his home and left me to merciless boys of the alleys.

"Oh son of Adam, I see the similarity between me and your fellow men when age disables them. There are soldiers who fought for their country when they were in the prime of life, and who later tilled its soil. But now that the winter of their life has come and they are useful no longer, they are cast aside.

"I also see a resemblance between my lot and that of a woman who, during the days of her lovely maidenhood enlivened the heart of a young man; and who then, as a mother, devoted her life to her children. But now, grown old, she is ignored and avoided. How oppressive you are, son of Adam, and how cruel!"

Thus spoke the speechless animal whom my heart had understood.

Poets and Poems

IF MY FELLOW POETS had imagined that the necklaces of verses they composed, and the stanzas whose meters they had strengthened and joined together, would some day become reins to hold back talent, they would have torn up their manuscripts.

If Al-Mutanabbi,* the prophet, had prophesied, and Al-Farid,** the seer, had foreseen that what they had written would become a source for the barren and a forced guide to our poets of today, they would have poured out their inks in the wells of Oblivion, and broken their quills with the hands of Negligence.

If the spirits of Homer, Virgil, Al-Maary,*** and Milton had known that poetry would become a lapdog of the rich, they would have forsaken a world in which this could occur.

* The word Al-Mutanabbi means the one who divines or predicts. He was a famous Arabian poet whose poems were translated into several languages.
** An outstanding Arabian poet and philosopher.
*** A ninth century Arabian poet who became blind at the age of four and was looked upon as a genius.

I grieve to hear the language of the spirits prattled by the tongues of the ignorant. It slays my soul to see the wine of the muses flow over the pens of the pretenders.

Neither am I found alone in the vale of Resentment. Say that I am one of the many who see the frog puffed up to imitate the buffalo.

Poetry, my dear friends, is a sacred incarnation of a smile. Poetry is a sigh that dries the tears. Poetry is a spirit who dwells in the soul, whose nourishment is the heart, whose wine is affection. Poetry that comes not in this form is a false messiah.

Oh spirits of the poets, who watch over us from the heaven of Eternity, we go to the altars you have adorned with the pearls of your thoughts and the gems of your souls because we are oppressed by the clang of steel and the clamor of factories. Therefore our poems are as heavy as freight trains and as annoying as steam whistles.

And you, the real poets, forgive us. We belong in the New World where men run after worldly goods; and poetry, too, is a commodity today, and not a breath of immortality.

Among the Ruins

THE MOON DROPPED its gauzy veil over the gardens of the City of the Sun,* and silence swathed all beings. The fallen palaces looked menacing, like sneering monsters.

At that hour two phantoms, like vapor rising from the blue water of a lake, sat on a marble pillar pondering the scene which was like a realm of magic. One lifted his head, and with a voice that set echoes reverberating, said:

"These are the remnants of temples I built for you, my beloved, and this is the rubble of a palace I erected for your enjoyment. Nothing else remains to tell the nations of the glory to which I devoted my life, and of the pomp for which I exploited the weak.

"Think and ponder, my beloved, upon the elements that triumphed over my city, and upon Time that thus belittled my efforts.

"Oblivion has submerged the empire I established, and naught is left save atoms of love which your beauty has created, and effects of beauty which your love has enlivened.

* The ruined City of Baalbek.

"I erected a temple in Jerusalem and the priests sanctified it, but time has destroyed it. But in my heart the altar I built for Love was consecrated by God and sustained against the powers of destruction.

"Men said of me, 'What a wise king he is!' The angels said, 'How trifling is his wisdom.' But the angels rejoiced when I found you, my beloved, and sang for you the song of Love and longing; though men heard no notes of my hymn. . . .

"The days of my reign were barriers to my understanding of Love and of the beauty of life, but when I saw you, Love awoke and demolished those barriers, and I lamented the life I spent considering everything under the sun as vanity.

"As Love enlightened me, I became humble both before the tribes who had feared my military might and before my own people.

"But when death came, it buried my deadly weapons in earth and carried my love to God."

And the other phantom said, "As the flower obtains life and aromatic scent from earth, so the soul extracts wisdom and strength from the weakness and errors of matter."

Then the two fused into one and walked away, saying:

"Eternity keeps naught but Love,
For Love is like Eternity."

At the Door of the Temple

I PURIFIED MY LIPS with the sacred fire, to speak of Love, but could find no words.

When Love became known to me, the words lapsed into a faint gasping, and the song in my heart into deep silence.

Oh you who asked me about Love, whom I convinced of its mysteries and wonders, now since Love has wrapped me in its veil, I come to ask you about Love's course and merit.

Who can answer my questions? I ask about that which is in me; I seek to be informed about myself.

Who among you can reveal my inner self to myself and my soul to my soul?

Tell me, for Love's sake, what is that flame which burns in my heart and devours my strength and dissolves my will?

What are those hidden soft and rough hands that grasp my soul; what is that wine mixed of bitter joy and sweet pain that suffuses my heart?

What are those wings that hover over my pillow in the

silence of Night, and keep me awake, watching no one knows what?

What is the invisible thing I stare at, the incomprehensible thing that I ponder, the feeling that cannot be sensed?

In my sighs is a grief more beautiful than the echo of laughter and more rapturous than joy.

Why do I surrender myself to an unknown power that slays me and revives me until Dawn rises and fills my chamber with its light?

Phantoms of wakefulness tremble between my seared eyelids, and shadows of dreams hover over my stony bed.

What is that which we call Love? Tell me, what is that secret hidden within the ages yet which permeates all consciousness?

What is this consciousness that is at once origin and result of everything?

What is this vigil that fashions from Life and Death a dream, stranger than Life and deeper than Death?

Tell me, friends, is there one among you who would not awake from the slumber of Life if Love touched his soul with its fingertip?

Which one of you would not leave his father and mother at the call of the virgin whom his heart loves?

Who among you would not sail the distant seas, cross the deserts, and climb the topmost peak to meet the woman whom his soul has chosen?

What youth's heart would not follow to the ends of the world the maiden whose aromatic breath, sweet voice, and magic-soft hands have enraptured his soul?

What being would not burn his heart as incense before a god who listens to his supplications and grants his prayer?

Yesterday I stood at the temple door interrogating the passers-by about the mystery and merit of Love.

And before me passed an old man with an emaciated and melancholy face, who sighed and said:

"Love is a natural weakness bestowed upon us by the first man."

But a virile youth retorted:

"Love joins our present with the past and the future."

Then a woman with a tragic face sighed and said:

"Love is a deadly poison injected by black vipers, that crawl from the caves of hell. The poison seems fresh as dew and the thirsty soul eagerly drinks it; but after the first intoxication the drinker sickens and dies a slow death."

Then a beautiful, rosy-cheeked damsel smilingly said:

"Love is wine served by the brides of Dawn which strengthens strong souls and enables them to ascend to the stars."

After her a black-robed, bearded man, frowning, said:

"Love is the blind ignorance with which youth begins and ends."

Another, smiling, declared:

"Love is a divine knowledge that enables men to see as much as the gods."

Then said a blind man, feeling his way with a cane:

"Love is a blinding mist that keeps the soul from discerning the secret of existence, so that the heart sees only trembling phantoms of desire among the hills, and hears only echoes of cries from voiceless valleys."

A young man, playing on his viol, sang:

"Love is a magic ray emitted from the burning core of the soul and illuminating the surrounding earth. It enables us to perceive Life as a beautiful dream between one awakening and another."

And a feeble ancient, dragging his feet like two rags, said, in quavering tones:

"Love is the rest of the body in the quiet of the grave, the tranquility of the soul in the depth of Eternity."

And a five-year-old child, after him, said laughing:

"Love is my father and mother, and no one knows Love save my father and mother."

And so, all who passed spoke of Love as the image of their hopes and frustrations, leaving it a mystery as before.

Then I heard a voice within the temple:

"Life is divided into two halves, one frozen, the other aflame; the burning half is Love."

Thereupon I entered the temple, kneeling, rejoicing, and praying:

> "Make me, O Lord, nourishment
>   for the blazing flame . . .
> Make me, O God, food for the
>   sacred fire . . . Amen."

Narcotics and Dissecting Knives

"HE IS EXCESSIVE and fanatic to the point of madness. Though he is an idealist, his literary aim is to poison the mind of the youths. . . . If men and women were to follow Gibran's counsels on marriage, family ties would break, society would perish, and the world would become an inferno peopled by demons and devils.

"His style is seductively beautiful, magnifying the danger of this inveterate enemy of mankind. Our counsel to the inhabitants of this blessed Mountain (Mount Lebanon) is to reject the insidious teachings of this anarchist and heretic and to burn his books, that his doctrines may not lead the innocent astray. We have read *The Broken Wings* and found it to be honeyed poison."

Such is what people say of me and they are right, for I am indeed a fanatic and I am inclined toward destruction as well as construction. There is hatred in my heart for that which my detractors sanctify, and love for that which they reject. And if I could uproot certain customs, beliefs, and traditions of the people, I would do so without hesitation. When they said my books were poison, they were speaking truth about themselves, for what I say is poison to them. But they falsified when they said I mix honey into it, for I apply the poison full strength and pour it from transparent glass. Those who call me an idealist becalmed in clouds are the very ones who turn away from the transparent glass they call poison, knowing that their stomachs cannot digest it.

This may sound truculent, but is not truculence preferable to seductive pretense?

The people of the Orient demand that the writer be like a bee always making honey. They are gluttonous for honey and prefer it to all other food.

The people of the Orient want their poet to burn himself as incense before their sultans. The Eastern skies have become sickly with incense yet the people of the Orient have not had enough.

They ask the world to learn their history, to study their antiquities, customs and traditions, and acquire their languages. They also expect those who know them not to repeat the words of Baidaba the Philosopher, Ben Rished, Ephraim Al-Syriani, and John of Damascus.

In brief, the people of the Orient seek to make their past a justification and a bed of ease. They shun positive thinking and positive teachings and any knowledge of reality that might sting them and awake them from their slumber.

The Orient is ill, but it has become so inured to its infirmities that it has come to see them as natural and even noble qualities that distinguish them above others. They consider one who lacks such qualities as incomplete and unfit for the divine gift of perfection.

Numerous are the social healers in the Orient, and many

are their patients who remain uncured but appear eased of their ills because they are under the effects of social narcotics. But these tranquilizers merely mask the symptoms.

Such narcotics are distilled from many sources but the chief is the Oriental philosophy of submission to Destiny (the act of God). Another source is the cowardice of the social physicians who fear to aggravate pain by administration of drastic medicine.

Here are some samples of these social tranquilizers:

A husband and wife, for substantial reasons, find that hate has replaced love between them. After long mutual torment they separate. Immediately their parents meet and work out some agreement for the reconciliation of the estranged couple. First they ply the wife with falsehoods, then they work on the husband with similar deceits. Neither is convinced, but they are shamed into a pretense of peace. This cannot endure; soon the effects of the social narcotics have worn off, and the miserable pair return for further doses.

Or a group or party revolts against a despotic government and advocates political reforms to free the oppressed from their shackles. They distribute manifestoes and deliver fiery speeches and publish stinging articles. But a month later, we hear that the government has either imprisoned the leader or silenced him by giving him an important position. And nothing more is heard.

Or a sect rebels against its religious leader, accusing him of misdeeds and threatening to adopt another religion, more humane and free of superstition. But shortly we hear that the wise men of the country have reconciled the shepherd and the flock, through the application of social narcotics.

When a weak man complains of oppression by a strong,

his neighbor will quieten him, "Hush, the eye of the stubborn seer cannot withstand the blow of the spear."

When a villager doubts the holiness of the priest, he will be told, "Listen only to his teaching and disregard his shortcomings and misdeeds."

When a teacher rebukes a student, he will say, "The excuses that a lazy youth invents are often worse than the crime."

If a daughter refuses to adhere to her mother's customs, the mother will say, "The daughter is not better than the mother; she should follow in her mother's footsteps."

Should a young man ask a priest to enlighten him about an ancient rite, the preacher will reprove him, "Son, he who does not look at religion with the eyes of Faith, will see nothing save mist and smoke."

Thus the Orient lies upon its soft bed. The sleeper wakes for an instant when stung by a flea, and then resumes his narcotic slumber.

Whoever tries to awaken him is berated as a rude person who neither sleeps himself nor lets others sleep. Shutting their eyes again, they whisper into the ears of their souls, "He is an infidel poisoning the mind of the youths and undermining the foundation of the ages."

Many times I have asked my soul, "Am I one of those awakened rebels who reject narcotics?" And my soul answered with cryptic words. But hearing my name and principles reviled, I was assured that I was awake and could count myself among those who do not surrender themselves to pipe dreams, that I belong with the strong-hearted who walk narrow and thorny paths where flowers are also to be found, amidst howling wolves—and singing nightingales.

If awakening were a virtue, modesty would prevent me from claiming it. But it is not a virtue, but a reality that appears suddenly to those who have the strength to rise. To be modest in speaking truth is hypocrisy. Alas that the people of the Orient call it education.

I will not be surprised if the "thinkers" say of me, "He is a man of excess who looks upon life's seamy side and reports nothing but gloom and lamentation."

To them I declare, "I deplore our Oriental urge to evade the reality of weakness and sorrow.

"I grieve that my beloved country sings, not in joy, but to still the quakings of fear.

"In battling evil, excess is good; for he who is moderate in announcing the truth is presenting half-truth. He conceals the other half out of fear of the people's wrath.

"I loathe the carrion mind; its stench upsets my stomach. I will not serve it with sweets and cordials.

"Yet I will gladly exchange my outcries for cheerful laughter, speak eulogies instead of indictments, replace excess with moderation, provided you show me a just governor, a lawyer of integrity, a religous hierarch who practices what he preaches, a husband who looks upon his wife with the same eyes as he looks upon himself.

"If you prefer me to dance, to blow the trumpet or beat the drum, invite me to a wedding feast and lead me out of the graveyard."

The Giants

WE LIVE IN AN ERA whose humblest men are becoming greater than the greatest men of preceding ages. What once preoccupied our minds is now of no consequence. The veil of indifference covers it. The beautiful dreams that once hovered in our consciousness have been dispersed like mist. In their place are giants moving like tempests, raging like seas, breathing like volcanoes.

What destiny will the giants bring the world at the end of their struggles?

Will the farmer return to his field to sow where Death has planted the bones of the dead?

Will the shepherd pasture his flock on fields mown by the sword?

Will the sheep drink from springs whose waters are stained with blood?

Will the worshipper kneel in a profaned temple at whose altars Satanists have danced?

Will the poet compose his songs under stars veiled in gun smoke?

Will the musician strum his lute in a night whose silence was ravished by terror?

Will the mother at the cradle of her infant, brooding on the perils of tomorrow, be able to sing a lullaby?

Can lovers meet and exchange kisses on battlefields still acrid with bomb fumes?

Will Nisan* ever return to earth and dress the earth's wounds with its garment?

What will be the destiny of your country and mine? Which giant shall seize the mountains and valleys that produced us and reared us and made us men and women before the face of the sun?

Will Syria remain lying between the wolf lair and the pigsty? Or will it move with the tempest to the lion's den or soar to the eagle's eyrie?

Will the dawn of a new Time ever appear over Lebanon's peaks?

Every time I am alone I ask my soul these questions. But my soul is mute like Destiny.

Which one of you, people, does not ponder day and night on the fate of the world under the rule of the giants intoxicated with the tears of widows and orphans?

I am among those who believe in the Law of Evolution: I believe that ideal entities evolve, like brute beings, and that religions and governments are raised to higher planes.

The law of evolution has a severe and oppressive countenance and those of limited or fearful mind dread it; but its principles are just, and those who study them become enlightened. Through its Reason men are raised above themselves and can approach the sublime.

All around me are dwarves who see the giants emerging; and the dwarves croak like frogs:

* The month of April.

"The world has returned to savagery. What science and education have created is being destroyed by the new primitives. We are now like the prehistoric cave dwellers. Nothing distinguishes us from them save our machines of destruction and our improved techniques of slaughter."

Thus speak those who measure the world's conscience by their own. They measure the range of all Existence by the tiny span of their individual being. As if the sun did not exist but for their warmth, as if the sea was created for them to wash their feet.

From the heart of life, from deep within the universe where the secrets of Creation are stored, the giants rise like winds and ascend like clouds, and convene like mountains. In their struggles age-old problems are being brought to solution.

But man, in spite of all his knowledge and skills, and notwithstanding the love and hatred in his heart, and the torments he endures, is but a tool in the hands of the giants, to reach their goal and accomplish their inevitable high purpose.

The streams of blood shall some day become flowing rivers of wine; and the tears that bedewed the earth shall bring forth aromatic flowers; and the souls that left their abodes shall assemble and appear from behind the new horizon as a new Morn. Then man will realize that he had bought Justice and Reason in the slave market. He will understand that he who works and spends for the sake of Right will never lose.

Nisan shall come, but he who seeks Nisan without Winter's aid, will never find it.

Out of Earth

Wrathfully and violently earth comes out of earth;
and gracefully and majestically earth walks over
earth.
Earth from earth, builds palaces and erects towers
and temples,
And earth weaves on earth, legends, doctrines, and
laws.

Then earth becomes tired of the deeds of earth and
wreathes from its halo, dreams and fantasies.

And earth's eyes are then beguiled by earth's slumber
to enduring rest.
And earth calls unto earth:
"I am the womb and the sepulchre, and I shall
remain a womb and a sepulchre until the planets
exist no more and the sun turns into ashes."

O Night

O Night of lovers, inspirer of poets and singers,
O Night of phantoms, of spirits and fancies,
O Night of longing, of hopes and memories,
You are like a giant dwarfing the evening clouds
and towering over the dawn.
With the sword of fear you are armed, and with
the shining moon you are crowned, and with calm
and silence you are veiled.

With a thousand eyes you penetrate the depth
of life,
With a thousand ears you hear the moan
of death and non-existence.
The light of heaven shines through your darkness,
For Day is but light overwhelming us with the
obscurity of the earth.
Before the awe of eternity you open our eyes and
give us hope,
For Day is a deceiver that blinds us
with measures and quantities.

You are perfect silence revealing the secrets of
the awakened spirits in heaven,
But day is an uproar agitating the souls that
lie between the hooves of purpose and wonder.
You are Justice that brings unto the haven of
slumber the dreams of the weak, that they may be united
with the hopes of the strong.

You are a merciful monarch who closes with his
fingers of enchantment the eyes of the miserable,
and conveys their hearts into a gentler realm.

The lovers' spirits find refuge between the folds of
your blue garment,
And upon your feet, drenched with dew, the
forlorn shed their tears.

In the palms of your hands, where lies the fragrance
of the valleys, strangers find ease for their
yearnings.

You are the companion of lovers; you console the
desolate; you shelter the alien and the lonely.
In your shadow the poet's affections rest, and
the hearts of the prophets awaken,
And under your crown the
wisdom of the thinker takes form.
You inspire poets; you bring revelation to the
prophets; you instruct the philosophers.

When my soul wearies of humanity, when my
eyes tire of staring into the face of the day,
I wander where the phantoms
of past ages sleep.

There I pause before a dim presence who strode
with a thousand feet over the earth, setting it
atremble.

There I look into the eyes of shadow, and
listen to the rustle of invisible wings, and feel
the soft touch of the unseen garment of silence,
and withstand the terrors of black darkness.

There I see you, Night, awful and beautiful,
poised between heaven and earth, veiled in
mist, cloaked in cloud, laughing at
the sun, ridiculing the day, taunting the slaves
who sleeplessly worship before the idols.

I see your wrath against kings sleeping upon beds of
velvet and silk;
I see thieves flinching before your vigilant gaze as
you guard the babes in slumber;
I see you weeping over the forced smiles of prostitutes
and smiling over tears of true lovers;
I see your right hand raising up the good and your
feet trampling the wicked.

There, I see you and you see me, Night. And though
terrible, you are like a father to me, and I,
dreaming, envision myself as your son.

The screen of distrust has been removed
from between us, and you reveal to me
your secrets and designs.
And I disclose to you my hopes and my desires.
Your terrors have turned into a melody sweeter and
more soothing to the heart than the whisper of the
flowers.

My fears are vanished and I am more tranquil
than birds.
You have lifted me unto you and held me between
your arms and taught my eyes to see, and my ears
to hear, and my lips to speak, and my heart to
love that which others hate, and to hate that
which others love.

You touch my thoughts with your
gentle fingers, and my contemplation flows like a strong
stream.

With your burning lips you print a kiss
upon the lips of my soul
and set it aflame like a torch.

I have accompanied you, O Night, and followed you
until we became akin.

I loved you until my being became a diminutive image
of your being.

In my dark self are glittering stars strewn
by my emotions.
And in my heart shines a moon lighting the processions
of my dreams.
In my sleepless soul a silence reveals
the lover's secrets and echoes the
worshipper's prayers,
And my face wears a magic mask. Torn by
the agony of death, it is mended by the songs of youth.
We are both alike in every way, Night.

Will man consider me boastful if I liken myself
unto you?

Does not man boast of his resemblance to the day?
I am like you, Night, and we are both accused of
being what we are not.
I am like you even though twilight does not crown me
with its golden clouds.
I am like you although morn does not adorn the
hem of my garment with its rosy rays.
I am like you though I am not encircled by the milky
way.
I am night boundless and calm; there is no beginning
to my obscurity and no end to my depth.

When the souls rise in the
light of their joy, my soul ascends glorified by the
dark of grief.
I am like you, Night! And when my morn comes, then
my time will end.

Earth

How beautiful you are, Earth, and how sublime!
How perfect is your obedience to the light, and
how noble is your submission to the sun!

How lovely you are, veiled in shadow, and how
charming your face, masked with obscurity!

How soothing is the song of your dawn, and how
harsh are the praises of your eventide!
How perfect you are, Earth, and how majestic!

I have walked over your plains, I have climbed your
stony mountains; I have descended into your valleys;
I have entered into your caves.
In the plains, I found your dream; upon the mountain
I found your pride; in the valley I witnessed your
tranquility; in the rocks your resolution; in the
cave your secrecy.

You are weak and powerful and humble and haughty.

You are pliant and rigid, and clear and secret.
I have ridden your seas and explored your rivers and
followed your brooks.
I heard Eternity speak through your ebb and flow,
and the ages echoing your songs among your hills.
I listened to life calling to life in your mountain
passes and along your slopes.
You are the mouth and lips of Eternity, the strings
and fingers of Time, the mystery and solution of
Life.
Your Spring has awakened me and led me to your fields
where your aromatic breath ascends like
incense.
I have seen the fruits of your Summer labor.
In Autumn, in your vineyards, I saw your
blood flow as wine.
Your Winter carried me into your bed, where the snow
attested your purity.
In your Spring you are an aromatic essence; in your
Summer you are generous; in your Autumn you are
a source of plenty.

One calm and clear night I opened the windows and
doors of my soul and went out to see you, my
heart tense with lust and greed.
And I saw you staring at the stars that smiled at
you. So I cast away my fetters, for I
found out that the dwelling place of the soul is in
your space.
Its desires grow in your desires; its peace rests in
your peace; and its happiness is in the golden
dust which the stars sprinkle upon your body.

One night, as the skies turned gray, and my soul was
wearied and anxious, I went out to you.
And you appeared to me like a giant, armed with
raging tempests, fighting the past with the present,
replacing the old with the new, and letting the
strong disperse the weak.

Whereupon I learned that the law of the people is
your law.
I learned that he who does not break his dry branches
with his tempest, will die wearily,
And he who does not use revolution, to strip
his dry leaves, will slowly perish.

How generous you are, Earth, and how strong is your
yearning for your children lost between that which
they have attained and that which they could not
obtain.
We clamor and you smile; we flit
but you stay!
We blaspheme and you consecrate.
We defile and you sanctify.
We sleep without dreams; but you
dream in your eternal wakefulness.

We pierce your bosom with swords and spears,
And you dress our wounds with oil and balsam.
We plant your fields with skulls and bones,
and from them you rear cypress
and willow trees.

We empty our wastes in your bosom, and you fill
our threshing-floors with wheat sheaves, and
our winepresses with grapes.

We extract your elements to make cannons and
bombs, but out of our elements you create
lilies and roses.

How patient you are, Earth, and how merciful!
Are you an atom of dust raised by
the feet of God when He journeyed from the east
to the west of the Universe?
Or a spark projected from the furnace
of Eternity?
Are you a seed dropped in the field of the
firmament to become God's tree reaching above
the heavens with its celestial branches?
Or are you a drop of blood in the veins of the
giant of giants, or a bead of sweat upon his
brow?

Are you a fruit ripened by the sun?
Do you grow from the tree of Absolute
Knowledge, whose roots extend through
Eternity, and whose branches soar through
the Infinite?

Are you a jewel placed by the God of Time in the
palm of the God of Space?

Who are you, Earth, and what are you?
You are "I," Earth!

You are my sight and my discernment.
You are my knowledge and my
dream.
You are my hunger and my thirst.
You are my sorrow and my joy.

You are my inadvertence and my wakefulness.
You are the beauty that lives in my eyes,
the longing in my heart, the everlasting life
in my soul.

You are "I," Earth.
Had it not been for my being,
You would not have been.

Perfection

You ask me, my brother, when will man reach
perfection. Hear my answer:
Man approaches perfection when he
feels that he is an infinite space and a sea
without a shore,
An everlasting fire, an unquenchable
light,
A calm wind or a raging tempest, a thunder-
ing sky or a rainy heaven,
A singing brook or a wailing rivulet, a tree abloom
in Spring, or a naked sapling
in Autumn,
A rising mountain or a descending valley,
A fertile plain or a desert.

When man feels all these, he has already
reached halfway to perfection. To attain his goal
he must then perceive
that he is a child dependent upon his mother,
a father responsible for his family,

A youth lost in love,
An ancient wrestling against his past,
A worshipper in his temple, a criminal in
his prison,
A scholar amidst his parchments,
An ignorant soul stumbling between the darkness of his
night and the obscurity of his day,
A nun suffering between the flowers of her faith and
the thistles of her loneliness,
A prostitute caught between the fangs of her
weakness and the claws of her needs,
A poor man trapped between his bitterness and his
submission,
A rich man between his greed and his conscience,
A poet between the mist of his twilight and the
rays of his dawn.

Who can experience, see, and understand
these things can reach perfection and
become a shadow of God's Shadow.

Yesterday, Today, and Tomorrow

I said to my friend,
   "See her leaning over his arm?
   Yesterday she leaned over my arm."
And he said:
   "Tomorrow she will lean over mine."
And I said,
   "See her sitting at his side;
   And yesterday she sat at my side."
And he said:
   "Tomorrow she will sit at mine."
And I said,
   "Don't you see her drinking from his
   Cup?
   And yesterday she sipped from mine."
And he said:
   "Tomorrow she will drink from mine."
And I said,
   "Look how she glances at him with eyes
   full of love!

>And with just such love, yesterday
>she glanced at me."

And he said:

>"Tomorrow she will glance at me
>likewise."

And I said,

>"Listen to her whispering songs of
>love in his ears.
>And yesterday she whispered the same songs
>in mine."

And he said:

>"Tomorrow she will whisper them
>in mine."

And I said,

>"Look at her embracing him; and yes-
>terday she embraced me."

And he said:

>"Tomorrow she will lie in my arms."

And I said,

>"What a strange woman she is!!"

And he said:

>"She is Life."

A Story of a Friend

1

I KNEW HIM as a youth lost on the paths of life, goaded by wild impulse and following death in pursuit of his desires. I knew him as a tender flower borne by the winds of rashness into the sea of lust.

I knew him in that village as an ill-natured boy tearing with cruel hands at the birds' nests and slaying the nestlings and trampling with his feet the beautiful crowns of the sweet flowers.

I knew him at school as an adolescent averse to learning, arrogant, and an enemy of peace.

I knew him in the city as a young man trading his father's honor in sinister markets, spending his father's money in houses of ill-fame, and surrendering his mind to the fruit of the vine.

However, I loved him. And my love for him was a mingling of sorrow and sympathy. I loved him because his sins were not born of a small spirit, but rather the deeds of a lost and desperate soul.

The spirit, my dear people, strays from the path of wisdom unwillingly, but returns to it willingly. When the whirlwinds of youth blow dust and sand, the eyes are blind for a time.

I loved that youth because I saw the dove of his conscience struggling with the hawk of his evils. And I saw that the dove was subdued not by its own cowardice but by the strength of its enemy.

Conscience is a just but a weak judge. Weakness leaves it powerless to execute its judgment.

I said I loved him. And love comes in different shapes. Sometimes it comes in wisdom; at other times in justice; and oftentimes in hope. My love for him sustained my hope of seeing the light in him triumph over the darkness. But I knew not when and where would his defilement turn into purity, his brutality into meekness, his recklessness into wisdom. Man does not know in what manner the soul frees itself from the slavery of matter until after it is freed. Neither does man know how the flowers smile save after the coming of the morn.

2

The days passed, following the nights, and I remembered the youth with painful sighs; I repeated his name with affection that made the heart bleed. Then yesterday a letter came from him saying:

"Come to me, my friend, for I wish to unite you with a young man whom your heart will rejoice to meet, and your soul will be refreshed to know."

I said, "Woe is me! Does he intend to mingle his sad friendship with another one similar to it? Is he not alone a sufficient example to the world of error and sin? Does he now wish to re-enforce his misdeeds with those of his companion so that I may see them in double darkness?"

Then I said to myself, "I must go; perhaps the wise soul shall reap figs from the brambles, and the loving heart shall extract light from the darkness."

When night came I found him alone in his room reading a book of verses. "Where is the new friend?" I said, and he answered, "I am he, my friend." And he displayed a calmness I had never seen in him before. In his eyes I could now see a strange light that penetrated the heart. Those eyes in which I had seen cruelty before, were radiant with the light of kindness. Then with a voice that I thought came from another, he said, "The youth whom you knew during childhood and with whom you walked to school, is dead. With his death I was born. I am your new friend; take my hand."

As I shook his hand I felt the existence of a gentle spirit circulating with the blood. His iron hand had become soft and kind. His fingers which yesterday tore like a tiger's claws, today caress the heart.

Then I spoke again. "Who are you, and what has happened? How have you become this kind of person? Has the Holy Spirit entered your heart and sanctified your soul? Or are you playing a part, the invention of a poet?"

And he said, "Ay, my friend, the spirit descended upon me and blessed me. A great love has made my heart a pure altar. It is woman, my friend—woman that I thought yesterday a toy in the hands of man—who has delivered me from the darkness of hell and opened before me the gates of Paradise where I have entered. A true woman has taken me into the Jordan River of her love and baptized me. The woman whose sister I disrespected through my ignorance has exalted me to the throne of glory. The woman whose companion I have defiled with my wickedness has purified my heart with her affections. The woman whose kind I have enslaved with my father's gold has freed me with her beauty. The woman who had Adam driven from Paradise by the strength of her will has restored me to Paradise by her tenderness and my obedience."

Ashes of the Ages and Eternal Fire

I

SPRING OF THE YEAR 116 B. C.

NIGHT AND SILENCE had fallen over the slumbering City of the Sun.* The lamps were extinguished in the dwellings among the majestic temples standing amid olive and laurel groves. The moon's silver light laved the marble columns that stood like giant sentinels before the houses of the gods.

At that hour, while souls succumbed to slumber, Nathan, son of the High Priest, entered Ishtar's temple, bearing a torch in quaking hands. He lit the lamps and censers and soon the fragrance of myrrh and frankincense rose to the uppermost corners. Then he knelt before the altar, inlaid with ivory and gold, raised his hands toward Ishtar,** and with a choking voice cried out, "Have mercy

* Baalbek, or the City of Baal, the sun god of ancient Syria; in Graeco-Roman times its name was changed to Heliopolis, the Greek term for City of the Sun. It was considered the most beautiful city in the ancient Middle East. The ruins are mainly Roman.
** Ishtar, great goddess of the Phoenicians, was worshipped in the cities of Tyre, Sidon, Sur, Djabeïl and Baalbek, and there called Burner of the

upon me, O great Ishtar, goddess of Love and Beauty. Be merciful and hold back the hands of Death from my beloved, whom my soul has chosen by thy will. The potions of the physicians and spells of the wizards are of no avail. Naught is left save thy holy will. Thou art my guide and my aid. Gaze upon my crushed heart and aching soul with pity and grant my prayer. Spare my beloved's life so that together we may worship thee with the rites of love and devote to you our youth and beauty.

"Your servant Nathan, son of your High Priest Hiram, loves a maiden without peer and has made her his companion. But some female djin envied her loveliness and my passion for her and breathed into her a deadly plague, and now the messenger of Death stands at her bedside, spreading his black-ribbed wings over her, and unsheathing his sharp claws. Have mercy upon us, I beseech thee. Spare that flower which has not yet rejoiced in its summer.*

"Save her from the grasp of Death so that we may sing hymns of praise to thee and burn incense in thine honor and offer sacrifices at thine altar and fill thy vases with perfumed oil and spread roses and violets upon the portico of thy temple. Let Love overcome Death in this struggle of Joy against Sorrow."

And Nathan, exhausted, could say no more.

At that moment his slave entered the temple, hastened to him, and whispered, "Master, she calls for you."

Nathan ran to his palace and entered the chamber of his beloved. He leaned over her bed, held her frail hand, and

---

Torch of Life, and Guardian of Youth. She was the counterpart of Aphrodite, the Greek goddess of Love and Beauty, and of the Roman goddess, Venus.

* During the "Era of Ignorance," (the period before the coming of Mohammed), the Arabs believed that if a female genie loved a human youth, she would prevent him from marrying, and if he did wed, she would bewitch the bride and cause her to die. This superstition persists today in isolated villages in Lebanon.

kissed her lips as if striving to breathe life into her body from his. Slowly she opened her eyes, and upon her lips appeared a faint smile, herald of a last heartbeat. With a feeble voice she said, "The goddess calls me, Oh Life of my Soul. Her servant, Death has come. The will of the goddess is sacred, and the errand of Death is just. I depart now, and I hear the rustle of the whiteness descending. But the cups of Love and Youth remain in our hands, and flowery paths of beautiful Life extend before us. I embark, my Beloved, upon an ark of the spirit, but I shall return to you; for great Ishtar will restore those souls of lovers who have not enjoyed their share of sweet Love and happy Youth."*

Weeping, Nathan bent down to kiss her and found her lips already cold. He cried out and began tearing his raiment, and his lamentations awoke the sleeping. At dawn many came to Nathan's palace to offer their sympathy. But Nathan had disappeared. After a fortnight, the chief of a newly arrived caravan related that he had seen Nathan in the distant wilderness, wandering among a flock of gazelles.

The ages passed. In place of Ishtar, goddess of Love and Beauty, a destroying goddess reigned. She pulled down the magnificent temples of the City of the Sun; she demolished its beautiful palaces. She laid waste the orchards and fields. The land was scarred with ruins.

* This belief recurs in Asian thought. Mohammed said, "You were dead and He brought you back to life, and He will slay you again and revive you, whereupon you shall return to Him." Buddha said, "Yesterday we existed, and today, and we will return to this life, again and again, until we become perfect like God."

II

SPRING OF THE YEAR 1890 A. D.

The sun withdrew its golden rays from the plain of Baal-bek. Ali El Hosseini* brought his sheep back to the sheds in the ruins of the temples. He sat among the ancient columns and piped to his flock.

Midnight came and heaven sowed the seeds of the following day in the deep furrows of the darkness. Ali's eyes became heavy and sleep captured his senses. He encountered his invisible self, who dwelt in a higher realm and the range of his vision broadened, bringing Life's hidden secrets to his view. His soul stood aside from Time rushing toward nothingness; it stood amid symmetrical thoughts and crystal ideas. For the first time in his life, Ali became aware of the causes of the spiritual hunger of his youth, the longing which neither the glory of the world nor passing time can still. Ali felt the ache of a centuries-old Memory, kindling like incense placed upon white-hot firebrands. A magic love touched his heart as a musician's delicate fingers touch quivering strings.

Ali looked at the ruins and then, like a blind man whose sight is suddenly restored, he recalled the lamps and the silver censers before the shrine of a goddess. . . . He recalled sacrifices at an altar of gold and ivory. . . . He saw again dancing maidens, tambourine players, singers who chanted hymns to the goddess of Love . . . and Beauty. . . . But how could such memories live in the heart of a simple shepherd youth born in a nomad's tent?

Suddenly the memories tore away the veil of oblivion and he rose and walked to the temple. At the cavernous

* The Hosseinese are an Arabian tribe, living in tents pitched in the plains surrounding the ruins of Baalbek.

entrance he halted as if a magnetic power had gripped his feet. Looking down, he saw a smashed statue on the ground, and the sight freed his soul's tears and they poured like blood from a deep wound. He also felt a stabbing loneliness and remoteness like an abyss between his heart and the heart from whom he had been torn before he entered upon this life.

"Who are you," Ali cried in anguish, "who stand close to my heart but unseen by my eyes? Are you a phantom from Eternity to show me the vanity of Life and the weakness of mankind? Or the spirit of a genie stolen out of earth's crevices to enslave me and render me an object of mockery? What is your strange power which at one time prostrates and enlivens my heart? Who am I and what is this strange self whom I call "Myself"? Has the Water of Life which I have drunk made me an angel in communion with the universe and its mysteries? Or is it inebriating wine that blinds me to myself?

"Oh, what the soul reveals, and the night conceals. . . . Oh, beautiful spirit, hovering in the firmament of my dream, disclose yourself to me if you are human or command Slumber to shut my eyes so I can view your divine vastness. If you are human, let me touch you; let me hear your voice. Tear away this veil that conceals you from me. If I am worthy, place your hand upon my heart and possess me."

Thus an hour passed, with Ali shedding tears and voicing his yearnings.

Then Dawn appeared and the morning breeze stirred. The birds left their nests and sang their morning prayers.

Ali placed his cupped hand over his forehead. Like Adam, when God opened his eyes with his all-creating breath, Ali saw new objects, strange and fantastic. He called to his sheep and they followed him quietly toward the meadow. As he led them, he felt like a philosopher with the power to divine the secrets of the Universe. He reached a brook whose murmuring was soothing to his spirit, and sat under a willow tree whose branches dipped over the water as if drinking from the cool depths.

Here Ali felt the beating of his heart increase and through his soul throbbed a strong and almost visible vibration. He sprang up like a mother suddenly awakened from her slumber by the scream of her child, and his eyes were magnetized by the sight of a beautiful maiden approaching from the opposite side, with a water jar on her shoulder. As she leaned over to fill the jar, her eyes and Ali's met. She cried out, distraught, dropped the jar, and ran off, but glanced back in agonizing disbelief.

Ali, compelled by the mysterious power, leaped across the brook, caught the maiden and embraced her. As if this caress had subdued her will she did not move, yielding to him as the fragrance of jasmine submits to the breeze. Both felt it to be the reunion of souls long separated by earth and now brought together by God.

The enamored pair walked amidst the willow trees, and the unity of the two selves was a speaking tongue for them; an eye to see the glory of Happiness; a silent auditor of the tremendous revelation of Love.

The sheep grazed; the birds of the sky hovered above their heads; the sun spread a golden garment upon the hills; and they sat by the side of a rock where the violets hid. The maiden looked into Ali's black eyes while the breeze caressed her hair, as though the shimmering wisps were fingertips craving kisses. Then she said: "Ishtar, oh my beloved, has restored both our spirits to this life from another, so that we shall not be denied the joy of Love and the glory of Youth."

Ali closed his eyes, as though her melodious voice had

brought to him images of a dream. Invisible wings bore him to a strange chamber where, upon her deathbed, lay the corpse of a maiden whose beauty had been claimed by Death. He uttered a fearful cry, then opened his eyes and found the maiden sitting by his side, a smile upon her lips and her eyes bright with the rays of Life. Then his heart was refreshed, and the phantom of his vision withdrew and the past and its cares vanished. The lovers embraced and drank the wine of sweet kisses. They slumbered, wrapped in each other's arms, until the last remnant of the shadow was dispersed by the Eternal Power which had awakened them.

book 4

a
self-portrait

Contents

CONTENTS

CONTENTS

Preface

Kahlil Gibran (1883-1931), known to the world as the Immortal Prophet of Lebanon and the Savant of His Age, was born in the famous town of Bsharré, which prides itself on being the guardian of the forest of the Holy Cedars of Lebanon from whose lumber King Solomon built his temple in Jerusalem. His parents were Kahlil Gibran and Camila, the daughter of Father Estephan Rahmé, a Maronite Catholic priest.

When Gibran was born his parents baptized him in the Maronite Church and named him after his paternal grandfather, Gibran, according to the Lebanese custom at that time. So Gibran became known as Gibran Kahlil Gibran, the name which he signed in Arabic, although in English he used the name of Kahlil Gibran.

He received his early education in his native town beginning with the study of Arabic and Syriac. Then at the age of twelve, accompanied by his mother, brother Peter, and his two sisters, Miriana and Sultana, he came to the United States and settled in the City of Boston in June, 1895.

While in Boston he attended a public school for

boys for two and a half years, after which he switched to a night school where he took general courses for a period of one year. At his insistence, his mother sent him back to Lebanon to enter the famous Madrasat Al-Hikmat, "The School of Wisdom," founded by the Savant Maronite Bishop Joseph Debs in the City of Beirut. After receiving his baccalaureate he travelled all over Syria and Lebanon visiting the historical places, ruins, and relics of the old civilization.

In 1902 he left Lebanon, never to return, for the United States, to dedicate himself to the art of painting, a hobby which he had acquired as a child.

Gibran was rather timid and unsociable; he shunned the company of his friends and neighbors in order to be left alone to devote himself to reading and meditation. As a boy, he spent most of his time reading, writing or drawing. If the other children succeeded in engaging him in conversation, he would tell them strange things which they could not understand and led them to believe that he was an odd child.

In 1908 he entered the Academy of Fine Arts in Paris where he spent three years studying under the supervision and guidance of the famous sculptor Auguste Rodin. The great man predicted a brilliant future for Gibran. Gibran's genius also inspired his friend Henri de Boufort to say, "The world must expect a lot of this Lebanese poet-artist who is today the William Blake of the twentieth century."

Upon the completion of his studies in Paris, Gibran returned to New York to stay, but each year he went to Boston, his refuge, to spend his vacation with his sister Miriana and, at the same time, to write and paint leisurely.

The note of sorrow that appears so frequently in the poems, stories, and letters of Kahlil Gibran can be traced to the frequent misfortunes that befell him in his youth. In April, 1902, his sister Sultana died; in February, 1903, his brother Peter passed away while in the spring of life; and three months later he lost his mother whom he loved to the point of veneration.

"The most beautiful word on the lips of mankind," said Gibran, "is the word 'Mother,' and the most beautiful call is the call of 'my mother.' It is a word full of hope and love, a sweet and kind word coming from the depths of the heart. The mother is everything—she is our consolation in sorrow, our hope in misery, and our strength in weakness. She is the source of love, mercy, sympathy, and forgiveness. He who loses his mother loses a pure soul who blesses and guards him constantly.

"Everything in nature bespeaks the mother. The sun is the mother of earth and gives it its nourishment of heat; it never leaves the universe at night until it has put the earth to sleep to the song of the sea and the hymn of birds and brooks. And this earth is the mother of trees and flowers. It produces them, nurses them, and weans them. The trees and flowers become mothers of their great fruits and seeds. And the mother, the prototype of all existence, is the eternal spirit, full of beauty and love."

As has been observed in his many published works, widely read in several languages, the early promise Gibran showed was sustained throughout his life. In the Arabic letters which I have gathered together and translated for this book, the reader will become reacquainted with the rich symbolism which marks Gibran's unique style. Moreover, Gibran enthusiasts will be rewarded with insights that can only come through an examination of real-life relationships. Many of Gibran's closest ones can be explored through these letters. As do his poetical and philosophical works, these letters reveal the curious blending of Oriental and Occidental philosophy characteristic of Gibran's thought—a combination occasionally disconcerting to the Western mind. Sometimes one has the feeling that the emotions expressed were almost too deep for words, which seem to be wrenched from him reluctantly at the agency of some compulsive force within him.

Recent world developments have heightened interest in Arabic literature and English-speaking peoples today are making deep, exploratory studies of these venerable writings, as yet unspoiled by Western influence.

The Arabs, despite centuries of internal political turbulence and external interference, have retained and refined their strong individuality. While the Western world has been seeking practical solutions to its problems through science, the various peoples comprising the Arabic-speaking world have preferred to look at life in poetic and philosophical terms. In a cultural climate dominated by the doctrines of Mohammed and his followers, Arab writers have captured the spirit of their people, portraying their devotion to the home, and their blind fidelity to their rulers, right or wrong. Not having been exposed to religious bias or disillusioned by scientific theories, Arabic writers have felt a freedom of expression which the Western literati may well envy. They set their own unconventional pattern, and no amount of outside pressure or criticism has been able to divert them from it. In the present climate of interest in Arabic writings, no author of the East offers greater rewards than Kahlil Gibran, for he stands alone on the summit of all that is fine in Oriental literature.

It is the translator's sincerest hope that those who have read Gibran and enjoyed his works will add to their enjoyment through the perusal of this book which is a portrait of Kahlil Gibran as revealed in his letters.

ANTHONY R. FERRIS

Austin, Texas,
May 13, 1959

opposite: Facsimile of a letter from Gibran to May Ziadeh, as it appeared in the Arabic edition. For the translation, see bottom of page 348.

من جبران الى مي زياده

عزيزتي مي

انا مدين بكل ما هو « انا » الى المرأة منذ كنت طفلاً حتى الساعة . والمرأة تفتح النوافذ في بصري والابواب في روحي . ولولا المرأة الام ، والمرأة الشقيقة ، والمرأة الصديقـــة لبقيت هاجعاً مع هؤلاء.النائمين الذين ينشدون سكينة العالم بغطيطهم .

... لقد وجدت في المرض لذة نفسية تختلف بتأثيرها عن كل لذة اخرى ، بل وجدت نوعاً من الطمأنينة يكاد يحبب اليّ الاعتلال . ان المريض لفي مأمن من منازع واغراض الناس والوعود والمواعيد والمخالطة والمنازعة والكلام الكثير ورنين جرس التلفون... وقد اكتشفت شيئاً آخر اهم ، مما لا يقاس ، من اللذة والطمأنينـــة ، وهو هذا : اني في اعتلالي ادنى الى الكليات المجردة مني اليها في صحتي . فاذا ما اسندت رأسي الى هذه المساند واغمضت عيني عن هذا المحيط وجدتني سابحاً كالطير فوق اودية وغابات هادئة متشحة بنقاب لطيف ووجدتني قريباً ممن احبهم اناجيهم واحدثهم ، ولكن بدون غضب ، واشعر شعورهم واقتكر افكارهم . يلومونني ولا يسخطون عليّ ، بل

٩٩

KHALIL GIBRAN
A Self-Portrait

Gibran wrote this letter to his father in Bsharré to reassure him of the health of his two sisters, Miriana and Sultana. One of their relatives in the United States had written to Gibran's father and told him that both of his daughters were ill and the old man conveyed his worry to his son. Gibran's father had not noticed the date of the letter: April first, or April Fool's Day.

GIBRAN TO HIS FATHER

Beirut,
April, 1904

Dear Father:

I received your letter in which you express to me your anxiety over "sad and unexpected news." I would have felt the same way had I not known the intention of the writer and the purpose of the letter. They (may God forgive them) tell you in the letter that one of my sisters is critically ill, and again they say that the illness will involve a great deal of expense, which will make it difficult for my sisters to send you money. I have immediately found an explanation in noting that the letter was written on the first day of April. Our aunt has been accustomed to such funny and gentle jokes. Her saying that my sister has been ill for six months is as far from the truth as we are from her. During the last seven months I have received five letters from Mr. Ray who assures me that both of my sisters, Miriana and Sultana, are in excellent health. He extols their fine characters, marking Sultana's refined manners; and speaks of the resemblance between her and me both in physique and in character.

These words came from the most honest man I have ever known; from a man who loathes April Fool jokes and dislikes any fabrication which saddens the heart of another. You may rest assured that all is well and let your mind be at ease.

I am still in Beirut, although I might be away from home for a whole month touring Syria and Palestine or Egypt and Sudan with an American family for whom I have great respect. For this reason I do not know how long my stay will last in Beirut. However, I am here for personal benefit which makes it necessary for me to remain in this country a while in order to please those who care for my future. Do not ever doubt my judgment regarding what is good for me and for the fortification and betterment of my future.

This is all I can tell you—with my affection to all my relatives and loving friends, and my respect to whoever inquires about me. May God prolong your life and protect you—

Your son,
GIBRAN

Jamil Malouf, a young Lebanese poet-writer, was a great admirer of Gibran. In this letter, Gibran reveals his concern and admiration for the young poet who had left Paris to live in São Paul, Brazil. Gibran pictures his friend Jamil as a torch from heaven illuminating the path of mankind, at the same time expressing his amazemnt at learning of his friend's move. He presses him for a revelation of the motive that prompted him to go to São Paul and place himself among the "living dead."

TO JAMIL MALOUF

1908

Dear Brother Jamil:

When I read your letters I feel the existence of an enchanting spirit moving in this room—a beautiful and sorrowful spirit that attracts me by its undulation and makes me see you as two persons: one hovers over humanity with enormous wings similar to the wings of the seraphim whom Saint John saw standing before the Throne by the seven lamps; the other person is chained to a huge rock like Prometheus, who, in giving man the first torch of fire, brought on himself the wrath of the gods. The first person enlivens my heart and soothes my spirit because he sways with the sun rays and the frolicsome breeze of dawn; while the second person makes my heart suffer, for he is a prisoner of the vicissitudes of time. . . .

You have always been and still are capable of causing the torch of fire to come from heaven and light the path of mankind, but tell me what law or force has brought you to São Paul and fettered your body and placed you among those who died on the day of their birth and have not yet been buried? Do the Greek gods still practice their power in these days?

I have heard that you are going to return to Paris to live there. I, too, would like to go there. Is it possible that we both could meet in the City of Arts? Will we meet in the Heart of the World and visit the Opera and the French theatre and talk about the plays of Racine, Corneille, Molière, Hugo, and Sardou? Will we meet there and walk together to where the Bastille was erected and then return to our quarters feeling the gentle spirit of Rousseau and Voltaire and write about Liberty and Tyranny and destroy every Bastille that stands in every city in the Orient? Will we go to the Louvre and stand before the paintings of Raphael, Da Vinci and Corot, and write about Beauty and Love and their influence on man's heart?

Oh, brother, I feel a gnawing hunger in my heart for the approach of the great works of art, and I have a profound longing for the eternal sayings; however, this hunger and longing come out of a great power that exists in the depth of my heart—a power that wishes to announce itself hurriedly but is unable to do so, for the time has not come, and the people who died on the day of their birth are still walking and standing as a barrier in the way of the living.

My health is, as you know, like a violin in the hands of one that does not know how to play it, for it makes him hear harsh melody. My sentiments are like an ocean with their ebb and flow; my soul is like a quail with broken wings. She suffers immensely when she sees the swarms of birds hovering in the sky, for she finds herself unable to do likewise. But like all other birds, she enjoys the silence of Night, the coming of Dawn, the rays of Sun, and the beauty of the valley. I paint and write now and then, and in the midst of my paintings and writings, I am like a small boat sailing between an ocean of an endless depth and a sky of limitless blue—strange dreams, sublime desires, great hopes, broken and mended thoughts; and between all these there is something which the people call Despair, and which I call Inferno.

GIBRAN

In the month of May, 1903, Ameen Guraieb, editor and owner of *Almuhager*, daily Arabic newspaper published in New York, visited the city of Boston. Among the people who received Ameen was the young Kahlil Gibran who captured the journalist's regard with his kind manner and intelligence.

The following day Gibran invited Guraieb to his home. He showed him his paintings and presented him with an old notebook in which he had set down his thoughts and meditations. When Ameen saw the paintings and read the poems in the notebook he realized he had discovered a genius artist, poet, and philospher. Thrilled by his discovery, the journalist offered to Gibran a position as columnist on his daily newspaper.

Thus Ameen Guraieb extracted Kahlil Gibran from his retreat in Boston and introduced him to his Arabic readers. "This newspaper is very fortunate," said Guraieb in one of his editorials, "to be able to present to the Arabic-speaking world the first literary fruit of a young artist whose drawings are admired by the American public. This young man is Kahlil Gibran of Bsharré, the famous city of the braves. We publish this essay without comments under the caption of *Tears and Laughter*, leaving it up to the readers to judge it according to their tastes." This was the first time that Gibran saw his name in print in a daily Arabic newspaper.

When Gibran wrote *Spirits Rebellious*, the book containing the story of Rose El Hanie which caused Gibran's expulsion from Lebanon and excommunication from the Church, it was his friend Ameen Guraieb who wrote the preface for the book.

As revealed in the following letter, Gibran's appreciation and love for Ameen went very deep. He wishes his friend *bon voyage*—Ameen was preparing for a trip to Lebanon—and confides in his friend traveling plans of his own.

TO AMEEN GURAIEB

Boston,
Feb. 12, 1908

Dear Ameen:

Only my sister Miriana knows something about this bit of news which I am going to tell you and which will make you and your neighbors rather happy: I am going to Paris, the capital of fine arts, in the late part of the coming spring, and I shall remain there one whole year. The twelve months which I am going to spend in Paris will play an important part in my every day life, for the time which I will spend in the City of Light will be, with the help of God, the beginning of a new chapter in the story of my life. I shall join a group of great artists in that great city and work under their supervision and gain a lot from their observation and benefit myself from their constructive criticism in the field of fine arts. It matters not whether they benefit me or not, because after my return from Paris to the United States, my drawings will gain more prestige, which makes the blind-rich buy more of them, not because of their artistic beauty, but because of their being painted by an artist who has spent a full year in Paris among the great European painters.

I never dreamed of this voyage before, and the thought of it never did enter into my mind, for the expense of the trip would make it impossible for a man like me to undertake such a venture. But heaven, my dear Ameen, has arranged for this trip, without my being aware of it, and opened before me the way to Paris. I shall spend one whole cycle of my life there at the expense of heaven, the source of plenty.

And now, since you have heard my story you will know that my stay in Boston is neither due to my love for this city, nor to my dislike for New York. My being here is due to the presence of a she-angel who is ushering me towards a splendid future and paving for me the path to intellectual and financial success. But it makes no difference whether I am in Boston or in Paris, *Almuhager* will remain the paradise in which my soul dwells and the stage upon which my heart dances. My trip to Paris will offer me an opportunity to write about things which I cannot find or imagine in this mechanical and commercial country whose skies are replete with clamor and noise. I shall be enlightened by the social studies which I will undertake in the capital of capitals of the world where Rousseau, Lamartine and Hugo lived; and where the people love art as much as the Americans adore the Almighty Dollar.

During your absence I shall continue to contribute to every issue of *Almuhager*. I shall pour upon its pages all the affections, hopes and ideas that my heart, soul and mind contain. I am not looking forward to receiving any compensation. All I want from you is your friendship. But if you feel like adding a material debt to the many moral debts which I owe you, you may tell your editorial staff to get behind my book *Tears and Laughter* and help me reap the harvest of the many nights I have spent on its writing. Tell them to assist me in selling the book to the Arabic readers and to the merchants in New York and other states. As you know, I cannot promote the book without the help of *Almuhager*.

Be at ease and do not occupy your mind with anything other than the joy of seeing your family and beholding the beautiful scenery of Lebanon. You have worked hard enough in the last five years and you deserve a little rest. Let not your worrying about the future interfere with your tranquility. No matter what happens, *Almuhager* will ever remain the pride of all Arabic papers. A message from you, a poem from Assad Rustum, and an article from Gibran every week will be sufficient to open the eyes of the Arab world and direct their attention to Twenty-one Washington Street.*

Your introduction to my book *Spirits Rebellious* made me happy because it was free from personal comment. Monday I sent you an article for *Almuhager*; has it arrived yet? Write me a few lines in answer to this letter. I shall write you more than one letter before you leave for Lebanon. Let nothing dampen your enthusiasm for your trip. We will be unable to meet and shake hands, but we will join each other in thoughts and spirits. Seven thousand miles are but one mile, and one thousand years are but one year in the eyes of the spirit.

Miriana sends you her regards and wishes you success. May God bless you and bring you back safe to me, and may heaven shower upon you blessings, the amount of which will equal the love and respect I have in my heart for you.

GIBRAN

It is a custom among the people of the Near East to call each other "brother" or "sister." Close friends and relatives other than those actually so related are often referred to in this manner.

This letter was written to Nakhli, Gibran's first cousin whom he addresses as brother. Gibran and Nakhli were inseparable companions in their early

* Address of the office and publishing house of *Almuhager*.

youth. They lived, slept, played, and ate together in their home town, Bsharré, close by the Holy Cedars of Lebanon.

Peter, Gibran's half-brother, a good singer and lute player, entertained Gibran and Nakhli and took good care of them. When Nakhli left Bsharré for Brazil in search of a livelihood, Gibran kept in close touch with him.

In the following letter, Gibran speaks to Nakhli of his struggles and complains of the Arabic-speaking conservative class which was accusing him of heresy because of their feeling that his writings were poisoning the mind of the youth. Gibran later published a story which he called "Kahlil the Heretic."

TO NAKHLI GIBRAN

Boston,
March 15, 1908

Dear Brother Nakhli:

I have just received your letter which filled my soul with joy and sadness at the same time, for it brought back to my memory pictures of those days that passed like dreams, leaving behind phantoms that come with the daylight and go with the darkness. How did those days undo themselves, and where did those nights, in which Peter lived, go? How did those hours, which Peter filled with his sweet songs and handsomeness pass away? Those days, nights and hours have disappeared like open flowers when dawn descends from the gray sky. I know that you remember those days with pain and I have noticed the phantoms of your affections between the lines of your missive, as if they came from Brazil to restore to my heart the echo of the valleys, the mountains and the rivulets surrounding Bsharré.

Life, my dear Nakhli, is like the seasons of the year. The sorrowful Autumn comes after the joyful Summer, and the raging Winter comes behind the sad Autumn, and the beautiful Spring appears after the passing of the awful Winter. Will the Spring of our life ever return so we may be happy again with the trees, smiling with the flowers, running with the brooks, and singing with the birds like we used to do in Bsharré when Peter was still alive? Will the tempest that dispersed us ever reunite us? Will we ever go back to Bsharré and meet by Saint George Church? I do not know, but I feel that life is a sort of debt and payment. It gives us today in order to take from us tomorrow. Then it gives us again and takes from us anew until we get tired of the giving and receiving and surrender to the final sleep.

You know that Gibran, who spends most of his life writing, finds enchanting pleasure in corresponding with the people he loves most. You also know that Gibran, who was very fond of Nakhli when he was a child, will never forget the man that Nakhli has become. The things which the child loves remain in the domain of the heart until old age. The most beautiful thing in life is that our souls remain hovering over the places where we once enjoyed ourselves. I am one of those who remembers such places regardless of distance or time. I do not let one single phantom disappear with the cloud, and it is my everlasting remembrance of the past that causes my sorrow sometimes. But if I had to choose between joy and sorrow, I would not exchange the sorrows of my heart for the joys of the whole world.

And now let me drop the curtain upon the past and tell you something about my present and my future,

for I know that you would like to hear something about
the boy you have always loved. Listen to me, and I will
read to you the first chapter of Gibran's story: I am a man
of weak constitution, but my health is good because I
neither think about it nor have time to worry about it. I
love to smoke and drink coffee. If you were to come to see
me now and enter my room, you would find me behind a
screen of thick smoke mingled with the aromatic scent of
Yamanite coffee.

       I love to work and I do not let one moment pass
without working. But the days in which I find myself
dormant and my thought slothful are more bitter than
quinine and more severe than the teeth of the wolf. I
spend my life writing and painting, and my enjoyment in
these two arts is above all other enjoyments. I feel that the
fires that feed the affection within me would like to dress
themselves with ink and paper, but I am not sure whether
the Arabic-speaking world would remain as friendly to me
as it has been in the past three years. I say this because the
apparition of enmity has already appeared. The people
in Syria are calling me heretic, and the intelligentsia in
Egypt vilifies me, saying, "He is the enemy of just laws,
of family ties, and of old traditions." Those writers are
telling the truth, because I do not love man-made laws and
I abhor the traditions that our ancestors left us. This
hatred is the fruit of my love for the sacred and spiritual
kindness which should be the source of every law upon the
earth, for kindness is the shadow of God in man. I know
that the principles upon which I base my writings are
echoes of the spirit of the great majority of the people of
the world, because the tendency toward a spiritual independence is to our life as the heart is to the body. . . .
Will my teaching ever be received by the Arab world, or
will it die away and disappear like a shadow?

Will Gibran ever be able to deflect the people's eyes from the skulls and thorns towards the light and the truth? Or will Gibran be like so many others who returned from this world to Eternity without leaving behind any reminders of their existence? I do not know, but I feel that there is a great power in the depth of my heart that wishes to come out, and it is going to come out some day with the help of God.

I have an important news for you. On the first day of the coming June I will be leaving for Paris to join a committee of artists, and I shall remain there a whole year after which I shall return to this country. My stay there will be filled with study and research and hard work; at the same time it will be the beginning of a new life.

Remember me when you and the family gather at the table to partake of your meals, and tell your wife and the children that a certain relative, whose name is Gibran, has a loving place in his heart for every one of you.

My sister Miriana joins me in sending her regards. When I read your letter to her, it made her so happy that she was unable to hold back her tears when I ran across certain phrases. May God bless you and give you the best of health and keep you as a dear brother to

GIBRAN

TO AMEEN GURAIEB

Boston
March 28, 1908

Dear Ameen:

I have just locked myself up in my room behind a screen of cigarette smoke mingled with aromatic scent

294

of Yamanite coffee to spend one hour talking to you. I am now enjoying my coffee and my smoke as well as our conversation.

You are now in the other part of the great, but small, globe, while I am still here. You are now in beautiful and peaceful Lebanon and I am in clamorous and noisy Boston. You are in the East and I am in the West, but no matter how far away you are from me, I feel that you are closer to me than ever. Man finds the expatriation of his beloved friends difficult to bear because his pleasure comes through the five senses. But Gibran's soul has already grown beyond that to a plane of higher enjoyment which does not require the mediation of the five senses. His soul sees, hears, and feels, but not through the medium of eyes, ears, and fingers. His soul roams the whole world and returns without the use of feet, cars, and ships. I see Ameen far and near and I perceive everything around him as the soul regards many other invisible and voiceless objects. The subtlest beauties in our life are unseen and unheard.

How did you find Lebanon? Is it as beautiful as your yearnings promised? Or is it an arid spot where slothfulness dwells? Is Lebanon the same glorious Mountain whose beauty was sung and praised by poets like David, Isaiah, Farhat, Lamartine, and Haddad? Or is it a chain of mountains and valleys empty of geniality, aloof from beauty, and surrounded by loneliness?

Undoubtedly you shall answer all these questions in long articles to *Almuhager* and I shall read every word. But if there is something that you do not feel can be discussed publicly, tell it to me in a personal letter so that I may share your thoughts and see the reality of Lebanon through your eyes.

I am in these days like a man observing Lent and awaiting the coming of the dawn of the feast. My planned trip to Paris causes my dreams to hover around the great achievements I hope will be mine during my year in the City of Knowledge and Arts. I told you ere your departure to Lebanon that I would spend a whole year in Paris, and now I have also decided to visit Italy after the expiration of my time in Paris. I intend to spend another year visiting Italy's great museums and ruins and cities. I shall visit Venice, Florence, Rome, and Genoa; then I will return to Naples and board a boat to the United States. It will be a wonderful journey, for it will forge a golden chain connecting Gibran's sorrowful past with his happy future.

I am sure that you will pass through Paris on your way back to the United States. In Paris we shall meet and be merry; in Paris we shall quench our soul's thirst for beautiful things created by famous artists. In Paris we shall visit the Panthéon and stop for a few minutes by the tombs of Victor Hugo, Rousseau, Chateaubriand, and Renan. In Paris we shall roam the Palace of the Louvre and look upon the paintings of Raphael, Michelangelo, and Da Vinci. In Paris we shall go to the Opera and hear songs and hymns revealed by the deity to Beethoven, Wagner, Mozart, and Rossini. . . . These names, whose pronunciation is rather difficult to an Arabic-speaking person, are names of great men who founded the civilization of Europe; these are the names of men whom the earth has swallowed, but whose deeds it could not fold or engulf. The tempest is capable of laying waste the flowers but unable to harm the seeds. This is the consolation that heaven delivers to the hearts of great men who love great deeds, and this is the light which causes us—the sons of knowledge—to walk proudly upon the path of life.

I was thrilled to receive your letter from Alexandria, Egypt, and I was proud to read in *Almuhager* about the reception you and our brother Assad Rustum met in Cairo. My heart and soul rejoice every time I hear a word from you or about you. But tell me, Ameen, did you mention my name when you met with the intelligentsia of Lebanon and Egypt? Did you speak of the third name in the Trinity who is still behind the ocean? I believe that my friend Saleem Sarkis had told you about the criticism I had received from Lutfi Al-Manfaluti concerning my story about Madame Rose Hanie. It was published in *Al Muayad*. I was well pleased with the criticism because I feel that such persecution is a diet for new principles, especially when it comes from a learned man like Al-Manfaluti.

My work in these days is like a chain of many rings connected with one another. I have changed my way of living and I miss some of the joys of loneliness that embraced my soul before I dreamed about going to Paris. Yesterday I was contented with playing minor parts upon the limited stage of life, but today I have realized that such contentment is a sort of sluggishness. I used to look upon life through tears and laughter, but today I see life through golden and enchanting rays of light that impart strength to the soul and courage to the heart and motion to the body. I used to be like a bird imprisoned in a cage, contenting myself with seeds dropped down to me by the hands of Destiny. But today I feel like a free bird who sees the beauty of the fields and prairies and wishes to fly in the spacious sky, mingling its affections, its fancy and its hopes with the ether.

There is something in our life which is nobler and more supreme than fame; and this *something* is the great deed that invokes fame. I feel, within me, a hidden power that wishes to dress its nakedness with a beautiful garment of great deeds. This makes me feel that I came to this world to write my name upon the face of life with big letters. Such emotion accompanies me day and night. It is this sort of sentiment that causes me to see the future surrounded by light and encircled by rapture and triumph which I have been dreaming about since I was fifteen years of age. My dreams have just begun to be realized, and I feel that my trip to Paris is going to be the first step on a ladder that reaches to heaven. I am intending to publish my book *The Broken Wings* next summer. This book is the best one I have ever written. But the one that is going to create a great movement in the Arabic-speaking world is a book of philosophy named *Religion and Religiousness*,* which I started more than a year ago, and whose place to my heart is as the center to the circle. I shall finish this book in Paris, and probably will have it published at my own expense.

When you are in a beautiful spot or among learned people, or by the side of old ruins, or on the top of a high mountain, whisper my name so that my soul will go to Lebanon and hover around you and share with you the pleasure of life and all life's meanings and secrets. Remember me when you see the sun rising from behind Mount Sunnin or Fam El Mizab. Think of me when you see the sun coming down toward its setting, spreading its red garment upon the mountains and the valleys as if shedding blood instead of tears as it bids Lebanon farewell. Recall my name when you see the shepherds sitting in the shadow of the trees and blowing their reeds and filling the silent field with soothing music as did Apollo when he was exiled to this world. Think of me when you see the damsels carrying their earthenware jars filled with water upon their shoulders. Remember me when you see the Lebanese villager plowing the earth before the face of the sun, with beads of sweat adorning his forehead while

* This book was never finished or published.

his back is bent under the heavy duty of labor. Remember me when you hear the songs and hymns that Nature has woven from the sinews of moonlight, mingled with the aromatic scent of the valleys, mixed with the frolicsome breeze of the Holy Cedars, and poured into the hearts of the Lebanese. Remember me when the people invite you to their festivities, for your remembrance of me will bring to you pictures of my love and longing for your person and will add spiritual overtones and deeper meaning to your words and your speeches. Love and longing, my dear Ameen, are the beginning and the end of our deeds.

Now that I have written these lines to you, I feel like a child who wants to scoop the ocean water with a sea shell and place it in a small ditch he has dug in the sand of the shore. But do you not see between these lines other lines whose secrets you should inquire? They were written with the finger of the soul and the ink of the heart upon the face of love that hangs between the earth and the stars and hovers between the East and the West.

Remember me to your father, whom I admire and respect, and give my regards to your respected mother —that dear mother who gave the Arabic-speaking world a powerful figure, and bestowed upon Lebanon a brilliant torch, and enriched Gibran with a very dear and beloved brother. Kindly spread my salaam among your brothers, neighbors and admirers like the frolicsome breeze of Lebanon spreads its blossoms upon the apple trees in the month of Nisan.

Miriana greets you from behind the ocean and wishes you the best of health. My relative Melhem and his daughter Zahieh asked me to send you their regards. Everybody misses you and longs to see you, oh beloved brother of

GIBRAN

TO NAKHLI GIBRAN

Paris, France,
Sept. 27, 1910

My Beloved Brother Nakhli:

Do you recall those interesting tales we used to hear during the cold rainy days while sitting around the hearth with the snow falling outside and the wind blowing between the dwellings? Do you still remember the story about the gorgeous garden with beautiful trees bearing delicious fruits? Do you also remember the end of the story which tells how those bewitched trees turned into young men whom destiny had brought into the garden? I am sure you remember all these things even without knowing that Gibran is like those bewitched young men tied with unseen chains and ruled by invisible power.

I am, my dear, Nakhli, a bewitched tree, but Sid Aladin has not yet come from behind the Seven Seas to unshackle me and loosen the magic ties and make me free and independent.

On the 14th day of the coming month I shall leave Paris, but now I am busy arranging my work and planning for the future. I am like a spinning wheel turning day and night. God only knows how busy I am. Thus heaven directs my life, and thus destiny rotates me around a certain point from which I cannot get away.

Your letter just reached me this morning, and since then I have been thinking and thinking, but I do not know what to do. Do you believe that you can help me with your thoughts and affections? Can you look into the depth of my heart and understand the misery which God has placed in it? All I ask of you is to feel with me and have faith and believe me when I tell you that I am a prisoner of time and circumstances. I am not lamenting my luck because I prefer to be like I am, and I refuse to exchange my plight for another one because I have chosen the literary life while being aware of all the obstacles and pains surrounding it.

Just think, my dear Nakhli, and ponder upon Gibran's life, for it reveals to you a sort of struggle and strife. It is a chain of connected links of misery and distress. I can say these things to you because I am very patient and glad of the existence of hardships in my life, for I hope to overcome all these difficulties. Had it not been for the presence of calamities, work and struggle would not have existed, and life would have been cold, barren and boresome.

GIBRAN

The ties of friendship were developed between Kahlil Gibran and the Lebanese artist, Yousif Howayek while they were studying art in Paris. Gibran was Howayek's inseparable friend who accompanied him to the opera, theatres, museums, galleries and other places of interest. Howayek was a great admirer of Gibran, and as a token of his admiration for the Prophet of Lebanon he worked several months on a beautiful oil portrait of Gibran and presented it to him.

TO YOUSIF HOWAYEK

Boston, 1911

Although this city is full of friends and acquaintances, I feel as if I had been exiled into a distant land where life is as cold as ice and as gray as ashes and as silent as the Sphynx.

My sister is close by me, and the loving kinfolks are around me everywhere I go, and the people visit us every day and every night, but I am not happy. My work is progressing rapidly, my thoughts are calm, and I am enjoying perfect health, but I still lack happiness. My soul is hungry and thirsty for some sort of nourishment, but I don't know where to find it. The soul is a heavenly flower that cannot live in the shade, but the thorns can live everywhere.

This is the life of the oriental people who are afflicted with the disease of fine arts. This is the life of the children of Apolon who are exiled into this foreign land, whose work is strange, whose walk is slow, and whose laughter is cry.

How are you, Yousif? Are you happy among the human ghosts you witness every day on both sides of the road?

GIBRAN

In the preface of his Arabic book *May and Gibran*, Dr. Jamil Jabre wrote: "It is difficult to imagine a man and a woman falling in love without having known or met one another except by correspondence. But artists have their own unusual way of life which they themselves can only understand. This was the case of the great Lebanese woman writer, May Ziadeh and Kahlil Gibran.

"The literary and love relationship between Kahlil Gibran and May Ziadeh was not a myth or presumption, but a proven fact which was revealed to the public through some letters published by May Ziadeh after Gibran's death."

When *The Broken Wings* made its first appearance in Arabic, Gibran presented May Ziadeh with a copy of his novel and asked her to criticize it. Complying with his request, she wrote him the following letter:

FROM MAY ZIADEH

Cairo, Egypt,
May 12, 1912

. . . I do not agree with you on the subject of marriage, Gibran. I respect your thoughts, and I revere your ideas, for I know that you are honest and sincere in the defense of your principles that aim at a noble purpose. I am in full accord with you on the fundamental principle that advocates the freedom of woman. The woman should be free, like the man, to choose her own spouse guided not by the advice and aid of neighbors and acquaintances, but by her own personal inclinations. After choosing her life partner, a woman must bind herself completely to the duties of that partnership upon which she has embarked. You refer to these as heavy chains fabricated by the ages. Yes, I agree with you and I say that these *are* heavy chains; but remember that these chains were made by nature who made the woman what she is today. Though man's mind has reached the point of breaking the chains of customs and traditions, it has not yet reached the point of breaking the natural chains because the law of nature is above all laws. Why can't a married woman meet secretly with the man she loves? Because by thus doing she will be betraying her husband and disgracing the name she has willingly accepted, and will be lowering herself in the eyes of the society of which she is a member.

At the time of marriage the woman promises to be faithful, and spiritual faithfulness is as important as physical faithfulness. At the time of matrimony she also declares and guarantees the happiness and well-being of her husband; and when she meets secretly with another man, she is already guilty of betraying society, family and duty. You may counter with, "Duty is a vague word that is hard to define in many circumstances." In a case like this we need to know "what is a family" in order to be able to ascertain the duties of its members. The role which the woman plays in the family is the most difficult, the most humble, and the most bitter.

I myself feel the pangs of the strings that tie the woman down—those fine silky strings are like those of a spider's web, but they are as strong as golden wires. Suppose we let Selma Karamy,* the heroine of your novel, and every woman that resembles her in affections and intelligence, meet secretly with an honest man of noble character; would not this condone any woman's selecting for herself a friend, other than her husband, to meet with secretly? This would not work, even if the purpose of their secret meeting was to pray together before the shrine of the Crucified.

MAY

Sarkis Effandi, one of Gibran's best friends, was considered a scholar among the intelligentsia of Lebanon. He owned a publishing house and a daily Arabic newspaper called *Lisan-Ul-Hal*. In the year 1912 the Arab League of Progress, an organization composed of many literary figures joined together for the purpose of promoting Arab unity and culture, decided to honor the

* The beautiful girl of Beirut in Gibran's *The Broken Wings*.

great Lebanese poet Khalil Effandi Mutran, who a few years later became the poet laureate of Egypt and Syria.

Since Sarkis was the head of the committe honoring the poet, he extended an invitation to his friend Gibran in New York to join them on the honor day in Beirut. Gibran could not make the trip, but he sent to Sarkis a prose poem with instructions to read it in his behalf before the poet on the day of the event. The story, which is not published in this book, was entitled "The Poet from Baalbeck." It was a eulogy in which Gibran pictured the poet laureate of the two sister countries as a prince sitting on his golden throne and receiving wise men from the East. In the story, Gibran expressed his belief in the transmigration of souls and praises the great soul that was incarnated in the honored poet's body.

TO SALEEM SARKIS

New York,
Oct. 6, 1912

Dear Sarkis Effandi,

I am sending you a story that was revealed to me by the devilish muses to honor the poet Khalil Effandi Mutran. As you notice, the story is rather short compared with the dignity of the great prince and outstanding poet. But at the same time it is long in comparison to the ones written by other poets and writers who, of course, are inclined to be brief and clever, especially when it comes to honoring poets. What shall I do when the muses inspire me to write on such a subject that needs a little expatiation?

Please accept my sincerest thanks for your invitation to join you in honoring a great poet who pours his soul as wine into the cups of the Arab League of Progress, and who burns his heart as incense before the two countries [Syria and Egypt] by strengthening the ties of friendship and love between them.

To you goes my salaam mingled with my sincerest respect and admiration.

GIBRAN

TO AMEEN GURAIEB

Boston,
Feb. 18, 1913

Brother Ameen:

This is the last word I say to you while you are in this country. It is a word emanating from the holy of holies of the heart, mingled with a sigh of longing and a smile of hope:

Be healthy every hour of the day, and every day of the month. Enjoy beautiful things wherever you see them, and let their memory and their echo remain in your heart until the day you return to your friends and well-wishers. Meet the admirers of *Almuhager* in Egypt, Syria, and Lebanon, and speak to them of the deeds of their immigrant brethren; unfold before them that which the long distance has folded between our hearts and their hearts; and strengthen the ties that connect our souls with their souls.

Take a walk in the morning and stand on the top of one of the mountains in Lebanon and meditate upon the sun when it is rising and pouring its golden rays upon the villages and the valleys. Let these heavenly pictures remain inscribed upon your heart so that we can share them when you come back to us. Be kind enough to convey the longing of our souls and the wishes of our hearts to the youth of Lebanon. Tell the elderly men of Syria that our thoughts, affections, and dreams never leave our hearts and souls except when they fly towards them. When your boat reaches Beirut, stand on its prow and look towards Mount Sunnin and Fam El-Mizab and greet our forefathers who are sleeping under the layers of the earth, and salute the fathers and brothers who are living above the earth. Mention our works and endeavors in private and public meetings. Tell them that we are busy sowing seeds in America so that we may some day reap the harvest in Lebanon. Do and say whatever you wish provided you are happy, for your happiness is the wish and hope of every true Lebanese in the United States of America.

Miriana shakes your hand and wishes you happiness. Remember me to the well-wishers of *Almuhager* in Egypt, Syria, and Lebanon. Perchance when my name reaches their ears it will turn into a soothing tune. Goodbye, Ameen, goodbye, O dear brother of

GIBRAN

Every time Gibran published a book, he sent a copy to May for criticism. When *The Cortege* or *Procession*, and *The Madman* were published, May reviewed them in *Al-Hilal*, a magazine in Egypt, and wrote Gibran a special letter in which she discussed the above books. Gibran answered her and thanked her for the criticism, praising her cleverness, her vast knowledge, and her frankness. At the same time he tried to acquit himself

of being in agreement with Nietzsche and to deny some
ideas he wrote on passion in *The Madman.*

TO MAY ZIADEH

Dear May,

. . . All in all the madman is not I. The passion
which I sought to bring out through the lips of a person-
age I had created does not represent my own feelings. The
language that I found expressive of the desires of this madman is different from the language that I use when I sit
down to converse with a friend whom I love and respect.
If you really want to discover my reality through my writings, why don't you refer to the youth in the field and the
soothing tune of his flute instead of the madman and his
ugly cries? You will realize that the madman is no more
than a link in a long chain made of metal. I do not deny
that the madman was an unpolished link of rough iron,
but this does not mean that the whole chain is rough. For
every soul there is a season, May. The soul's winter is not
like her spring, and her summer is not like her autumn. . . .

> Then Gibran went on discussing his book *Tears and
> Laughter* whose dialogue May had criticized and en-
> quired of its author what prompted him to write such
> a childish work, to which Gibran bravely answered:

. . . Now let us discuss *Tears And Laughter* for a moment.
I am not afraid to tell you that this came out before the
World War. At that time I sent you a copy and never heard
from you whether you received it or not. The articles in
Tears And Laughter were the first ones that I wrote in
series and published them in *Almuhager* sixteen years

ago. Nasseeb Arida (may Allah forgive him) was the one who collected these articles, to which he added two more which I wrote in Paris, and published them in one book. During my childhood and the days of my youth, before the writings of *Tears And Laughter*, I wrote enough prose and poetry to fill many volumes, but I did not, and shall not, commit the crime of having them published.

GIBRAN

As the name of Kahlil Gibran was, and still is, dear to every Lebanese heart or Arabic-speaking person, so the name of Mikhail Naimy today is dear to the hearts of the sons and daughters of Lebanon.

Naimy, who is a leading literary figure in Lebanon and the Middle East, lives in seclusion in his home town, Biskinta, near Mount Sunnin in Lebanon. While in New York, Naimy and Gibran were inseparable friends, and it was to Naimy that Gibran complained and entrusted his secrets. Even on his deathbed Gibran called for Naimy, who came to stay with him at the hospital until he breathed his last.

Born in Biskinta, Lebanon, Mikhail Naimy received his early education at a parochial school conducted by the Imperial Russian Palestine Society. In 1906 he was granted a scholarship to the Seminary of Poltava in the Ukraine, where he made an extensive study of the Russian language in which he wrote poems and treatises that were widely admired. In 1916 Naimy received two degrees from the University of Washington. He wrote and published in Arabic many critical articles and stories while at the University. In 1916 he decided that the Arabic literary circle in New York, with the great Arabic writers, Ameen Rihani, Kahlil Gibran, Nasseeb Arida, and others, was to be his field.

In World War I, he served at the front with the

AEF. After his honorable discharge in 1919 he returned to his literary career. In 1932 at the height of his fame he decided to return to Lebanon.

Among the works he published are *Two Generations*, a popular play; *The Cribble*, a series of critical essays; *Stages*, dealing with inner and outer life; *Once Upon a Time*, a collection of short stories; *Food for the Godward Journey*, his famous discourses; *Eyelid Whisperings*, philosophical poems; *Encounter*, a novel; *Threshing Floor* and *Light and Darkness*, philosophical contemplations; *The Memoirs of a Pitted Face*, a self-portrait of a bizarre personality; *Vineyard by the Road*, sayings and parables; *Present-Day Idols*, an analytical essay; *The World's Voice*, thoughts and meditations of life; *The Book of Mirdad*, a book for seekers after spiritual emancipation.

In his letters Kahlil Gibran addresses Mikhail Naimy sometimes as "Dear Meesha"—a diminutive for Mikhail. The long trip that Gibran refers to in the following letter was one of his usual trips to Boston where his sister Miriana lived. He also refers to *Al-Funoon*, an Arabic magazine which Gibran started, but which did not last long.

TO MIKHAIL NAIMY

New York,
Sept. 14, 1919

Dear Mikhail:

May God's peace be upon you. I have returned from my long trip and met with our brother Nasseeb and had a long discussion with him about reviving *Al-Funoon*, and the ways and means of securing its future. I interviewed many educated and half-educated people in Boston and New York regarding this matter, but all of the talks stopped at a certain point. The point is this: Nasseeb Arida cannot take the responsibility alone. It is necessary that Mikhail Naimy return to New York and join Nasseeb in the project and put it on a working basis before the intelligentsia and the merchants of New York. By having these two men working together, the confidence of the Syrian people may be gained; for one alone cannot win. An entertainment should be given in New York, and the proceeds would go to the magazine. How can the entertainment be a success when the man who is capable of obtaining speakers and musicians is in Washington? A committee should be formed to start the work. The treasurer must be known to the Syrians in other states who will ask themselves a thousand and one questions before they answer the circular. But who else other than Mikhail Naimy is capable of forming this committee?

There are numerous things, Mikhail, that begin and end with you each time we discuss the subject of *Al-Funoon*. If you wish to revive the magazine, you should come to New York and be the trigger behind every move. Nasseeb is unable to do anything at present, and of all the admirers and well-wishers of *Al-Funoon* in New York, there is no one who is capable of taking the responsibility upon himself. It is my belief that five thousand dollars would be sufficient to guarantee the future of the magazine. However, I presume that a circular without the entertainment would not bring half of the proposed amount. In short, the success of the project depends upon your presence in New York. If your return to New York means a sacrifice on your part, that sacrifice must be considered as placing that which is dear, and offering the important upon the altar of that which is more important. To me the dearest thing in your life is the realization of your dreams, and the most important thing is the reaping of the fruit of your talents.

Write me if you will; and may God protect you for your brother

GIBRAN

Emil Zaidan was an outstanding scholar and well known throughout the Arabic-speaking world for his great works in the field of Arabic literature. Being a Lebanese and owner and editor of one of the best Arabic magazines in Egypt, he admired Gibran and looked upon him as a genius. He devoted many pages to him in his monthly magazine *Al-Hilal*, the Crescent. It was through this magazine and many others that Gibran won fame and became known as poet, artist, and philosopher.

In the following letter to his friend Zaidan, Gibran speaks of the circumstances that made it necessary for him to work ten hours a day despite his doctor's orders that he work no more than five. Gibran at that time was working on several projects that required many hours of daily work. He tells his friend that there is nothing more difficult than the existence of a strong spirit in a weak body.

TO EMIL ZAIDAN

1919

My Brother Emil:

. . . My health is better now than it used to be. Yet it is still like a violin with broken strings. What is bothering me most now is that circumstances have placed me in a position that require of me ten hours of daily work while I am forbidden to spend more than four or five hours writing or painting. There is nothing more difficult than the existence of a strong spirit in a weak body. I feel—I am not modest—that I am just at the beginning of a mountain road. The twenty years which I have spent as a writer and painter were but an era of preparation and desire. Up to the present time I have not yet done anything worthy of remaining before the face of the sun. My ideas have not ripened yet, and my net is still submerged in water.

GIBRAN

In this letter Gibran mentions his two friends, Abdul-Masseh and Nasseeb Arida. The former was the owner and editor of *As-Sayeh*, an Arabic newspaper published in New York, and the latter was a famous poet and owner and editor of *Al-Akhlak*, the Character, a monthly magazine published also in New York. Both Abdul-Masseh and Nasseeb were members of Arrabitah, a literary circle limited in membership to ten or thirteen, organized in New York with Gibran as president and Mikhail Naimy as secretary. Other members of Arrabitah were Catzeflis, an intimate of Gibran and an essayist of recognized accomplishments in the field of Arabian thought and literature, Ayoub, Hawie, Rihani, Abu-Mady, Nadra, Alkazin, Bahut, Atalla. Each one of these pioneers from Syria or Lebanon made a worthy contribution to poetry and literature. Gibran was the first of eight now dead. Arrabitah brought about a real renaissance in modern Arabic literature. Many books in Arabic have already been written about it, and many more will be written.

TO MIKHAIL NAIMY

Boston, 1920

My Brother Mikhail:

Peace be unto you and unto your big heart and pure soul. I would like to know how you are and where you are. Are you in the forest of your dreams or in the knolls and hills of your thoughts? Or are you on the top of that mountain where all dreams turn into one vision, and all thoughts into a single ambition? Tell me where you are, Mikhail.

As to myself, I am, between my confounded health and the will of the people, like an out-of-tune musical instrument in the hands of a giant who plays on it strange melodies devoid of harmony. God help me, Mikhail, with those Americans! May God take both of us away from them to the placid valleys of Lebanon.

I have just mailed to Abdul-Masseh a short article for publication. Examine it, brother, and if it is not fit for publishing, tell Abdul-Masseh to keep it for me in an obscure corner until I return.

This article was written between midnight and dawn, and I do not know whether it is good or not. But the basic idea in it is not strange to the subject matter we discuss during our evening gathering. Tell me, how is Nasseeb and where is he? Each time I think of you and him, I feel peaceful, calm and enchantingly tranquil, and I say to myself, "Nothing is vanity under the sun."

A thousand greetings and salaams to our brethren in the spirit of truth. May God protect you and watch over you, and keep you a dear brother to your brother

GIBRAN

314

When Gibran published his Arabic book *The Tempest* in 1920, Naimy came out with an article praising the author and the outstanding works included in the volume.

TO MIKHAIL NAIMY

Boston, 1920

Brother Mikhail:

I have just read your article on *The Tempest*. What shall I say to you, Mikhail?

You have put between your eyes and the pages of my book a magnifying glass which made them appear greater than they really are. This made me feel ashamed of myself. You have placed, through your article, a great responsibility upon me. Will I ever be able to live up to it? Will I be able to vindicate the basic thought in the vision you have revealed of me? It seems to me that you wrote that wonderful article while looking upon my future, and not upon my past. For my past has consisted only of threads, not woven. It has also been stones of various sizes and shapes, but not a structure. I could see you looking upon me with the eye of hope, not of criticism, which makes me regret much of my past and at the same time dream about my future with a new enthusiasm in my heart. If that was what you wanted to do for me, you have succeeded, Mikhail.

I liked the stationery for Arrabitah very much, but the motto "To God many a treasure beneath the throne, etc." should be more obvious. The printing of the names of the officers and members is necessary if we wish to create the desired result. Everyone looking at a missive from Arrabitah would wonder who the members of Arrabitah are. However, I prefer that the names be printed in the smallest Arabic type.

I am sorry, Mikhail, that I shall not return to New York before the middle of next week, for I am tied up with some important problems in this abominable city. What shall I do? You all go to Milford, and replenish your cups with the wine of the spirit and the wine of the grapes, but do not forget your loving brother who is longing to see you

GIBRAN

In the following letter Gibran speaks of the meeting he and other members of Arrabitah had at the home of Rasheed Ayoub. Plans had been made at the meeting for the publication of the *Anthology of Arrabitah*, an Arabic book containing a history of the literary organization as well as a collection of stories, articles, and poems written by its members.

Gibran refers to *Barren* and *Memoirs of a Pitted Face*. These were manuscripts of Mikhail Naimy, who had asked Gibran to inquire of Nasseeb Arida as to their whereabouts.

The word *inshallah* means "God willing."

TO MIKHAIL NAIMY

New York,
October 8, 1920

Dear Mikhail:

Each time I think of you traveling as a salesman in the interior for a business firm, I feel somehow hurt.

Yet I know that this pain is the residue of an old philosophy. Today I believe in Life and in all that she brings upon us, and I confirm that all that the days and nights bring is good, and beautiful and useful.

We met last night at Rasheed's home, and we drank and ate and listened to songs and poetry. But our evening was not complete because you were not with us in person.

The materials for the *Anthology of Arrabitah* are all ready, if only in spirit! And they are all arranged, but only in words. When I ask for something from any of our brethren, he answers me saying, "In two days" or "At the end of this week," or "Next week." The philosophy of postponement, which is oriental, almost chokes me. And the strange thing about it, Meesha, is that some people consider coquettishness as a sign of intelligence!

I have asked Nasseeb through Abdul-Masseh to look for *Barren* and *Memoirs of a Pitted Face*, and he promised to do so, *inshallah*.

I was glad to hear that your absence will not be prolonged. Perhaps I should not be glad. Come back to us, Meesha, when you want, and you shall find us as you want us to be.

May God watch over you and keep you for your brother

GIBRAN

TO MIKHAIL NAIMY

Boston,
May 24, 1920

Dear Mikhail:

May God shower your good soul and big heart with peace. Arrabitah shall hold its official meeting tomorrow (Wednesday) evening. Unfortunately I shall be far away from you. Had it not been for a lecture I am going to give Thursday night, I would return to New York for the sake of Arrabitah's love. If you consider the lecture a legal excuse, I will be grateful for your generosity and consideration; otherwise you will find me willing to pay the fine of five dollars with pleasure.

This city was called in the past the city of science and art, but today it is the city of traditions. The souls of its inhabitants are petrified; even their thoughts are old and worn-out. The strange thing about this city, Mikhail, is that the petrified is always proud and boastful, and the worn-out and old holds its chin high. Many a time I have sat and conversed with Harvard professors in whose presence I felt as if I were talking to a sheik from Al-Azhar.*

On several occasions I have talked with Bostonian ladies and heard them say things which I used to hear from the ignorant and simple old ladies in Syria. Life is all the same, Mikhail; it declares itself in the villages of Lebanon as in Boston, New York, and San Francisco.

Remember me with best wishes to my brethren

* According to historians, Al-Azhar is the oldest university in the world whose sheiks (professors) stick to old traditions.

and fellow workers in Arrabitah. May God keep you as a dear brother to

GIBRAN

In many places throughout his writings Gibran refers to his studio in New York as "the hermitage." In this letter he speaks of his meeting there with Nasseeb Arida and Abdul-Masseh.

TO MIKHAIL NAIMY

New York, 1920

My Dear Meesha:

Good morning to you, oh wondering soul between the intent of the earth and the claim of heaven. I heard your voice calling the people's attention to "your goods" in the markets and squares. I heard you shouting softly, "We sell denims, we sell muslins," and I loved the soothing tone of your voice, Meesha, and I know that the angels hear you and record your calls in the Eternal Book. I was happy to hear about your great success. However, I fear this success! I am afraid it is going to lead you into the heart of the business world. He who reaches that heart will find it very difficult to return to our world!

I shall meet with Nasseeb and Abdul-Masseh at the hermitage tonight and we shall discuss the *Anthology*. Wish you were with us.

I am in these days a man with a thousand and one things to do. I am like a sick bee in a garden of flowers. The nectar is ample and the sun is beautiful upon the flowers.

Pray for me and receive God's blessing, and remain a dear brother to

GIBRAN

TO MIKHAIL NAIMY

New York, 1920

Dear Meesha:

We have already missed you, though you have barely said goodby. What would happen to us if you stayed away three weeks?

The *Anthology*: What of it? It is a chain whose rings are made of postponement and hesitation. Every time I mention it to Nasseeb or Abdul-Masseh, the first will say to me, "Tomorrow," and the second will respond "You are right." But in spite of all these delays, the *Anthology* will appear at the end of the year, *Inshallah*.

Write to me when you have nothing better to do. If your new poem has already been completed, send me a copy of it. You have not given me a copy of your poem "Oh, Cup-Bearer." May God forgive you. Be as you wish and remain a dear brother to your brother

GIBRAN

TO MAY ZIADEH

Nov. 1, 1920

Dear May:

The soul, May, does not see anything in life save that which is in the soul itself. It does not believe except in its own private event, and when it experiences something, the outcome becomes a part of it. I experienced something last year that I intended to keep a secret, but I did not do so. In fact, I revealed it to a friend of mine to whom I was accustomed to reveal my secrets because I felt that I was in dire need of talking to someone. But do you know what she told me? She said to me without thinking, "This is a musical song." Suppose someone had told a mother holding her babe in her arms that she was carrying a wooden statue, what would be the answer, and how would that mother feel about it?

Many months had passed and the words ("a musical song") were still ringing in my ears, but my friend was not satisfied with what she had told me, but kept on watching me and reprimanding me for every word I uttered, hiding everything away from me and piercing my hand with a nail every time I attempted to touch her. Consequently I became desperate, but despair, May, is an ebb for every flow in the heart; it's a mute affection. For this reason I have been sitting before you recently and gazing at your face without uttering a word or without having a chance to write you, for I said in my heart, "I have no chance."

Yet in every winter's heart there is a quivering spring, and behind the veil of each night there is a smiling dawn. Now my despair has turned into hope.

GIBRAN

May asked Gibran once how he wrote and how he ate and how he spent his everyday life, etc. She also inquired about his home and office and everything he did. Gibran answered some of her questions in the letter which follows.

TO MAY ZIADEH

1920

. . . How sweet are your questions, and how happy I am to answer them, May. Today is a day of smoking; since this morning I have already burned one million cigarettes. Smoking to me is a pleasure and not a habit. Sometimes I go for one week without smoking one single cigarette. I said that I burned one million cigarettes. It is all your fault and you are to blame. If I were by myself in this valley, I would never return . . .

As to the suit I am wearing today, it is customary to wear two suits at the same time; one suit woven by the weaver and made by the tailor and another one made out of flesh, blood, and bones. But today I am wearing one long and wide garment spotted with ink of different colors. This garment does not differ much from the ones worn by the dervishes save that it is cleaner. When I go back to the Orient I shall not wear anything but old-fashioned Oriental clothes.

. . . As regards my office, it is still without ceiling and without walls, but the seas of sands and the seas of ether are still like they were yesterday, deep with many waves and no shores. But the boat in which I sail these seas has no masts. Do you think you can provide masts for my boat?

The book *Towards God* is still in the mist factory, and its best drawing is in *The Forerunner* of which I sent you a copy two weeks ago.

After answering some of her questions he began to describe himself to her symbolically.

What shall I tell you about a man whom God has arrested between two women, one of whom turns his dream into awakeness, and the other his awakeness into dream? What shall I say of a man whom God has placed between two lamps? Is he melancholy or is he happy? Is he a stranger in this world? I do not know. But I would like to ask you if you wish for this man to remain a stranger whose language no one in the universe speaks. I do not know. But I ask you if you would like to talk to this man in the tongue he speaks, which you can understand better than anyone else. In this world there are many who do not understand the language of my soul. And in this world there are also many who do not understand the language of your soul. I am, May, one of those upon whom life bestowed many friends and well-wishers. But tell me: is there any one among those sincere friends to whom we can say, "Please carry our cross for us only one day"? Is there any person who knows that there is one song behind our songs that cannot be sung by voices or uttered by quivering strings? Is there anyone who sees joy in our sorrow and sorrow in our joy?

. . . Do you recall, May, your telling me about a journalist in Buenos Aires who wrote and asked for what every newspaperman asks for—your picture? I have thought of this newspaperman's request many times, and each time I said to myself, "I am not a journalist; therefore I shall not ask for what the newspaperman asks for. No I am not a journalist. If I were the owner or editor of a magazine or newspaper, I would frankly and simply and without abashment ask her for her picture. No, I am not a journalist; what shall I do?"

GIBRAN

As-Sayeh was the name of an Arabic newspaper owned and edited by Abdul-Masseh who was a member of Arrabitah, the literary circle. In that year Abdul-Masseh was preparing a special issue of *As-Sayeh* and he called on Gibran and all the members of Arrabitah to contribute, which they did.

In that same year Gibran must have written an article under the caption of "The Lost One" and sent it to his friend Emil Zaidan to have it published in his magazine, *Al-Hilal*, in Egypt. The translator of these letters has not yet succeeded in finding the article which Gibran speaks of in this letter. Gibran also refers to Salloum Mokarzel. He was at that time the owner of a publishing house in New York where he published his English magazine, *The Syrian World*.

TO MIKHAIL NAIMY

Boston,
Jan. 1, 1921

Dear Meesha:

Good morning, and a happy New Year. May the Lord burden your vines with bunches of grapes, and fill your bins with wheat, and replenish your jars with oil, honey, and wine; and may Providence place your hand upon the heart of Life in order to feel the pulse of Life's heart.

This is my first letter to you in the New Year. Were I in New York, I would ask you to spend the evening with me in the peaceful hermitage. But how far am I from New York, and how far is the hermitage from me!

How are you, and what are you writing or composing, and what are you thinking? Is the special issue of *As-Sayeh* about to come out, or is it still waiting for those machines which run fast when we wish them to slow down, and slow down when we wish them to run fast? The West is a machine and everything in it is at the mercy of the machine. Yes, Meesha, even your poem, "Do the Brambles Know," is at the mercy of Salloum Mokarzel's wheels. I was indisposed last week, and for this reason I did not write anything new. But I have reviewed my article, "The Lost One," smoothed it out, and mailed it to *Al-Hilal*.

Remember me, Meesha, with love and affection to our comrades, and may God protect you as a dear brother to

GIBRAN

TO MIKHAIL NAIMY

Boston, 1921

Brother Meesha:

After I read the last number of the Arrabitah's magazine and reviewed the previous issues, I was convinced that there is a deep abyss between us and them. We cannot go to them nor can they come to us. No matter what we endeavor to do, Mikhail, we cannot free them from the slavery of superficial literary words. Spiritual freedom comes from within and not from without. You know more about this truth than any man.

Do not endeavor to awaken those whose hearts God has put to sleep for some hidden wisdom. Do whatever you wish for them, and send them whatever you like, but do not forget that you shall place a veil of doubt and suspicion upon the face of our Arrabitah. If we have any power, this power exists in our unity and aloneness. If we must cooperate and work with other people, let our cooperation be with our equals who say what we say.

     . . . So you are on the brink of madness. This is a good bit of news, majestic in its fearfulness, fearful in its majesty and beauty. I say that madness is the first step towards unselfishness. Be mad, Meesha. Be mad and tell us what is behind the veil of "sanity." The purpose of life is to bring us closer to those secrets, and madness is the only means. Be mad, and remain a mad brother to your mad brother

GIBRAN

TO MIKHAIL NAIMY

Boston, 1921

Dear Meesha:

     Here is a gentle missive from Emil Zaidan. Read it thoroughly and take care of it to the best of your knowledge as you have always done. The heat is killing in this city and its environs. How is it in New York, and what are you doing?

     In my heart, Meesha, there are shadows and images that sway, walk, and expand like mist, but I am unable to give them the form of words. Peradventure it would be better for me to keep silent until this heart returns to what it used to be a year ago. Possibly silence is better for me, but, alas! How difficult and how bitter is silence in the heart of one who has become accustomed to talking and singing.

     A thousand salaams to you and to our dear brothers. May you remain a dear brother to

GIBRAN

In this letter Gibran speaks of *Al-Barq* (The Lightning), which was one of the leading Arabic newspapers in Beirut. Beshara El-Khoury, the editor and owner of *Al-Barq*, was a great admirer of Gibran, and he devoted many columns in his paper to him. Gibran also threatens his friend Naimy, saying that if he (Naimy) did not mail him the snapshots which they had taken at Cahoonzie he would file two suits against him: one in the court of friendship and the other in the court of El-Jazzar, a Turkish ruler known for his despotism during his reign in Syria.

TO MIKHAIL NAIMY

Boston, 1921

Dear Mikhail:

Peace be unto you. Enclosing herewith a letter addressed to the counsellor of Arrabitah from Beshara El-Khoury editor of *Al-Barq*. As you notice, it is a brief and gentle missive, and it demonstrates at the same time a sort of pain in the soul of its author—and pain is a good sign.

What happened to the snapshots we took at Cahoonzie? You are hereby notified that I want a copy of each. If I do not obtain my rights, I shall file two suits against you—one with the court of friendship, the other with the court of Ahmad Pasha El-Jazzar.

Remember me, Meesha, to our brethren and comrades, and may God keep you dear to your brother

GIBRAN

327

William Catzeflis has already been identified as one of Gibran's intimates and an essayist of recognized accomplishments in the field of Arabic thought and literature. He also was one of the members of Arra-bitah.

The farewell party which Gibran refers to in this letter was given in Catzeflis' honor on the occasion of the latter's departure to Lebanon on a pleasure trip. He also refers to a special Arabic dish prepared by Nasseeb Arida consisting of meat, vegetables and spices.

TO MIKHAIL NAIMY

Boston, 1921

Dear Meesha:

A thousand salaams to your heart that neither beats, nor pities, nor palpitates, nor glitters. It seems that you are ridiculing me for that which has turned my hair white and my poetry black; and you blame me for my briefness in writing and my silence about myself; and you proceed gradually to scold me, entering through the door of blasphemy. Allah be my rescue!

As to myself, I do not see any fault in you. You are perfect with your black hair covering your temples and the top of your head, and with the abundance of your poetry and prose. It seems as if you were born just as you wished to be born when you were in the state of embryo, and that you attained your wish while in the cradle. From God we came and to God we return!

I regret to be absent while Nasseeb's *meddeh* (spread) is being prepared. But what can I do if the *meddeh* cannot be spread from one city to another? It is a shame that some people can be filled with delicious things while others are hungry even for the grace of God, unable to obtain even a mouthful of it.

I am glad that Nasseeb insisted on your writing the preface to the *Anthology of Arrabitah*. Undoubtedly you have written or shall write that which shall be "a necklace about the neck of the *Anthology* and a bracelet about its wrist." May you remain, oh brother of the Arabs, a gem in the crown of literature, and a glittering star in its sky.

My health is better than it was last week. But I must keep away from working, from thinking, and even from feeling for a period of three months in order to regain my full health. As you know, Meesha, to quit working is harder than to work; and he who is accustomed to work finds rest the severest punishment.

I have done my duty towards William Catzeflis and those who wish to honor him by giving him a farewell party. I sent a telegram to William and another one to Anton Semman in response to their invitation to attend the reception in New York.

May God keep you and your brethren and mine, and may you remain a dear brother to

GIBRAN

TO MIKHAIL NAIMY

Boston, 1921

My Dear Meesha:

Good morning and good evening to you, and may God fill your days with songs and your nights with dreams. I am enclosing herewith a good letter and a check, which is still better, from an adherent member of Arra-bitah. Will you answer the first in your good taste and perfect literary style, and accept the second as a burned incense and oil offering. Hoping that you do so, *inshallah*.

You say in your letter that you have told George* to send me the Spanish magazine and newspaper, but George has not sent them yet. May God forgive George, and may He mend George's memory with the threads of my patience and self-control. It seems to me, brother, that George has thrown the *Republic of Chile* [name of a magazine] into the waste-basket.

The cold in Boston is terrible. Everything is frozen, even the thoughts of the people are frozen. But in spite of the cold and the severe wind I am enjoying good health. My voice (or yell) is like the thunder of a volcano! And the tramping of my feet upon the ground is like a falling meteor that makes a big hollow in the ground. As to my stomach, it is like a mill whose lower stone is a file and whose upper one is a rattler! Hoping that your yell, your tramping, and your stomach are just as you like them to be whenever and wherever you want.

Give my regards to our brethren mingled with my love, my prayers, and longing. May God keep you dear to your brother

GIBRAN

When the doctors ordered Gibran in 1921 to leave New York for Boston to stay with his sister Miriana and rest at home for a while, he carried with him on his way to Boston the English manuscript of *The Prophet* which he intended to publish that same year.

* A clerk in the office of *As-Sayeh*.

When he arrived in Boston he was so sick that he had to postpone the publication of *The Prophet* until 1923. In the year 1918 he had published his first work in English, *The Madman*, and in 1920 *The Forerunner*. In this letter Gibran speaks of these two books and also of *Ad-Deewan*, which must have been an Arabic magazine or newspaper.

TO MIKHAIL NAIMY

Boston, 1921

Brother Meesha:

Ever since I arrived in this city I have been going from one specialist to another, and from one exhaustive examination to a more exhaustive one. It all happened because this heart of mine has lost its meter and its rhyme. And you know, Mikhail, the meter of this heart never did conform to the meters and rhymes of other hearts. But since the accidental must follow the constant as the shadow follows the substance, it was definitely decided that this lump within my chest should be in unison with that trembling mist in the firmament—that mist which is myself—called "I."

Never mind, Meesha, whatever is destined shall be. But I feel that I shall not leave the slope of this mountain before daybreak. And dawn shall throw a veil of light and gleam on everything.

When I left New York I put nothing in my valise except the manuscript of *The Prophet* and some raiments. But my old copy-books are still in the corners of that silent room. What shall I do to please you and to please the Damascus Arrabitah? The doctors have ordered me to leave all mental work. Should I be inspired within the next two weeks, I shall take my pen and jot down the inspiration; otherwise my excuse should be accepted.

I do not know when I may return to New York. The doctors say I should not return until my health returns to me. They say I must go to the country and surrender myself to simple living free from every thought and purpose and dispute. In other words, they want me to be converted into a trifling plant. For that reason I see fit that you send the picture of Arrabitah to Damascus without me in it. Or you may send the old picture after you stain my face with ink. If it is necessary, however, that Arrabitah in New York should appear in full before the Damascus Arrabitah, how would you like for Nasseeb, or Abdul-Masseh or you (if that were possible) to translate a piece from *The Madman* or *The Forerunner*? This may seem to be a silly suggestion. But what can I do, Mikhail, when I am in such a plight? He who is unable to sew for himself a new garment must go back and mend the old one. Do you know, brother, that this ailment has caused me to postpone indefinitely the publication of *The Prophet*? I shall read with interest your article in *Ad-Deewan*. I know it is going to be just and beautiful like everything else you have written.

Remember me to my brother workers of Arrabitah. Tell them that my love for them in the fog of night is not any less than in the plain light of the day. May God protect you and watch over you and keep you a dear brother to

GIBRAN

Gibran had always expressed his desire for and love of death. Although he wished at all times to attain such a goal, he was extremely affected when a dear friend of his or someone that he knew passed away. Saba, who was an intimate of Gibran and a dear friend of Naimy, was taken away by death while Gibran was in Boston suffering the pangs of a severe ailment. As soon as he heard of the death of his good friend Saba he wrote to Naimy expressing his sentiments toward his departed friend.

He also tells his friend Naimy of his dream of a hermitage, a small garden, and a spring of water on the edge of one of the Lebanese valleys. He loathed this false civilization and wished to be left alone in a solitary place like Yousif El-Fakhri, one of the characters of a story that he wrote under the name of "The Tempest." Yousif at thirty years of age withdrew himself from society and departed to live in an isolated hermitage in the vicinity of Kadeesha Valley in North Lebanon.

TO MIKHAIL NAIMY

Boston, 1922

Dear Meesha:

Saba's death affected me immensely. I know that he has reached his goal, and that he has now fortified himself against things we complain of. I also know that he has attained what I wish at all times to attain. I know all that, yet it is strange that this knowledge cannot lighten my burden of sorrow. What could be the meaning of this sorrow? Saba had hopes he wanted to fulfill. His lot of hopes and dreams was equal to the lot of each one of us. Is there something in his departure, before his hopes blossomed and his dreams became fruitful, that creates this deep sorrow in our hearts? Is not my sorrow over him truly my grief over a dream I had in my youth when that youth passed away before my dream came true? Are not sorrow and regret at bereavement really forms of human selfishness?

I must not go back to New York, Meesha. The doctor has ordered me to stay away from cities. For this reason I rented a small cottage near the sea and I shall move to it with my sister in two days. I shall remain there until this heart returns to its order, or else becomes a part of the Higher Order. However, I hope to see you before summer is over. I know not how, where, or when, but things can be arranged somehow.

Your thoughts on "repudiating" the world are exactly like mine.* For a long time I have been dreaming of a hermitage, a small garden, and a spring of water. Do you recall Yousif El-Fakhri? Do you recall his obscure thoughts and his glowing awakening? Do you remember his opinion on civilization and the civilized? I say, Meesha, that the future shall place us in a hermitage on the edge of one of the Lebanese valleys. This false civilization has tightened the strings of our spirits to the breaking point. We must leave before they break. But we must remain patient until the day of departure. We must be tolerant, Meesha.

Remember me to our brethren and tell them that I love them and long to see them, and live in thought with them.

May God protect you, Meesha, and watch over you, and keep you a dear brother to your brother

GIBRAN

* Naimy was living at this time in a hermitage on the edge of one of the Lebanese valleys.

Nasseeb has already been identified as a member of Arrabitah—poet, editor and owner of *Al-Akhlak*, (the Character) which was a monthly Arabic magazine published in New York.

TO MIKHAIL NAIMY

New York,
1922

Dear Meesha:

Good evening to you. I now bring you the glad tidings that our Nasseeb is remaining with us, in us, and of us indefinitely, and his voyage to Argentina has now become ancient history.

Arrabitah did not meet the last Wednesday of this month for two reasons: The first is that you are away, and second is the non-existence of anything that calls for a meeting. I believe that the first reason is sufficient, and is the creator of the second one.

I was glad to hear that you are coming back Thursday. You have stayed too long away from us, Meesha. In your absence our circle turns into something nebulous, misty, without form or shape.

I was not pleased with your saying, "May Izrael take Mikhail."* In my opinion Mikhail is stronger than Izrael. The first has authority over the second, but the second has no power over the first. There are secrets in names deeper than we imagine; and their symbols are more obvious and more important than that which we think of. Mikhail has been since the beginning more powerful and more exacting than Izrael.

* May the angel of death take Mikhail.

Till we meet again, brother. May God keep you dear to

GIBRAN

A glimpse at the following letter will reveal that Gibran was to give two readings from his books: the first from *The Madman* and *The Forerunner*, and the second from *The Prophet*. Since this letter was written in 1922 and *The Prophet* was not published until 1923, it is obvious that the second reading was from the unpublished manuscript of *The Prophet*.

The reader will also realize that the money which the Syrians and the Lebanese in Brazil had spent on the gift (the translator does not know what kind) which they sent to the President of the United States was a waste of money. In Gibran's opinion, the money should have been sent to Arrabitah for the revival of *Al-Funoon*, the short-lived Arabic magazine which Gibran founded.

TO MIKHAIL NAIMY

Boston, 1922

Dear Meesha:

Do not say that the climate of Boston so agreed with me that I surrendered myself to relaxation and forgot New York and my comrades and my work and duties in New York. God knows that never in my life did I spend a month more full of difficulties, disasters, problems, and sorrows than the last month. I have asked myself many times if my "djinnee" or my "follower" or my "double"

336

has turned into a devil who opposes me and shuts doors in my face and places obstacles in my way. Since my arrival in this crooked city I have been living in a hell of worldly enigmas. Had it not been for my sister, I would have left everything and returned to my hermitage, dusting the dirt of the world off my feet.

When I received your telegram this morning I felt as if I were awakened from a terrible dream. I remembered the joyful hours we spent together talking about things spiritual and artistic. I forgot that I was in a battle and that my troops were in a critical situation. Then I remembered my past troubles and the coming ones and recalled that I was obliged to remain here to fulfill my promise and carry out my engagements. I am committed, Mikhail, to giving two readings from my books this coming week—the first from *The Madman* and *The Forerunner*, and the second one from *The Prophet*, before a "respectable" audience who likes this kind of thinking and this style of expression. But the things that have kept me in this city, and that will oblige me to remain here ten more days, have nothing to do with what I have written or read, or shall write or read. They have to do with dull and wearisome things, filling the heart with thorns and gall and grasping the soul with an iron hand as rough as a steel file.

I have not forgotten that next Wednesday is the date set for Arrabitah's meeting, but what shall I do when "the eye is far of view and the hand is short of reach?" I hope that you will meet and decide what is useful, and that you will remember me with a kind word, for I am these days in dire need of good wishes from friends, and prayers from the devout. I am in need of a sweet glance from a sincere eye.

The gift from our brethren in Brazil will reach the White House, and the President of the United States will thank them for their generosity and kind intentions. All that shall be arranged in a beautiful manner. But a wave from the sea of oblivion shall submerge the matter from beginning to end. Meanwhile, *Al-Funoon* magazine is still asleep and Arrabitah is poor, and our brethren in Brazil and the United States neither remember the first, nor feel the presence of the second. How strange people are, Meesha, and what strangers we both are among them!

GIBRAN

Emil Zaidan was editor of *Al-Hilal*, an outstanding Arabic magazine published in Egypt, to which Gibran contributed many articles.

TO EMIL ZAIDAN

In the late
part of 1922

My Brother Emil,

. . . I have intended to visit Egypt and Lebanon this year, but the indisposition which kept me away from work for twelve months has set me back two years and caused me to postpone those literary and technical treatises which I once talked to you about. I must now remain in this country until my English book *The Prophet* comes out. At the same time I will be finishing some paintings that I promised to complete.

I am already longing for the Orient in spite of what some friends write to me, which sometimes makes me feel discouraged and causes me to prefer expatriation and

living among strangers to the exile of living among relatives. Nevertheless, I shall return to my "old home" to see
with my own eyes what has become of it.

Remain a dear brother to

GIBRAN

In introducing Mikhail Naimy, the translator referred
to *The Cribble*, a series of critical essays, called
Algourbal in Arabic.

Naimy and Nasseeb had written a poem together
and promised to send it to Gibran. At the same time
they must have asked Rasheed and Gibran to write
something for publication. Rasheed, however, kept
postponing, which made Gibran feel empty-handed
also.

TO MIKHAIL NAIMY

Boston,
August 11, 1923

Dear Brother Meesha:

Good morning to you. I was glad to learn that
your book *The Cribble* is out. But I do not mind telling
you that I did not like for it to come at this time of the
year, although I know that the value of the book, which
is unique of its kind, has nothing to do with the season or
decade. Never mind, whatever is published is published.

I have spent many long hours with Archman-
drite Beshir reviewing the translation of *The Madman*
and *The Forerunner*. In spite of my rebellion, I was
pleased with the man's enthusiasm and determination.

When we finished reviewing and correcting he said to me, "I shall submit the translations of the two books to Mikhail Naimy and Nasseeb Arida and ask them to be unmerciful in their criticism." I liked his tact and I knew that he was truly seeking enlightenment.

I have not done anything worth mentioning since I left New York other than writing down some headings and renovating some old ideas. It seems to me, Meesha, that the orderly life in my sister's home pulls me away from creative writing. It is strange that chaotic living is the best sharpener for my imagination.

I shall be happy to receive your and Nasseeb's new poem, but I shall stand ashamed and empty-handed before both of you. I may not be the only one if Rasheed keeps on postponing. If he keeps this up, I do not know how he is going to have his book of poems published.

Give my salaam and love to our comrades and tell them that life without them is miserable. May God bless you, Meesha, and keep you a dear brother to your brother

GIBRAN

TO MIKHAIL NAIMY

Boston, 1923

Beloved Brother Meesha:

Forgive my long silence and help me obtain forgiveness from your brethren and mine. Early this summer the doctor told me to abstain from all kinds of writing, and I submitted to him after a great struggle between me and my will and the will of my sister and some friends. The result turned out to be good, for I am now closer to being in normal health than at any time during the last two years. My being away from the city, living a simple, quiet, and orderly life near the sea and the woods, has stilled the palpitations of my heart and altered my trembling hand to one that writes these lines.

I shall return to New York in two or three weeks and present myself to my brethren. If they take me into their midst, I shall know how affectionate they are. A beggar should not be demanding, and a criminal should make no conditions.

This is the first letter I have written to you for three months!

A thousand salaams to all, and may God protect you and keep you for your brother

GIBRAN

TO MIKHAIL NAIMY

Boston, 1923

I congratulate you and offer my felicitations upon *The Cribble.* Undoubtedly it is the first living breeze of that divine tempest which shall weed out all the dead wood in our literary forests. I have read the book thoroughly, from Aleph to Yey,* and I was reassured of a truth that I had long believed and which I once expressed to you. It is this: had you not been a poet and writer, you would not have reached your goal of critic, and you would not have succeeded in lifting the curtain to reveal the truth about poetry, poets, writing and writers. I say, Meesha,

* Aleph to Yey means A to Z.

341

that had you not undertaken the task of poetry in your own heart, you could not have discovered the poetic experiences of others. And had you not taken a long walk in the garden of poetry, you would not have rebelled against those who walk only the dark and narrow paths of meters and rhymes. Sainte-Beuve, Ruskin and Walter Pater were artists before and after they criticised the artistic works of others and each one of them criticised through the help of the light of his own inner feelings, and not through the help of acquired taste. The spiritual light that comes from within is the source of everything beautiful and noble. This light turns criticism into a fine and magnificent art. Without this light, criticism is compulsive and boring and lacking the positive note of decisive persuasion.

Yes, Meesha, you are a poet and a thinker before everything else, and your unique power of criticism is the outcome of your keen poetic thinking and feeling. Don't give the example of the "egg"*—I shall never accept it—for it smacks of empty controversy rather than demonstrable logic.

GIBRAN

In 1924, the Syrians apparently raised funds and built an orphanage, which Gibran calls "the noblest Syrian institution in the United States." He had planned to attend the dedication of the orphanage, but when the time came, he was ill in Boston with a stomach ailment.

* Gibran refers here to the old Arabic inquiry as to which came first—the egg or the hen.

TO MIKHAIL NAIMY

Boston,
Sept. 7, 1924

Dear Mikhail:

I have been locked in my room for several days and I have just left the bed to write you this letter. You know that I was indisposed when I left New York, and I have been fighting the poisoning in my stomach ever since. Had it not been for this, I would not have hesitated to go to the orphanage on the day of its dedication.

You realize, Meesha, that no matter how important and pressing my work is, it cannot keep me from absenting myself two or three days, especially when I am to take part in the dedication of the noblest Syrian institution in the United States. I beg you to offer my excuse to the Archbishop and to explain to him the real reason for my failure to come.

GIBRAN

Abdul-Masseh, owner and editor of *As-Sayeh*, had called on Gibran to make a special design for the annual special issue which came out in the form of a magazine rather than a paper and contained articles, poems, stories and pictures of the members of Arrabitah and other Arab writers.

TO MIKHAIL NAIMY

Boston, 1925

Dear Meesha:

Peace be unto your soul. As per your request, I have just mailed you the design for the cover of the special issue of *As-Sayeh*. The requests of princes are the princes of requests! I beg you to urge Abdul-Masseh to keep the design for me after the engraver is finished with it.

I have been wondering if you have found solitude and peace in the hermitage! I was afraid that you might find it cold; and I should have told you of the electric apparatus which can warm one of its corners. Of course, warm hearts do not need outside heat.

I shall return to New York in a week, more or less, and we shall have long talks of things beneath the earth and above the clouds. May God keep you, Meesha, a beloved brother to

GIBRAN

P.S.   I shall return to New York in ten days, *inshallah*, and we shall have a long discussion and set the drawings for Rasheed's book and share many beautiful dreams.

Edmond Wehby translated "The Crucified" from the Arabic to French and published it in *La Syrie*, a daily French newspaper in Beirut. A copy of the translation was sent by the translator to the author accompanied

344

by a nice letter to which Gibran wrote the following answer:

TO EDMOND WEHBY

New York,
March 12, 1925

Dear Brother:

Peace be unto you. I was very happy to receive your very kind letter. It revealed to me the abundance of your learning and the beauty of your spirit and your zeal for the arts and artists. I wish I were worthy of the praises and honor which you have accorded me in your missive, and I hope that I will be able to live up to the beautiful things you have said about me.

I have read with admiration your French translation of "The Crucified"—however, I was sorry to learn about the spiritual condition of Syrian and Lebanese youth today and their tendency towards learning foreign languages and neglecting their own tongue, which prompted your zeal to translate a piece especially written for that young generation in the language of their forefathers.

But your enthusiasm for Arrabitah and the deeds of its workers shows eagerness in your heart and willingness in your spirit for renovation, growth and enlightenment. Now in behalf of my brethren and fellow-workers of Arrabitah I offer to you thanks and gratitude.

Please accept my sincerest respect accompanied with my best wishes, and may Allah protect you and keep you.

GIBRAN

345

P.S. Please remember me to my great literary brother Felix Farris and give him my salaam.

TO MAY ZIADEH

1925

Dear May:

     . . . What shall I say to you about my vicissitudes? A year ago I was living in peace and tranquility, but today my tranquility has turned into clamor, and my peace into strife. The people devour my days and my nights and submerge my life in their conflicts and desires. Many a time I have fled from this awful city* to a remote place to be away from the people and from the shadow of myself. The Americans are a mighty people who never give up or get tired or sleep or dream. If these people hate someone, they will kill him by negligence, and if they like or love a person, they will shower him with affection. He who wishes to live in New York must be a sharp sword in a sheath of honey. The sword is to repel those who are desirous of killing time, and the honey is to satisfy their hunger.

     The day will come when I will be leaving for the Orient. My longing for my country almost melts my heart. Had it not been for this cage which I have woven with my own hands, I would have caught the first boat sailing towards the Orient. But what man is capable of leaving an edifice on whose construction he has spent all his life, even though that edifice is his own prison? It is difficult to get rid of it in one day . . .

     . . . So you want me to smile and forgive. I have

* New York.

been smiling a lot since this morning, and I am now all smiles deep down in my heart. I smile as if I were born to smile. . . . But forgiveness is a horrible word which makes me stand in fear and shame. The noble soul that humbles herself to that extent is closer to the angels than to human beings. . . . I alone am to blame, and I have done wrong in my silence and despair. For this reason I ask you to forget what I have done and to forgive me.

GIBRAN

TO MAY ZIADEH

In the year 1926

Dear May:

. . . You say that I am an artist and a poet. I am neither an artist, May, nor a poet. I have spent my days writing and painting, but I am not in accord with my days and my nights. I am a cloud, May—a cloud that mingles with objects, but never becomes united with them. I am a cloud, and in the cloud is my solitude, my loneliness, my hunger, and my thirst. But my calamity is that the cloud, which is my reality, longs to hear someone say, "You are not alone in this world but we are two together, and I know who you are."

. . . Tell me, May, is there any other person over there capable of and willing to say to me, "I am another cloud; O, cloud, let us spread ourselves over the mountains and in the valleys: let us walk between and above the trees, let us cover the high rocks, let us penetrate the heart of the human race, let us roam the unknown and the fortified distant places." Tell me, May, is there anyone who is capable of and willing to say at least one of these words?

GIBRAN

TO MAY ZIADEH

1928

Dear May:

I am indebted for all that I call "I" to women, ever since I was an infant. Women opened the windows of my eyes and the doors of my spirit. Had it not been for the woman-mother, the woman-sister, and the woman-friend, I would have been sleeping among those who seek the tranquility of the world with their snoring.

. . . I have found pleasure in being ill. This pleasure differs with its effect from any other pleasure. I have found a sort of tranquility that makes me love illness. The sick man is safe from people's strife, demands, dates and appointments, excess of talking, and ringing of telephones . . . I have found another kind of enjoyment through illness which is more important and unmeasurable. I have found that I am closer to abstract things in my sickness than in health. When I lay my head upon the pillow and close my eyes and lose myself to the world, I find myself flying like a bird over serene valleys and forests, wrapped in a gentle veil. I see myself close to those whom my heart has loved, calling and talking to them, but without anger and with the same feelings they feel and the same thoughts they think. They lay their hands now and then upon my forehead to bless me.

. . . I wish I were sick in Egypt or in my country

so I might be close to the ones I love.* Do you know, May, that every morning and every evening I find myself in a home in Cairo with you sitting before me reading the last article I wrote or the one you wrote which has not yet been published.

. . . Do you realize, May, that whenever I think of the Departure which the people call Death, I find pleasure in such thinking and great longing for such departure. But then I return to myself and remember that there is one word I must say before I depart. I become perplexed between my disability and my obligation and I give up hope. No, I have not said my word yet, and nothing but smoke has come out from this light. This is what makes me feel that cessation of work is more bitter than gall. I say this to you, May, and I don't say it to anyone else: If I don't depart before I spell and pronounce my word, I will return to say the word which is now hanging like a cloud in the sky of my heart.

. . . Does this sound strange to you? The strangest things are the closest to the real truth. In the will of man there is a power of longing which turns the mist in ourselves into sun.

GIBRAN

This letter was written in the year 1928 when Gibran's book, *Jesus the Son of Man*, was published by Alfred A. Knopf. In this book Gibran speaks of Jesus in behalf of seventy-nine persons who saw him. The last man who speaks of Jesus in the book is a man from Lebanon who lives in the twentieth century.

* At the writing of this letter May was living in Cairo, Egypt.

As we notice in the following letter, Gibran wrote this book while he was ill.

TO MIKHAIL NAIMY

Boston, 1928

Dear Meesha:

Peace be unto your soul. How nice of you and typical of your big heart to inquire about my health. I was inflicted with a disease called summer rheumatism which departed from me with the departure of the summer and its heat.

I have learned that you returned to New Babylon* three weeks ago. Tell us, O Spring of Youth, what kind of treasures have you brought back with you as a result of your bodily and spiritual absence? I shall return to New York in a week, and I shall search your pockets to find out what you have brought with you.

The book of *Jesus* has taken all my summer, with me ill one day and well another. And I might as well tell you that my heart is still in it in spite of the fact that it has already been published and has flown away from this cage.

GIBRAN

The Garden of the Prophet, which Gibran speaks of in this letter, was published by Alfred A. Knopf in the year 1933, two years after Gibran's death. Gibran

* New York.

did not live to complete it. The book was later finished by Barbara Young, the author of *This Man from Lebanon*, a study of Kahlil Gibran.

TO MIKHAIL NAIMY

Boston,
March, 1929

Dear Meesha:

How sweet and how tender of you to ask about my health. I am at present in an "acceptable" state, Meesha. The pains of rheumatism are gone, and the swelling has turned to something opposite. But the ailment has settled in a place deeper than muscles and bones. I have always wondered if I was in a state of health or illness.

It is a plight, Meesha, to be always between health and illness. It is one of the seasons of my life; and in your life and my life there are winter and spring, and you and I cannot know truly which one is preferable to the other. When we meet again I shall tell you what happened to me, and then you shall know why I once cried out to you, saying, "You have your Lebanon, and I have mine."

There is nothing like lemon among all the fruits, and I take lemon every day. . . . I leave the rest to God!

I have told you in a previous letter that the doctors warned me against working. Yet there is nothing I can do but work, at least with my mind, or at least for spite . . . What do you think of a book composed of four stories on the lives of Michelangelo, Shakespeare, Spinoza and Beethoven? What would you say if I showed their achievements to be the unavoidable outcome of pain, ambition, "expatriation" and hope moving in the human heart? What is your opinion of a book of this kind?

So much for that. But as to the writing of *The Garden of the Prophet,* it is definitely decided, but I find it wise to get away from the publishers at present.

My salaams to our beloved brethren. May God keep you a brother to

GIBRAN

TO MIKHAIL NAIMY

Telegram dated
March 26, 1929

Dear Meesha:

I was deeply touched by your telegram. I am better. The return of health will be slow. That is worse than illness. All will be well with me gradually. My love to you and to all our comrades.

GIBRAN

TO MIKHAIL NAIMY

Boston,
May 22, 1929

Brother Meesha:

I feel better today than when I left New York. How great is my need for relaxation far away from the clamorous society and its problems. I shall rest and be away, but I would remain close to you and to my brethren in spirit and love. Do not forget me; keep in touch with me.

A thousand salaams to you, and Abdul-Masseh, and to Rasheed and William and Nasseeb and to each one connected with us in Arrabitah.*

May heaven protect you and bless you, brother.

GIBRAN

TO MAY ZIADEH

1930

Dear May:

. . . I have many things to discuss with you concerning the transparent element and other elements. But I must remain silent and say nothing about them until the cloud is dispersed and the doors of the ages are opened, whereupon the Angel of God will say to me: "Speak, for the days of silence are gone; walk, for you have tarried too long in the shadow of bewilderment." I wonder when will the doors open so that the cloud may be dispersed!

. . . We have already reached the summit, and the plains and the valleys and the forests have appeared before us. Let us rest, May, and talk a while. We cannot remain here long, for I see a higher peak from a distance, and we must reach it before sunset. We have already crossed the mountain road in confusion, and I confess to you that I was in a hurry and not always wise. But isn't there something in life which the hands of wisdom cannot reach? Isn't there something which petrifies wisdom?

* Arrabitah means "bond" in Arabic, and since this is a literary society, the meaning here is "pen bond."

Waiting is the hoofs of time, May, and I am always awaiting that which is unknown to me. It seems sometimes that
I am expecting something to happen which has not happened yet. I am like those infirms who used to sit by the
lake waiting for the coming of the angel to stir the water
for them. Now the angel has already stirred the water,
but who is going to drop me in it? I shall walk in that
awful and bewitched place with resolution in my eyes and
my feet.

GIBRAN

TO MAY ZIADEH

1930

Dear May:

. . . My health at present is worse than it was at
the beginning of the summer. The long months which I
spent between the sea and the country have prolonged the
distance between my body and my spirit. But this strange
heart that used to quiver more than one hundred times a
minute is now slowing down and is beginning to go back
to normal after having ruined my health and affected my
well-being. Rest will benefit me in a way, but the doctor's
medicines are to my ailment as the oil to the lamp. I am
in no need for the doctors and their remedies, nor for rest
and silence. I am in dire need for one who will relieve me
by lightening my burden. I am in need of a spiritual
remedy—for a helpful hand to alleviate my congested
spirit. I am in need of a strong wind that will fell my fruits
and my leaves.

. . . I am, May, a small volcano whose opening

has been closed. If I were able today to write something great and beautiful, I would be completely cured. If I could cry out, I would gain back my health. You may say to me, "Why don't you write in order to be cured; and why don't you cry out in order to gain back your health?" And my answer is: I don't know. I am unable to shout, and this is my very ailment; it's a spiritual ailment whose symptoms have appeared in the body . . . You may ask again, "Then what are you doing for this ailment, and what will be the outcome, and how long are you going to remain in this plight?" And I say to you that I shall be cured, and I shall sing my song and rest later, and I shall cry out with a loud voice that will emanate from the depth of my silence. Please, for God's sake, don't tell me, "You have sung a lot, and what you have already sung was beautiful." Don't mention to me my past deeds, for the remembrance of them makes me suffer, and their triviality turns my blood into a burning fire, and their dryness generates thirst in my heart, and their weakness keeps me up and down one thousand and one times a day. Why did I write all those articles and stories? I was born to live and to write a book—only one small book—I was born to live and suffer and to say one living and winged word, and I cannot remain silent until Life utters that word through my lips. I was unable to do this because I was a prattler. It's a shame, and I am filled with regret because I remained a chatterbox until my jabbering weakened my strength. And when I became able to utter the first letter of my word, I found myself down on my back with a stone in my mouth . . . However, my word is still in my heart, and it is a living and a winged word which I must utter in order to remove with its harmony the sins which my jabbering has created.

The torch must come forth.

GIBRAN

When Felix Farris, a prominent Lebanese writer, heard about his beloved Gibran's illness, he felt so bad that he forgot about his own illness, and wrote to Gibran the letter which follows. Gibran's answer is next included.

FROM FELIX FARRIS

1930

. . . Gibran, my seeing you ill was more painful to me than my own illness. Come let us go to the native land of the body and enliven it there. When the tempest of pain strikes a person, the body longs for its earth and the soul for its substance.

Come, my brother, let us discard what is broken, and fly away with the unbroken to the place where silence lives. There is a longing in my heart for you like the longing for the place in which I left my heart. There in Beirut, at the harbor, my eyes shall focus upon the heart of the Holy Cedars, the paradise of my country. With you by me, Gibran, my soul would look at its eternal Cedars as if it were on the shore of the true Universe. Let us triumph and remedy our ailments. This civilization which has tired you after many years, has exhausted me many months ago. Come, let us withdraw and exploit our suffering under the shade of the Cedars and the pine trees, for there we shall be closer to the earth and nearer to heaven. . . . My eyes are anxious to see the dust of the earth and all that is within it of importance in the hidden world.

Believe me, Gibran, I have not seen a blooming flower, nor have I smelled an aromatic scent, nor heard the singing of a nightingale, nor felt the passing of a frolicsome breeze since the last time my eyes saw the Orient, your home and mine.

Come, let us awaken the dormant pains—come and let the pure skies of your country hear your beautiful songs, and let your brush and pen draw from the original what you are drawing now from the prints of memory.

FELIX FARRIS

TO FELIX FARRIS

1930

My dear Felix,

. . . It is not strange that we are both struck by the same arrow at the same time. Pain, my brother, is an unseen and powerful hand that breaks the skin of the stone in order to extract the pulp. I am still at the mercy of the doctors and I shall remain subject to their weights and measures until my body rebels against them or my soul revolts against my body. Mutiny shall come in the form of surrender and surrender in the form of mutiny; but whether I rebel or not, I must go back to Lebanon, and I must withdraw myself from this civilization that runs on wheels. However, I deem it wise not to leave this country before I break the strings and chains that tie me down; and numerous are those strings and those chains! I wish to go back to Lebanon and remain there forever.

GIBRAN